IMAGES
of America

HOBART

I0806392

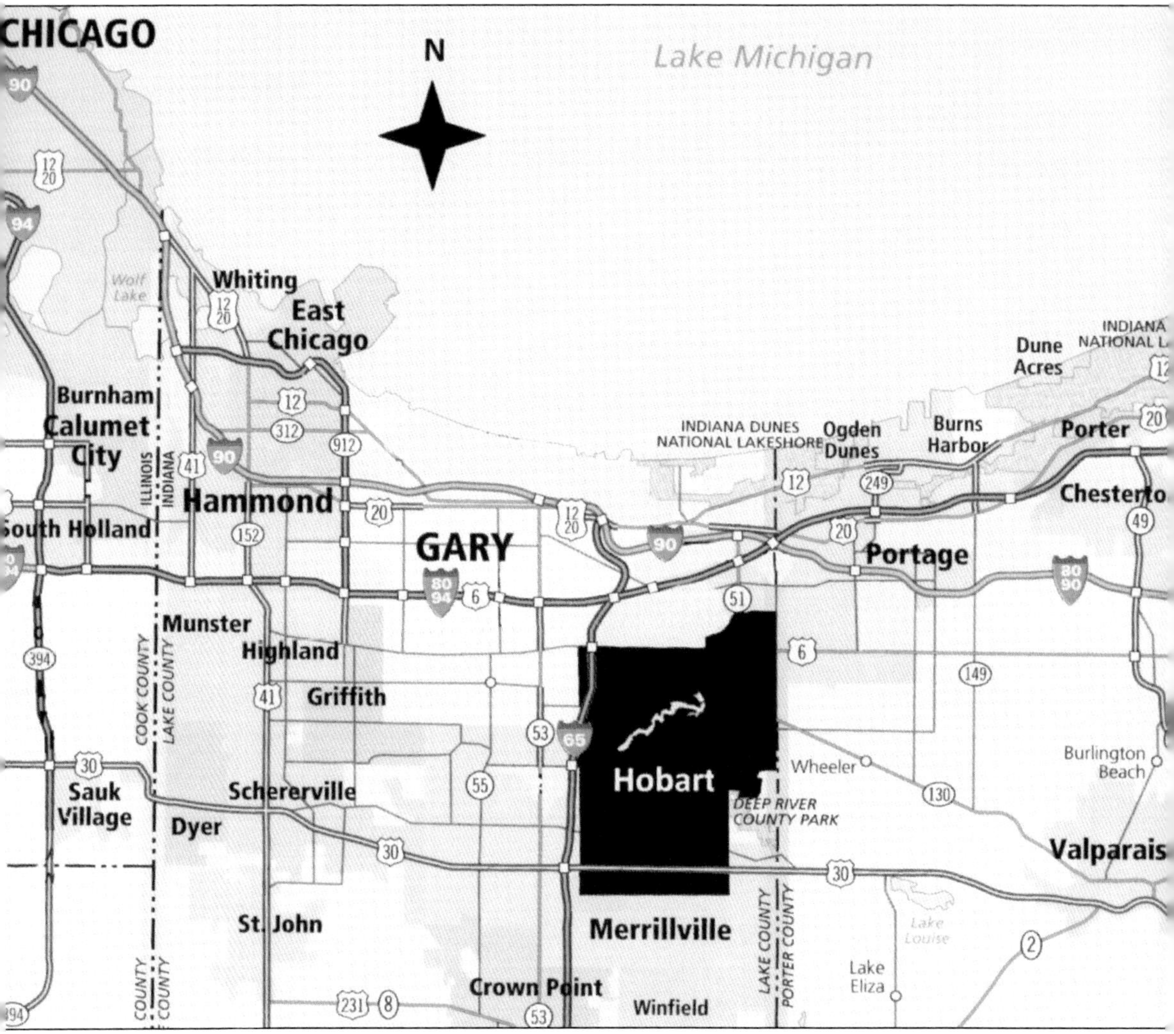

Location Map. The City of Hobart is located approximately 38 miles southeast of Chicago and near three major highways: I-65 to the west, I-80/I-94 to the north, and US 30 to the south. Hobart has nearly 30,000 residents and is approximately 27 square miles, making it the second-largest city in Lake County. Hobart has a mayor-council form of government that includes 10 elected officials: mayor, clerk-treasurer, judge, five district council representatives, and two at-large council representatives. Hobart dates its founding to 1847. In January 1889, Hobart incorporated as a town, and in November 1921 the town was converted into a city. (Courtesy of Rand McNally Street Maps, modified by Sergio Mendoza.)

On the Cover: This c. 1902 photograph offers a southeasterly view of downtown Hobart. The structures in the background stood along Main Street between Front and Second Streets. The "Old Mill" is seen on the left, and Trinity Lutheran Church is on the right. The individuals in the rowboat on Lake George are William and Mary Ballantyne with their two sons and grandson. James Ballantyne is at the oars, and John Ballantyne is at the prow. The young boy is Elmer Ballantyne, son of James. Another son, not pictured, is Donald Ballantyne. In 1934, Donald married Dorothy Dunning, and both are credited as charter members who helped establish the Hobart Historical Society. Donald and Dorothy's daughter, Elin Christianson, continues her parents' legacy as a preservation steward and president emeritus of the Hobart Historical Society.

IMAGES
of America

HOBART

Sergio Carrera Mendoza

ARCADIA
PUBLISHING

ISBN 978-1-4671-1064-8

Published by Arcadia Publishing
Charleston, South Carolina

Printed in the United States of America

Library of Congress Control Number: 2013934579

For all general information, please contact Arcadia Publishing:
Telephone 843-853-2070
Fax 843-853-0044
E-mail sales@arcadiapublishing.com
For customer service and orders:
Toll-Free 1-888-313-2665

Visit us on the Internet at www.arcadiapublishing.com

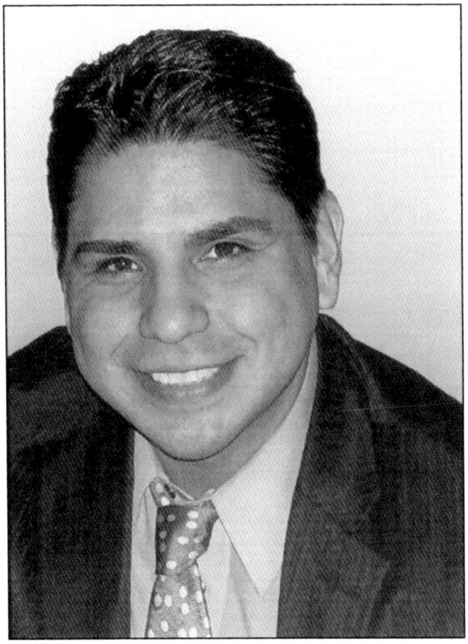

This book is dedicated to those in Hobart who walked before me, and to those who will walk after me; and for the one who walks beside me in this city, where we fell in love, my wife, Lisa. (Courtesy of Lisa Mendoza.)

Contents

Acknowledgments

I would like to express my gratitude to the many people who made this book possible. I would initially like to thank the person who inspired this book, Tiffany N. Tolbert, director of the Northwest Field Office of Indiana Landmarks, for encouraging me to take on this project. I would also like to thank Kelsey Jones, acquisitions editor at Arcadia Publishing, for her guidance and support through this process.

It is important to note that this book would not have come to fruition without the support of the Hobart Historical Society, with special thanks to Paula Isolampi, Rita McBride, and Karen Nelson for their assistance and for generously giving of their research time to help complete this book. Unless otherwise noted, all of the images in this book are courtesy of the Hobart Historical Society Museum.

Other community organizations that should be recognized for having contributed their time, shared their knowledge, or donated images for this book include: Hobart Chamber of Commerce, Mike Adams and Virginia Curtis; Maria Reiner Center, Pam Broadaway and Kristina Kuzma; Concept Marketing and Design, Dana Liss; St. Mary Medical Center, Mary Fetsch; College of Court Reporting, Nicky Rodriquez; Southlake Mall, Erin Webster; and Debbie Scurlock, assistant to the city engineer. Thanks go to community members Dr. James and Janet Herrick, Jay and Mona Scriba, Richard Smith, Cecelia Kenny, Bob Burns, Tom Ehrhardt Sr., and Ben Liss for sharing their enthusiasm and stories.

It is necessary to acknowledge those individuals who believed in my skills and talents. It is because of those early steps they afforded me that this book was possible. Thank you to former mayor Linda Buzinec, former city engineer Stephan Truchan, current mayor Brian Snedecor, and current clerk-treasurer Deborah Longer, for trusting me to serve the City of Hobart.

I would be remiss if I did not acknowledge the strength behind this book: my parents, Sergio Fernandez Mendoza and Yolanda (Villarreal) Carrera, for passing on to me their fortitude; and my wife, Lisa C. (Velazquez) Mendoza, for her unwavering encouragement and loving patience through this journey. Without her, my endeavors would only be half as intriguing.

INTRODUCTION

The area that became the City of Hobart once lay under a great ice cap that stood at what once was the shore of Lake Michigan. As the ice caps retreated, a diverse ecosystem of dune and swale was created, and natural drainage rivers along the southern rim of Lake Michigan were carved and great ridges were formed. In the area of what is now Hobart, Deep River and Turkey Creek took shape and an eight-mile ridge with rich soil and clay formed, setting the stage for Hobart to thrive as an exporting community.

Early European explorers found the area to be rich in flora and fauna. They reported open prairies, marshes, and heavily wooded acres of pine and cedar. The Robert LaSalle expedition of 1682 reported plentiful berries and nuts, large game, and valuable fur-bearing animals. The members of the expedition wrote in amazement of the variety of fowl the rivers attracted and the assortment of fish found in the rivers. The region was under the French flag from the late 1600s to 1763, when the French and Indian War ended with the Treaty of Paris. The British had control of the area from 1763 to 1783. In 1781, Spanish soldiers came through Northern Indiana, claiming the area for Spain. The Spanish quickly retreated, leaving artifacts, primarily muskets, along Deep River and in the area currently occupied by Indian Ridge Golf Course.

Prior to Indiana attaining statehood on December 11, 1816, what would become the City of Hobart was part of the Northwest Territory. The heavily wooded and unpredictable marshy region was home to the Potawatomi Tribe and fur traders. In 1800, Indiana became a territory. After the War of 1812, an interest in colonizing Indiana grew. By 1832, the US government had met with various Potawatomi chiefs and negotiated the Treaty of Tippecanoe. After 1835, many of the chiefs began to sell their granted land, known as "Indian Floats," to settlers and moved west of the Mississippi River. Some of these land sales occurred between George Earle and a few Potawatomi chiefs: Pokagon, Ben Ack, Wee Saw, and Meshowke-to-quah. The land grants sold by the chiefs included portions of current Hobart, from Old Ridge Road and Cleveland Avenue south to Tenth Street, and from Hobart Road west to Liverpool Road.

George Earle was a builder from Falmouth, England, who came to Philadelphia to fulfill a building contract. Upon his arrival, he came across three "western men" who spoke of a platted town with 455 lots "out west" in an area called Indiana, where Deep River meets the Calumet River and flows out to Lake Michigan. The western men spoke of heavy timber growth, and George Earle became intrigued with the possibility of a thriving western city. In 1836, he went to Liverpool and bought it and large tracts of land nearby. In 1837, rail lines from Michigan City to Joliet, and from Detroit to Chicago, passed through Liverpool. Earle used the rail lines and rivers to transport lumber and grain from Liverpool to the newly incorporated city of Chicago.

In 1837, Lake County was formed out of Porter County, and in 1839, the county seat was briefly located at Liverpool. In 1840, the Lake County Locating Commission decided to relocate the county seat to a more centralized site in Lake County, Crown Point. In 1845, Earle abandoned Liverpool, realizing that it would not be the thriving western city he dreamed of. He turned his attention to a new location, about five miles southeast along Deep River. He named the new location Hobart, after his brother Fredrick Hobart Earle. On September 5, 1849, Hobart Township was formed, and on December 6, 1853, sections 4, 5, and 6, township 35, range 7, were transferred from Ross Township to Hobart Township. The township was redefined in 1872 and again in 1883.

On September 7, 1860, according to Order No. 19, George Earle presented a petition asking that a part of Lake County be reorganized to form a new county. The boundary of the proposed county would start at the southeast corner of section 4, township 35, range 7 west, and extend west to the southwest quarter of section 3, township 35, range 8. The border would then extend north on the section line to the northwest corner of section 34, township 36, range 8, then west to the range line between ranges 8 and 9. Finally, the line would extend north to Lake Michigan, then east along the lake to the line between Lake and Porter Counties and then south to the starting place.

In December 1860, George Earle submitted a petition to create a Hobart County, but only two commissioners were present and they had a difference of opinion, so the matter was deferred to March 1861. The Hobart County proposal was brought to the attention of a Lake County representative in Indianapolis, who encouraged the state legislature to change the process for creating one county from another. When the Hobart County proposal reached the Lake County commissioners, the request was declared "dismissed." Earle's dream of establishing a Hobart County in Northwest Indiana, with the City of Hobart most likely as the county seat, would never happen.

One

Settlement in the Woods

In the wake of the Mexican-American War, which had little impact on a state that had been admitted to the union only 30 years earlier, George Earle made the decision to abandon Liverpool and move upstream along Deep River to establish a new community. As the United States prepared to go to war over the annexation of Texas and parts of Nebraska, Kansas, Oklahoma, and New Mexico, Daniel Tayor built a trading store and granary in Hobart near Front Street, and the Pennsylvania Railroad established Hobart as a trading community. Soon, Earle's grist- and sawmills were in full operation, advancing Hobart's status from a trading community to an exporting community.

In the 1850s, most homes were lit with oil lamps, and wood-plank roads, processed at Earle's sawmill, were the norm in Hobart. Also in the 1850s, a new steel manufacturing process, Bessemer, made steel more affordable and increased its output for railroads. George Earle took advantage of the low cost and high production of rail and timber ties and funded the Pennsylvania Railroad through Hobart, thereby increasing the settlement's viability. During the Civil War, Lake County was still viewed as a frontier; of Hobart Township's 800 residents, only about 50 volunteers enlisted in 1862.

After the Civil War, Congress created a plan to reconstruct the nation. Hobart was poised to contribute as a strong exporting community, with its brick and terra-cotta companies and its timber resources. The Great Chicago Fire of 1871 also created a demand on Hobart, in particular on the Isakson family, who owned large tracts of land near the intersection of Hobart and Ridge Roads. In 1877, Reconstruction came to an end, just as the railroad strike was beginning.

The 1877 railroad strike did not last long, but it slowed down the rail system throughout the nation. Eventually, additional rail lines crossed Hobart. The rail lines, two through Ross Township and two through downtown Hobart, helped increase local commercial opportunities. Local exporting opportunities in Hobart were also likely helped by the 1887 Interstate Commerce Act and the US tariffs on imported goods during the late 19th century.

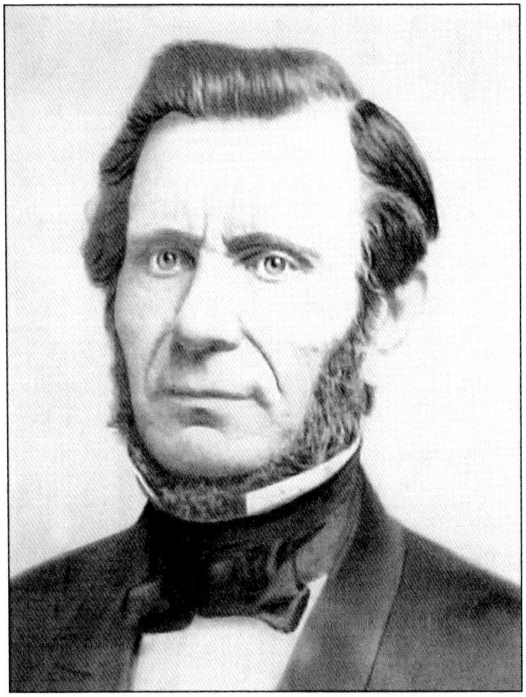

George Earle. Born in 1807, Earle, an architect, artist, and builder, was from Falmouth, England. He married Mary Devonshire, also from Falmouth, in 1832. Their marriage brought one son, John G.E. Earle, who was born in 1833. George came to Philadelphia, Pennsylvania, with his wife in 1835 to fulfill brick-building construction contracts. While in America, he became interested in discussion about land out west called Indiana. In 1836, George moved his family to a platted Indiana settlement called Liverpool. It was said that George Earle manifested the bearings of an American and English gentleman.

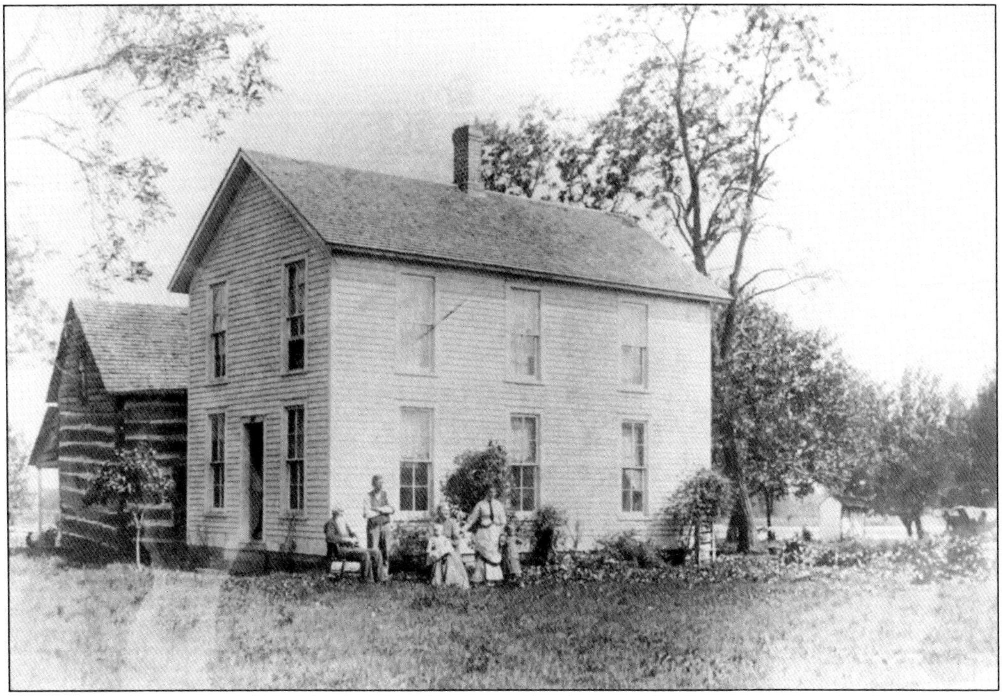

Mundell Homestead. Shown seated in this c. 1888 photograph are Joseph and Malvina (Sigler) Mundell. The Mundell home was a gable-front, wood frame structure. Adjacent to the building's entrance is the original log cabin, built around 1837. The Mundells are some of Hobart's earliest recorded settlers. In 1836, Joseph and Malvina arrived with her parents, Sam and Ann Sigler. Joseph and Malvina located their home on Old Ridge Road, just west of Wisconsin Street.

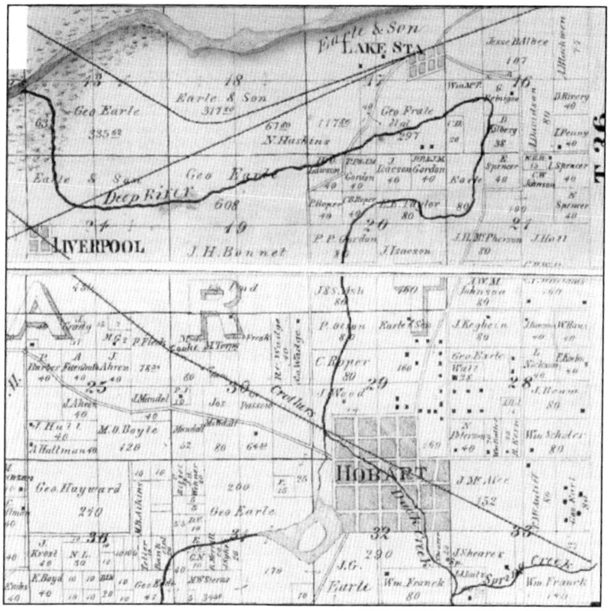

EARLY TOWNSHIP MAP. George Earle's community development interests are shown here. Upon his arrival in Indiana, he purchased vacant lots and acreage around a proposed community called Liverpool. After an unsuccessful attempt to secure the county seat in Liverpool, he abandoned the settlement. In 1845, Earle moved his interests upstream along Deep River to create another community. He named it Hobart, after his brother. In 1852, feeling secure with Hobart's prosperity, he initiated another settlement farther north and called it Lake Station, referencing the depot stop along the Michigan Central Railroad and its proximity to Lake Michigan.

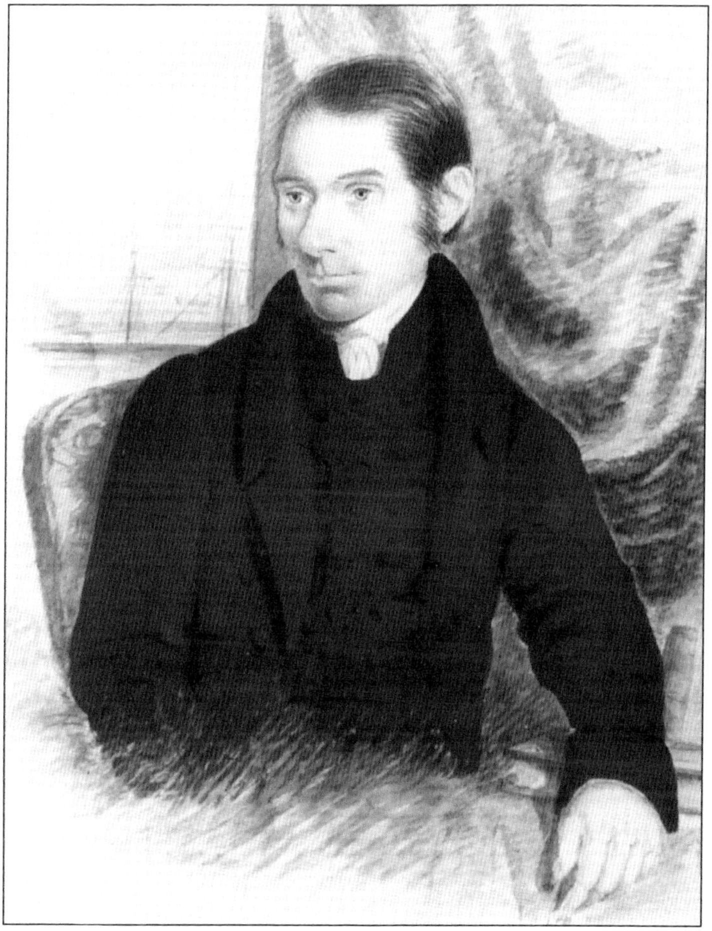

FREDERICK HOBART EARLE. George Earle's younger brother and namesake of the city, Frederick lived in Falmouth, England, with his wife and two children. He worked as a printer, quay master, and eventually as the first trustee of Earle's Retreat Complex for the Aged and Needy, a 20-room retirement home that George Earle constructed in his hometown of Falmouth. Earle's Retreat was dedicated in 1869. In 1876, George Earle passed away and was returned to Hobart for interment.

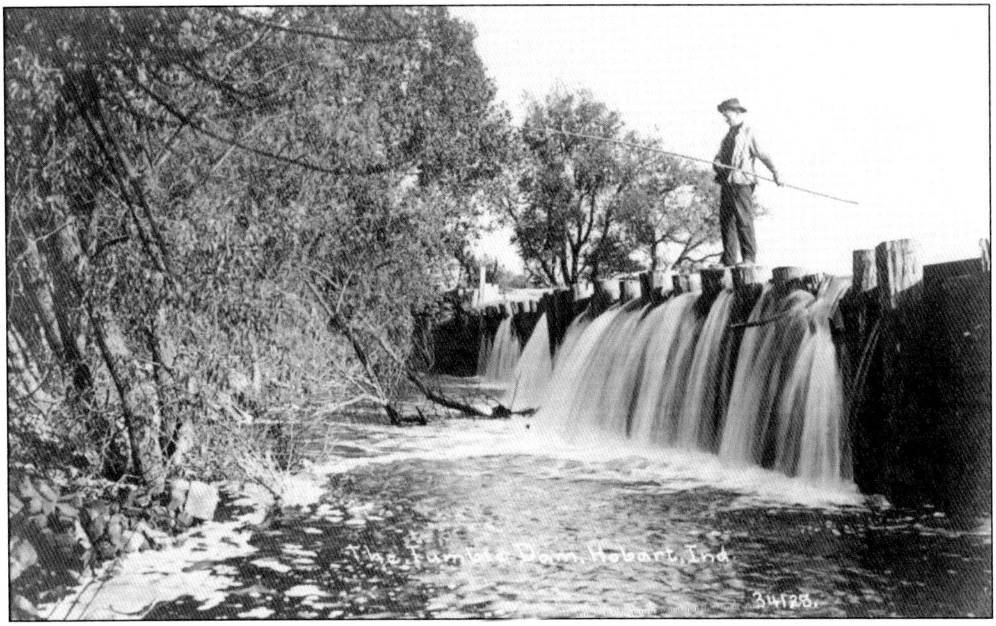

Early Hobart Dam. A fisherman stands on the "tumble dam" around 1913. In 1845, George Earle moved his community development interests upstream along Deep River to a site where Main and Front Streets now intersect. Here, he constructed an earthen dam across Deep River to help power future mills. This is where George Earle had visions of creating a settlement along Deep River, which he would later name Hobart.

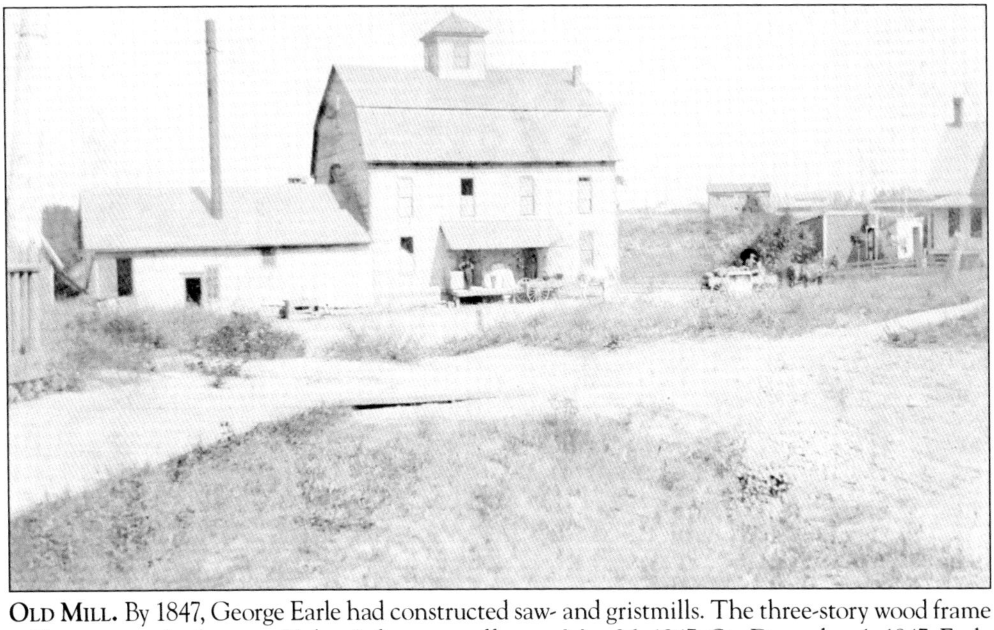

Old Mill. By 1847, George Earle had constructed saw- and gristmills. The three-story wood frame mill structure also became Hobart's first post office on May 26, 1847. On December 1, 1847, Earle printed notice that "his saw and grist mills are now in full operation." The mill structure sat on the shore of Deep River and used the river's water for power. On February 15, 1953, the mill was destroyed by fire. The blaze was so massive that it required six area fire departments to battle the inferno as embers rained across downtown. In 1955, this location became the site of a financial institution.

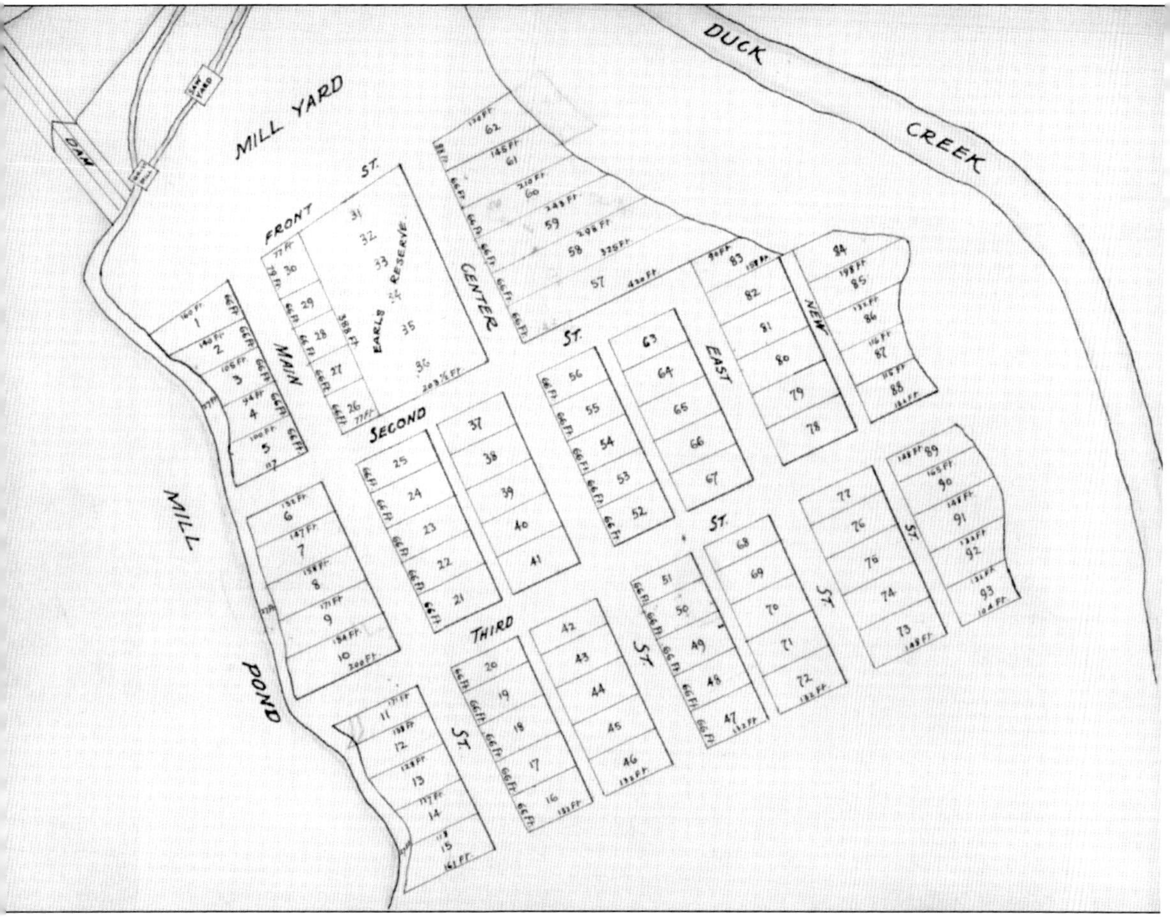

Early Hobart Plat. George Earle platted Hobart in 1848 and recorded it in May 1849. Before the plat was officially recorded and named after Frederick Hobart Earle, the area was referred to as Earle's Mills. The plat that George configured was a grid pattern, a common practice for new communities during that time in the United States. The newly annexed plat identifies 93 lots, including the mill yard; Front, Second, and Third Streets; Main, Center, East, and New Streets; and the mill pond, containing 1,000 acres. Over the next 30 years, Hobart grew with the acquisitions of the following properties: Wood's Addition, recorded January 25, 1851; Earle & Davis Addition and Hobart cemetery, recorded June 13, 1859; The Pittsburgh, Fort Wayne & Chicago Railway Company's Addition, recorded April 24, 1868; and John G. Earle's Addition to Hobart, recorded September 3, 1878. In 1908 and 1911, large rural areas were also annexed into the Town of Hobart.

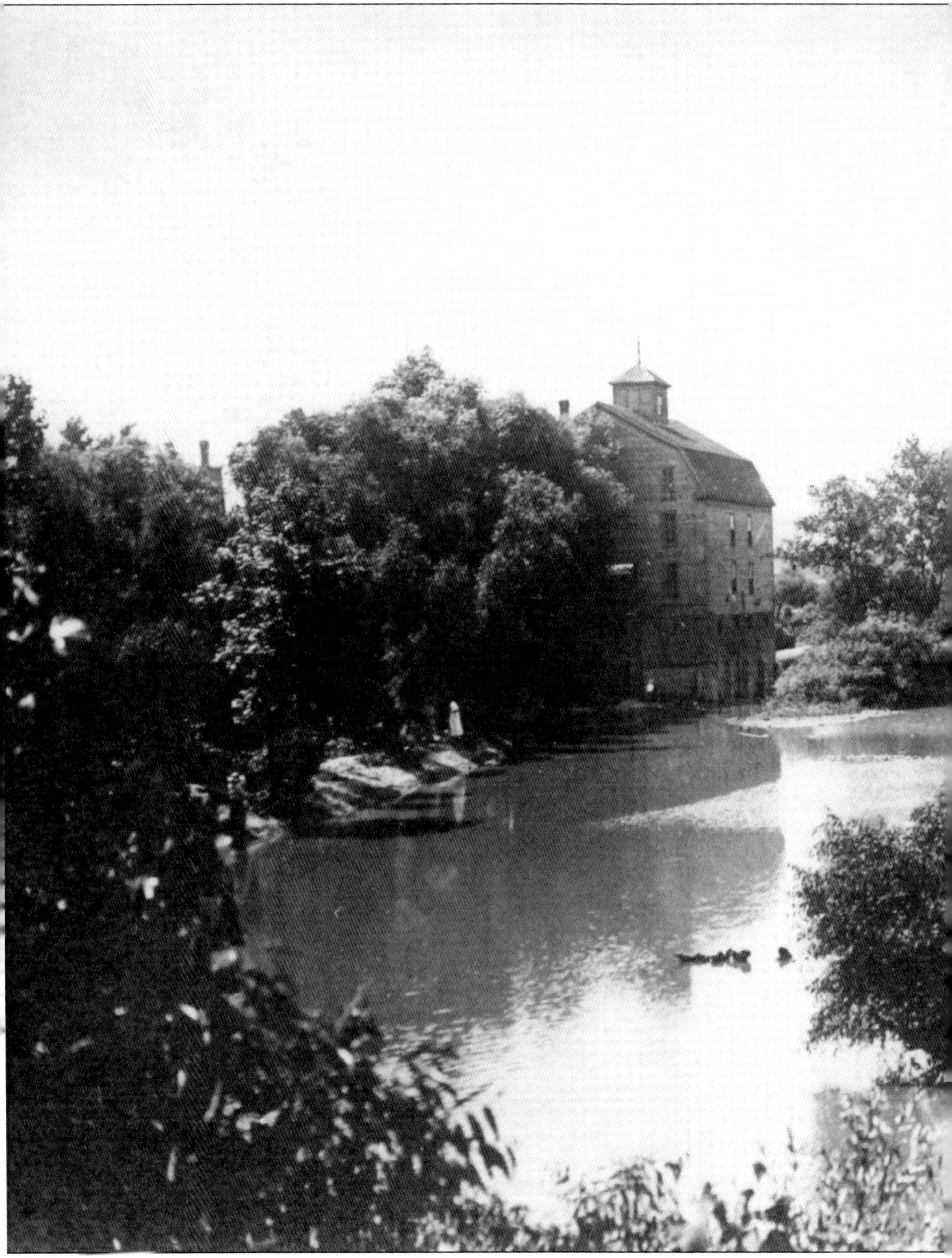

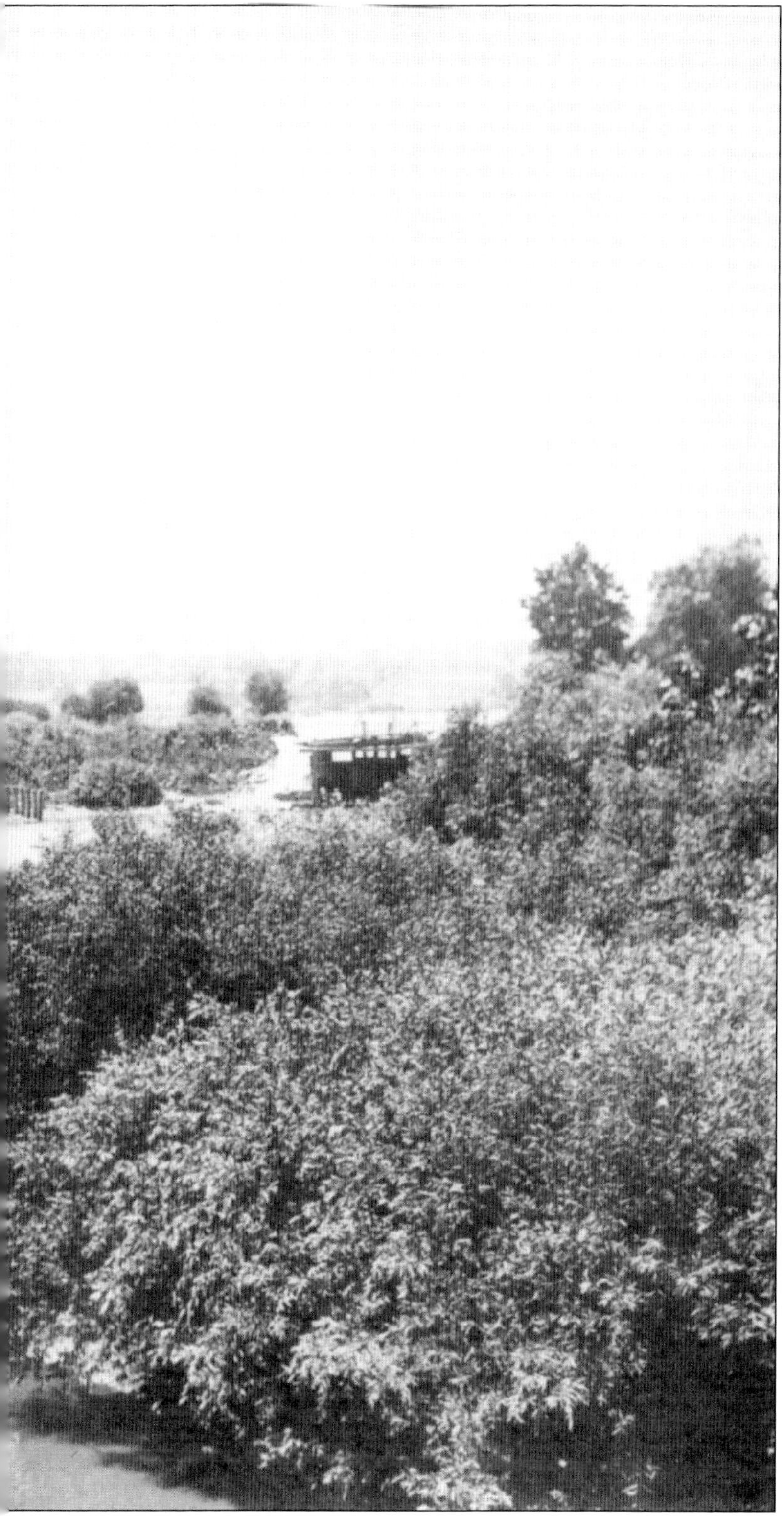

Millpond. The mill, dam, and lake have been associated with Hobart since its 1847 founding. This photograph is the most iconic of early Hobart. It depicts the Old Mill (left) and the dam (right). It has long been a favorite of artists, photographers, locals, and visitors. The mill was destroyed over 60 years ago, but its legacy continues as an image on the city's seal and flag. It was around the landscape seen here that a hamlet in the woods took hold and grew into a city of 30,000 people.

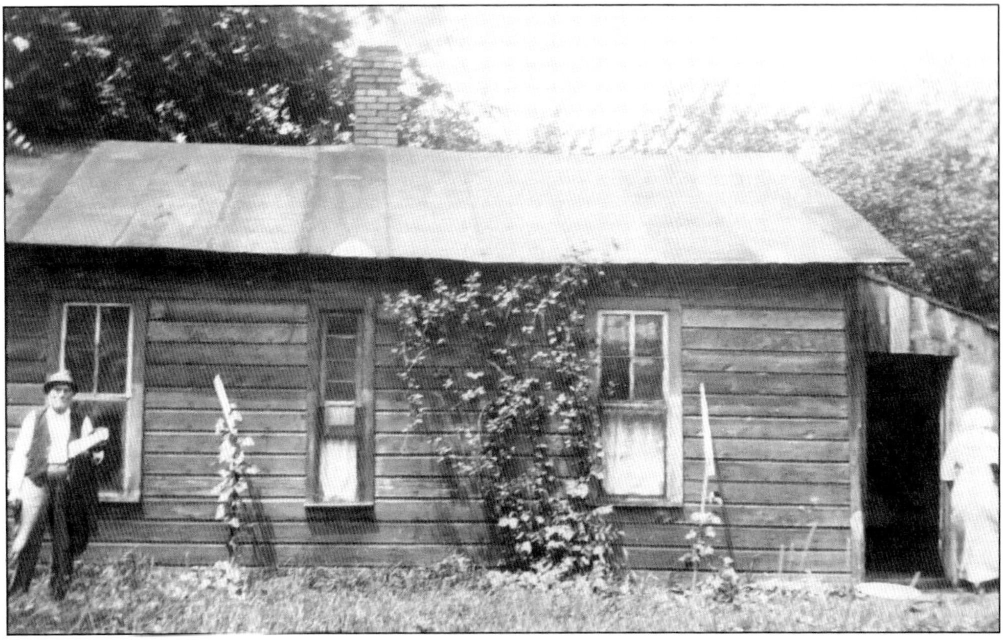

SCHOOLHOUSE. Township School No. 2 was constructed in 1845. The school was located on Center Street, on the east side of the 200 block, about where the current Masonic temple stands. It was said that local families helped build the school and that the wood used to construct and furnish it came from one oak tree. In 1850, the federal census showed Hobart Township as having 48 family groups and a population of 240 people. The school is seen here around 1884.

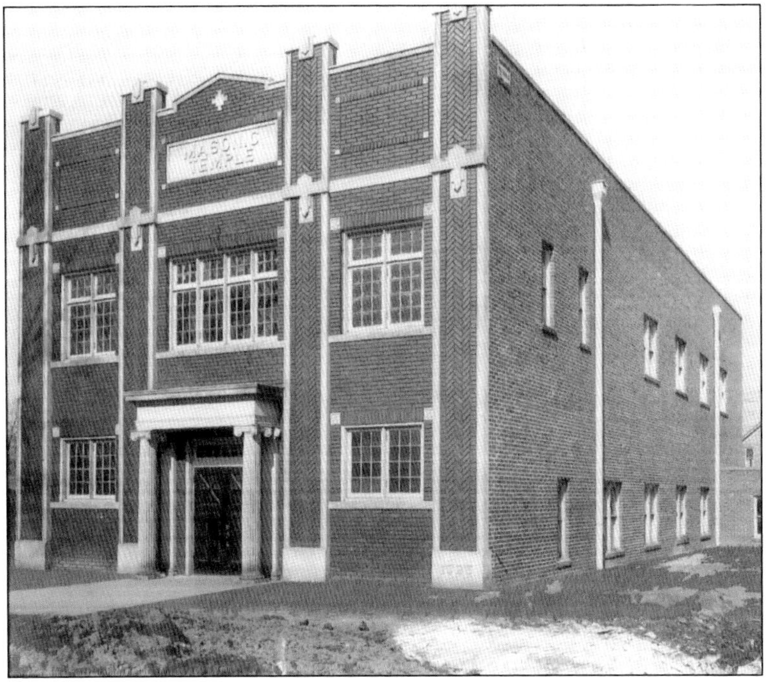

MASONIC TEMPLE. The oldest organization in Hobart arrived from the Wheeler, Indiana, settlement in May 1867. The members rented local space in Hobart for their meetings until they constructed this Colonial Revival building in 1925 on the east side of the 200 block of Center Street.

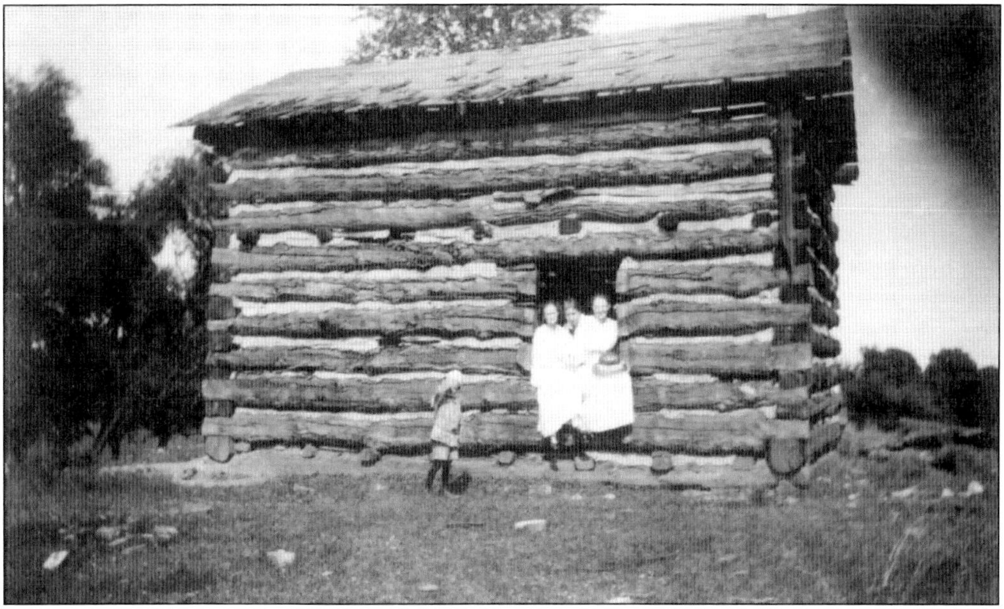

Roper Cabin. This mid-19th century Hobart log cabin house was said to be located on a bluff across Deep River, west of where Michigan Avenue and South Street intersect. The Roper cabin, seen here around 1890, is a common and coarse construction typical of early settlers' homes. Later, when dress lumber became available, log cabins were relegated to use as storage and stables.

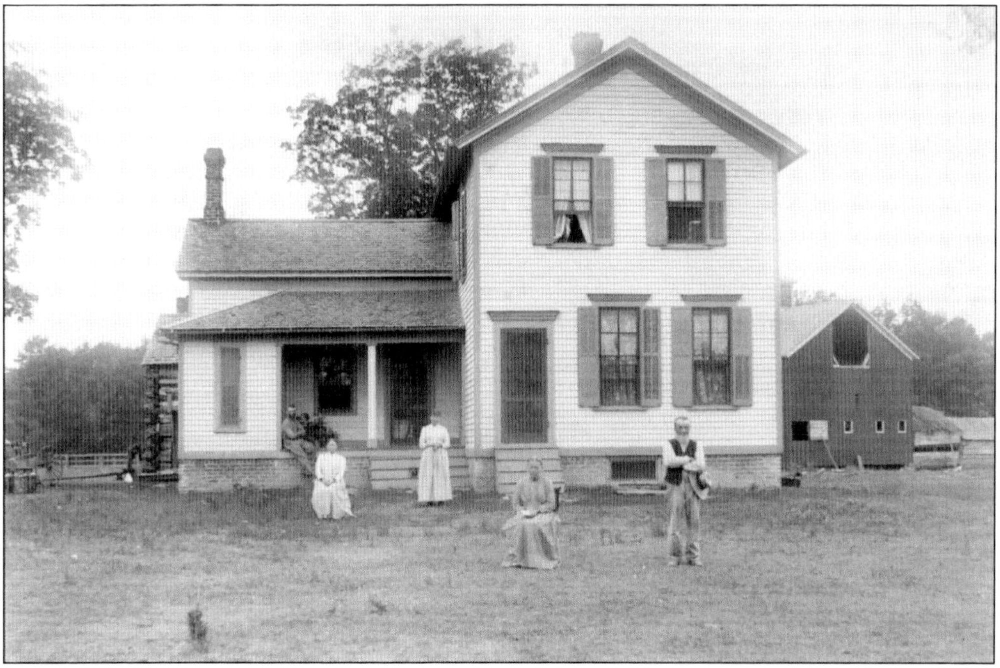

Schillo Homestead. This site was located in what was then rural west Hobart. It was said that Joseph Schillo assisted with the construction of the Hobart dam and sawmill. The Schillos' early log-cabin home can be seen to the left and rear of the wood frame, gabled-ell, one-and-a-half-story home. The dress lumber for the Schillo home most likely came from George Earle's sawmill, which allowed for Hobart homes to become more attractive and comfortable.

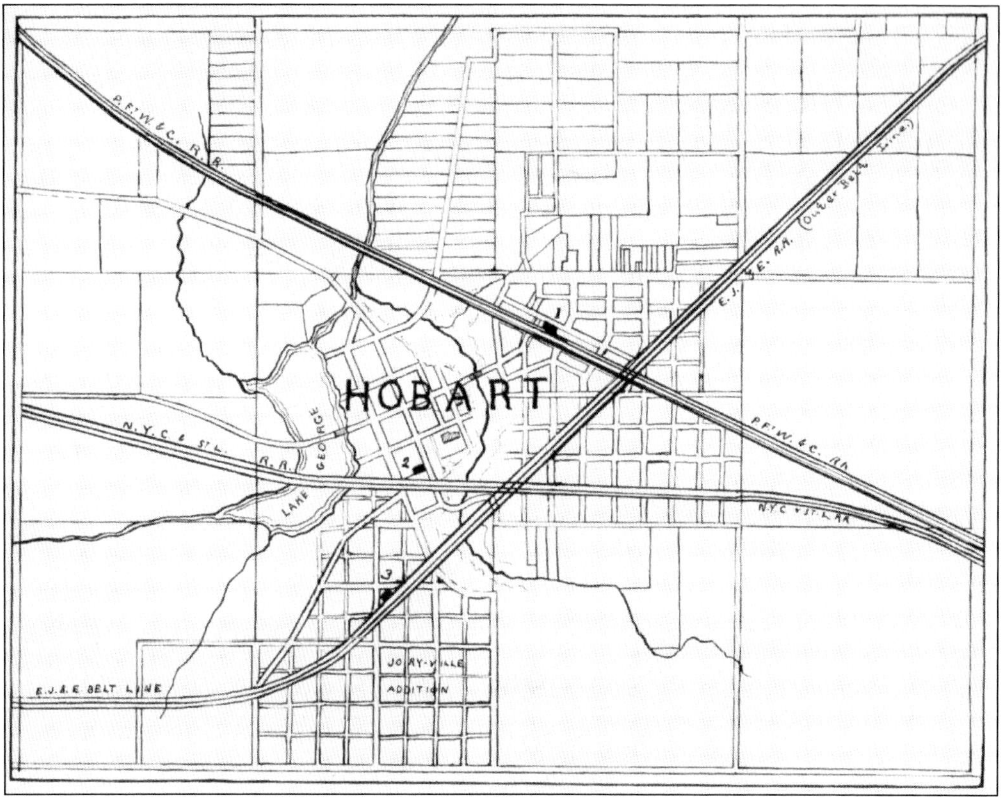

RAILWAY ROUTES. Hobart was successful in securing three rail lines through its early boundaries. This allowed the village to change from a strong producing settlement to a respected and competitive depot community. In 1858, George Earle made arrangements to have the Pennsylvania Railroad, eventually known as the Pittsburgh, Fort Wayne & Chicago Railway (PFW&C), come through Hobart. The New York, Chicago & St. Louis (NYC&StL) rail line, also known as the Nickel Plate, came in 1882, and the Elgin, Joliet & Eastern (EJ&E) line crossed Hobart in 1888. Each of these lines constructed depot stations in Hobart. EJ&E had two tower stations, "Ho Tower" at the Nickel Plate intersection, and "Bart Tower" at the PFW&C crossing.

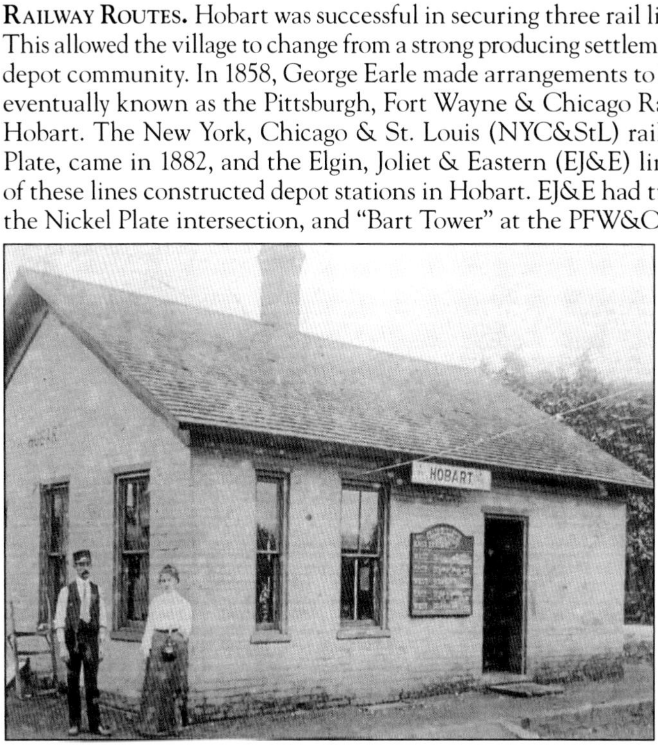

NICKEL PLATE DEPOT. This depot was located at the northwest intersection of Fourth Street and the Nickel Plate tracks, as identified in an 1895 Sanborn map. The name Nickel Plate was suggestive of the rail line's strong financial backing. Shown here are William and Jennie McClaren. William served as a Nickel Plate Railroad agent. Jennie was president of the Women's Reading Club in 1896 and also prepared and sold meals to Nickel Plate Depot patrons.

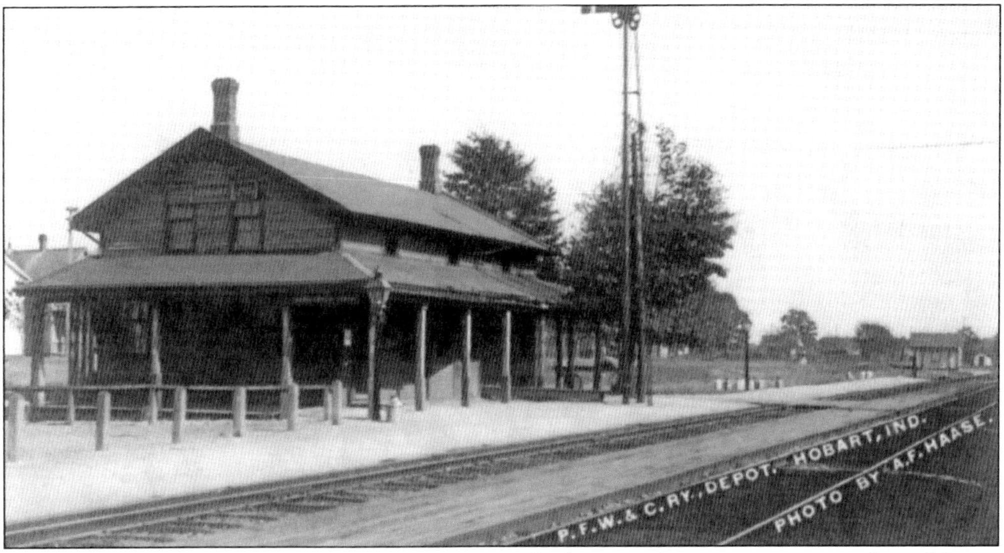

PITTSBURGH, FORT WAYNE & CHICAGO STATION. The first two depot stations were of wood frame construction. The first depot was built in 1858 and was destroyed by fire. The second station was removed around 1911 for the Third Street/Highway 51 road connection over the PFW&C tracks. The third and current "Pennsy Depot" was constructed from local brick. The Pennsy Depot was an important milestone for Hobart because it symbolized a step away from an era of settlers.

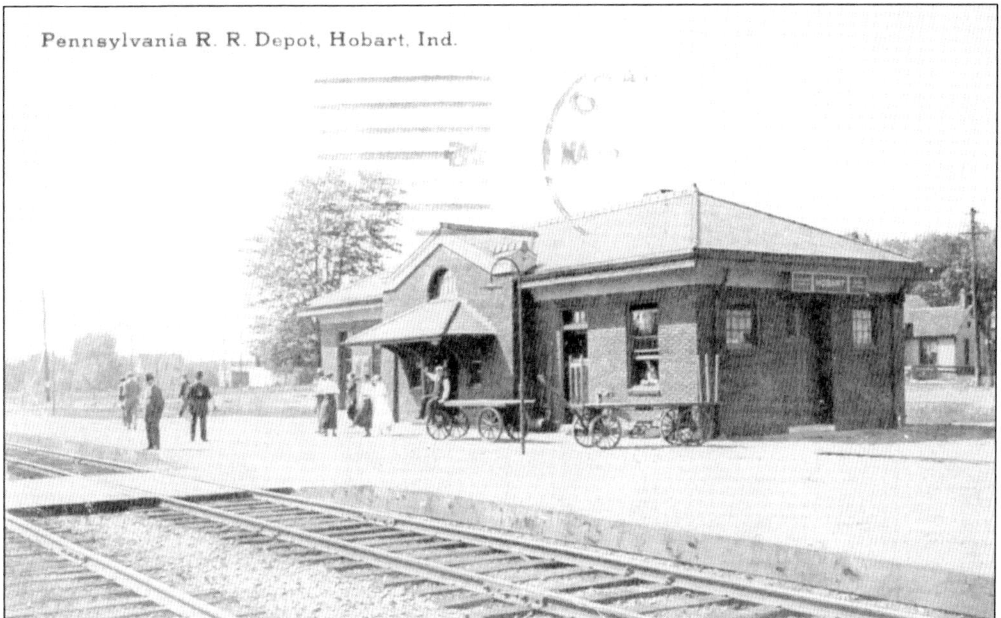

PENNSY STATION. This Colonial Revival station, designed by Price & McDanahan, opened in 1912 and was constructed using local pressed brick. The depot has gabled porticoes, curved soffits, ceramic-tile inserts, and semicircular transom windows. On February 23, 1983, ownership of the depot was transferred to the Save Our Station Committee of the Hobart Historical Society. In 2004, the Hobart Historical Society turned the station over to the City of Hobart. Both transfers occurred through a ceremonial English common-law practice of splitting a twig from the property. On March 1, 1984, the depot was listed in the National Register of Historic Places.

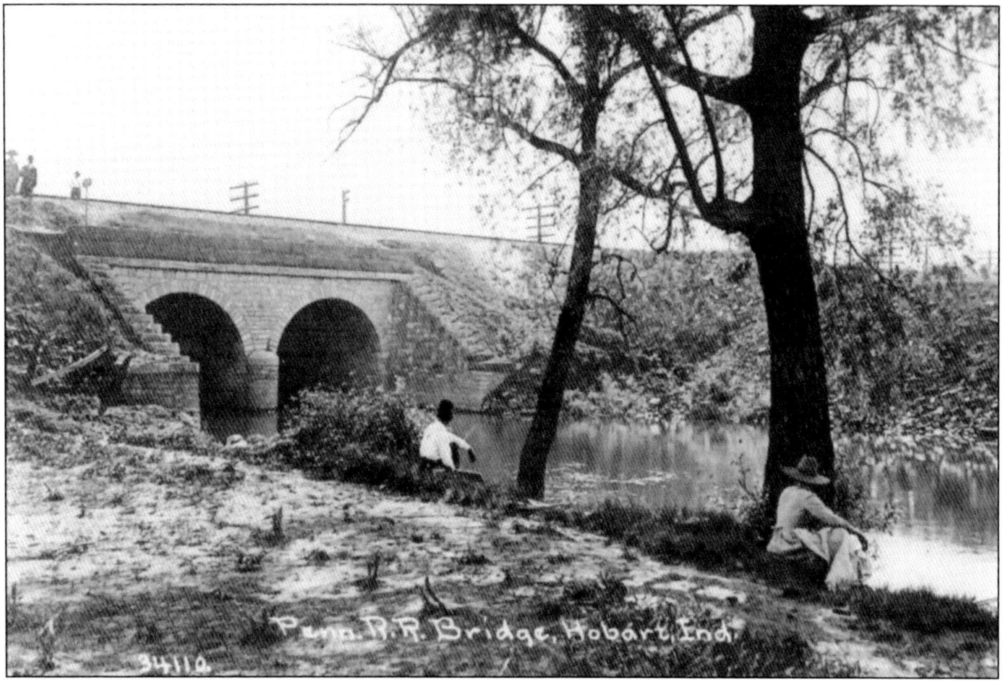

PENNSY BRIDGE. In preparation for the Pennsylvania Railroad crossing though Hobart, a bridge was constructed over Deep River around 1857. The architectural detail of the bridge's arches is striking, but the bridge's true importance lay in the fact that it allowed Hobart to become a competitive manufacturing town at the turn of the last century.

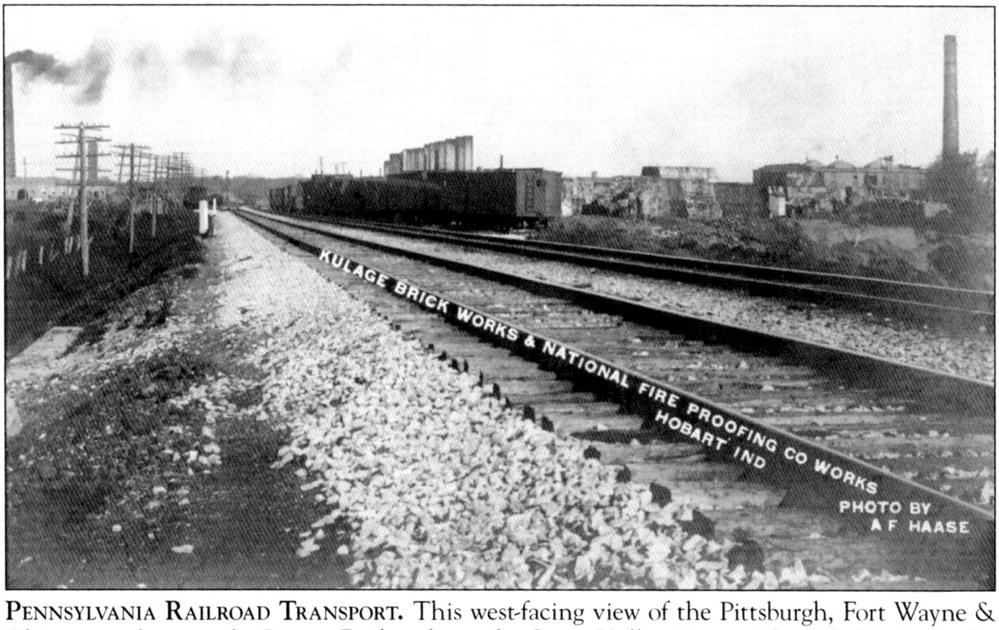

PENNSYLVANIA RAILROAD TRANSPORT. This west-facing view of the Pittsburgh, Fort Wayne & Chicago tracks, near the Pennsy Bridge, shows the Owen Hollow Porous Clay Tile Works on the right (north). At left (south), in the distance, is the Kulage Brick Works. This rail line proved vital to Hobart's continued prosperity. In 1896, it was reported that the rail line's valuation reduced the town's tax burden, making the Town of Hobart a desirable place to live.

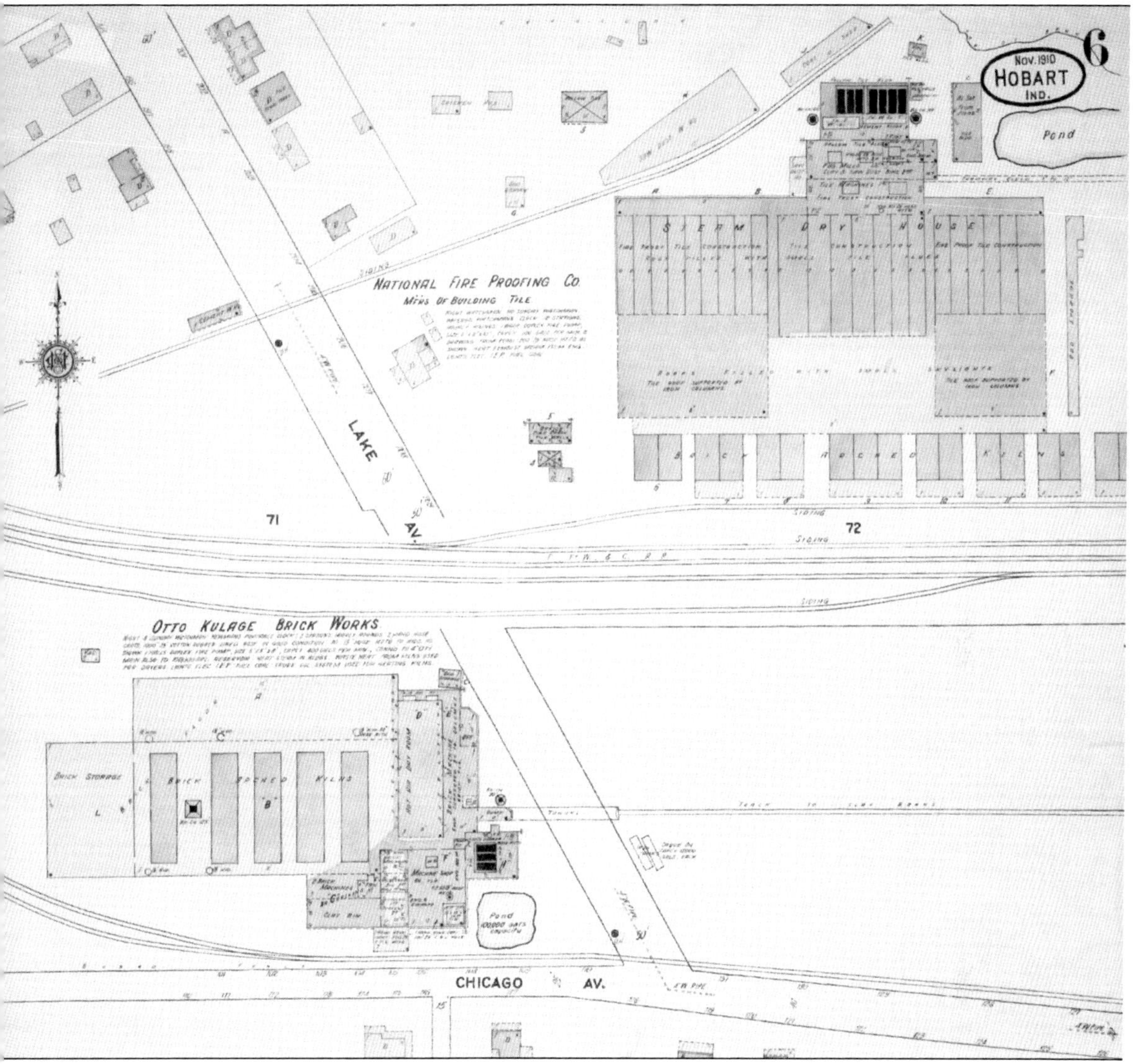

BRICKYARDS MAP. Bricks and brick products were the largest export items for the town of Hobart. At the intersection of Lake and Chicago Avenues, today known as Lake Park Avenue and Old Ridge Road, was an industry with products in high demand. Assisting with the export of these goods was the Pittsburgh, Fort Wayne & Chicago Railroad, which crossed through what seemed an inexhaustible supply of blue, lake, and boulder clay. Hobart, and the entire nation, profited from its natural resources for the next 100 years. Small brickyards began appearing in and around Hobart in the mid-1800s. But it was not until 1863, when Joseph Nash established the first large brickyard near Front Street and Michigan Avenue where the PFW&C Railway crossed, that the Hobart brick industry began. By the early 1960s, manufacturing regulations and standards started to change, resulting in the Hobart brick industry ending by 1965.

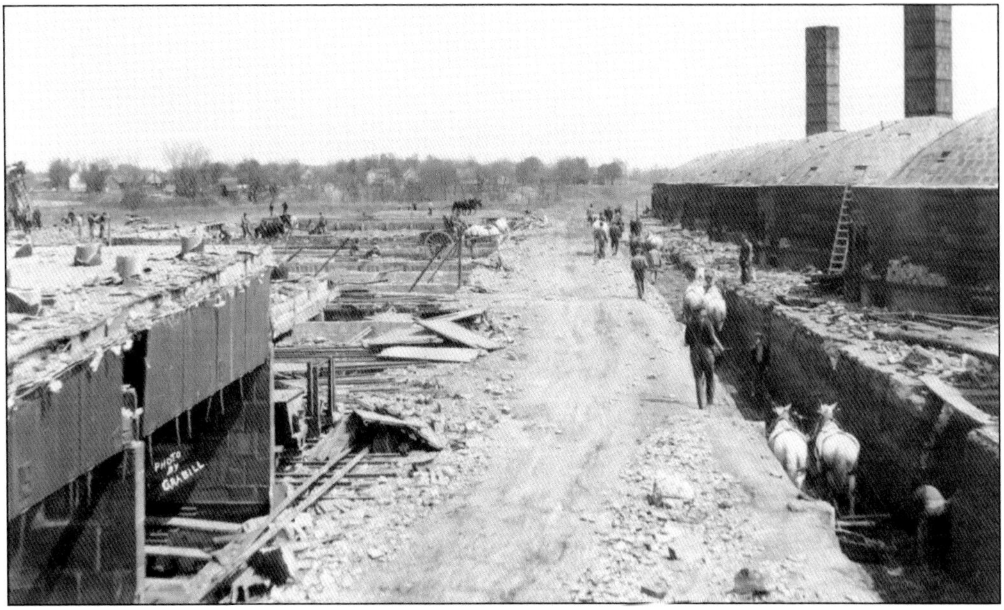

Owen Hollow Porous Clay Tile Works. In 1881, William B. Owen began manufacturing bricks on the northeast corner of Lake Park Avenue and the PFW&C tracks. In 1886, he converted the business to its primary operations of manufacturing hollow porous tile for fireproof building construction. The tile was initially known as "terra-cotta lumber" because it could be sawed and nailed like lumber. In 1902, a year after Owen's death, his company was sold to the National Fire Proofing Company.

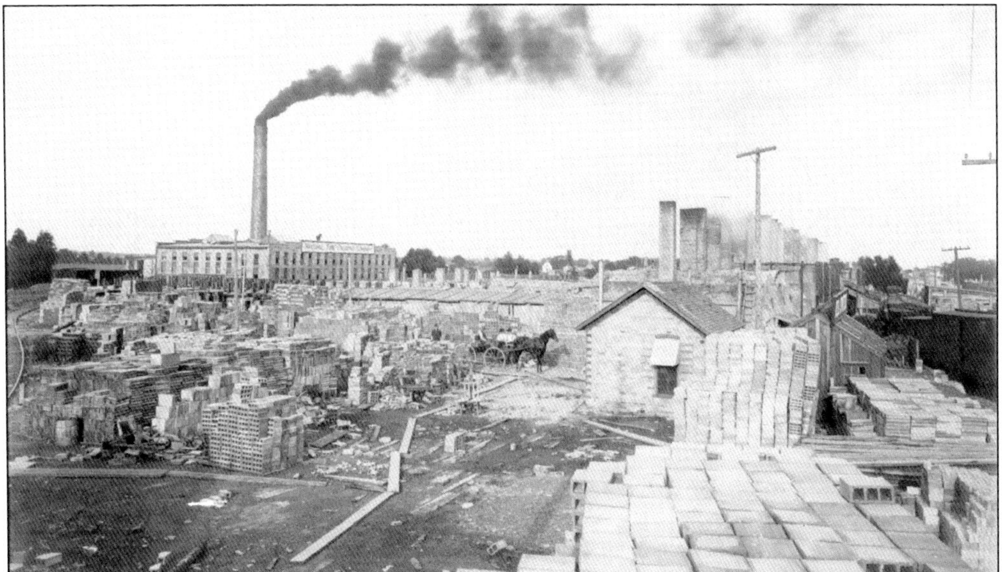

National Fire Proofing Company. National Fire Proofing Company continued the work of Owen Hollow Porous Tile Works. Located on the east side of Lake Park Avenue, the site consisted of 147 acres. In 1910, its main plant burned down due to a boiler explosion, and in 1920, the company rebuilt its facility and expanded operations to other states. In 1957, Great Lakes Industry acquired National Fire Proofing and changed the name to Natco Corporation. In 1965, the site was decommissioned under the management of Fugge Industries.

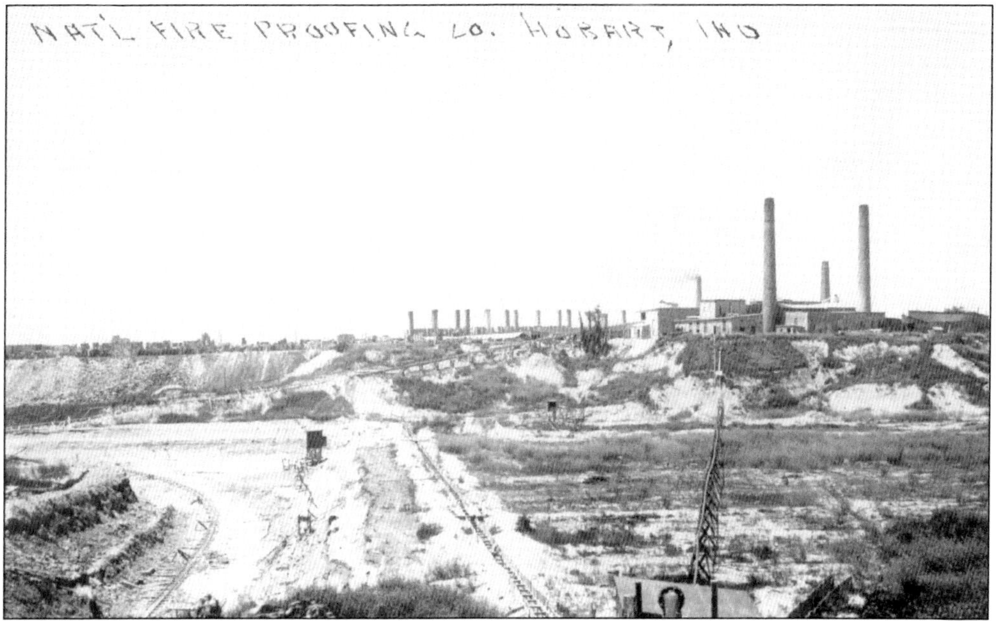

BRICKYARD EXCAVATION. Owen Hollow Porous Tile Works and the National Fire Proofing Company utilized over 85 acres for production. Their operation was so massive that a state geologist remarked that, each month, 60 freight cars of the industry's goods were shipped to all parts of the United States. Eventually, when the industry left the community, the excavation operations left behind large clay pits in the Hobart landscape, as seen here.

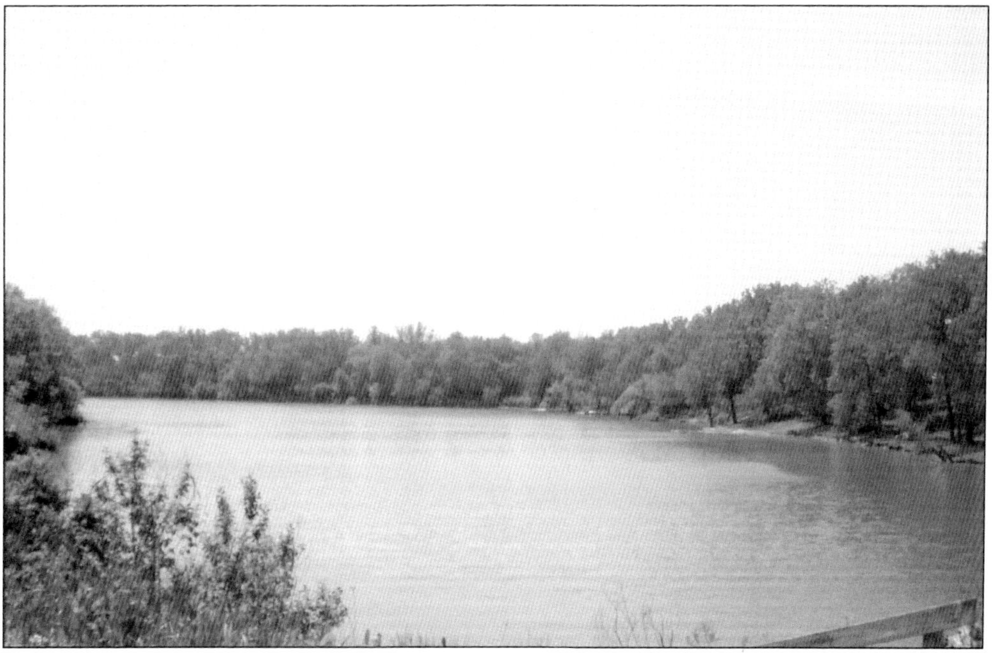

HIDDEN LAKE. In 1966, the former brick and terra-cotta industry site along the east side of Lake Park Avenue and north of the PFW&C line was sold for residential development. The former clay quarry pit was transformed into a 26-acre, spring-fed artificial lake known as Hidden Lake, also called Amber Lake.

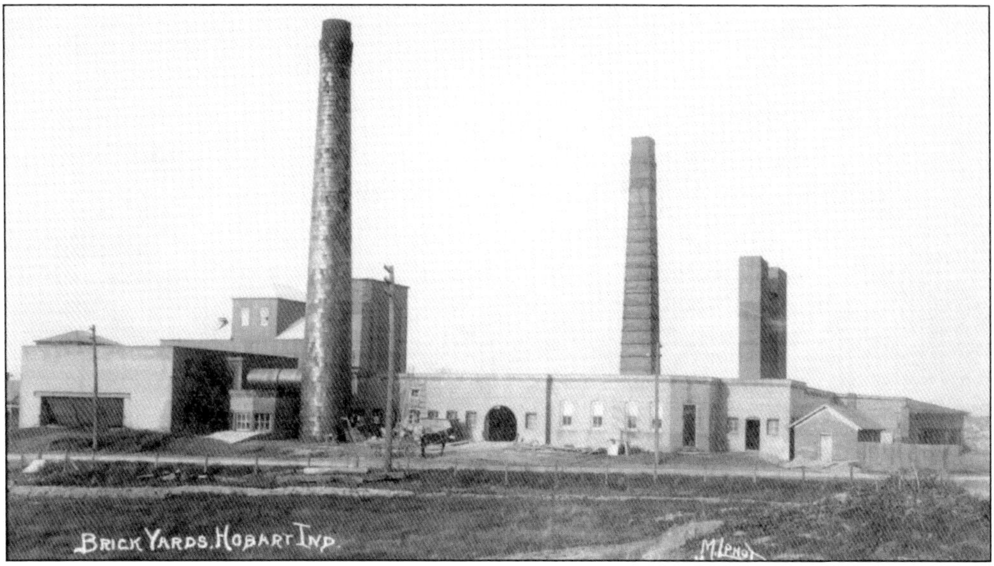

KULLAGE BRICK WORKS. The brickyard owned by Otto Kullage was located at the northwest corner of Lake Park Avenue and Old Ridge Road. Kullage Brick Works flourished from 1893 to the early 1920s. The brickyard excavation operation was located north of the Old Ridge Road, extending to the PFW&C, and east of Lake Park Avenue to Deep River. A second excavation site was located south of Old Ridge Road to Lake George, and west of Deep River to South Lake Park Avenue. In 1929, the Kullage Brick Works closed.

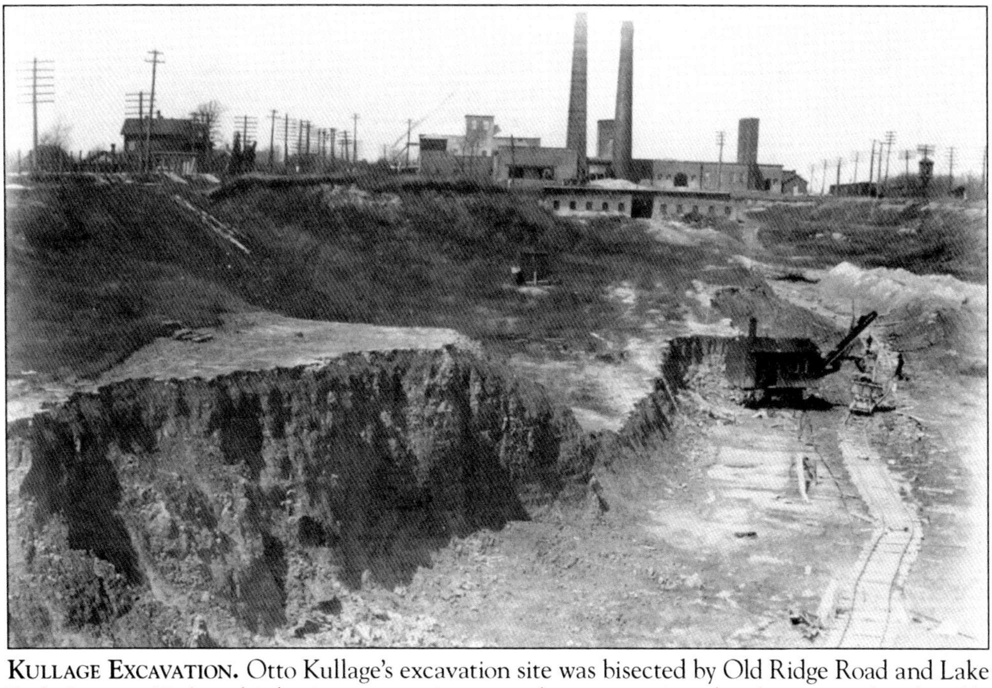

KULLAGE EXCAVATION. Otto Kullage's excavation site was bisected by Old Ridge Road and Lake Park Avenue. He kept his business operation intact by transporting the clay material with cable cars via tunnels. This west-facing photograph of the Kullage building was taken from within a clay pit that is the current site of the rugby field (city park). Formerly the city landfill site, it was purchased in 1957 and filled by 1971.

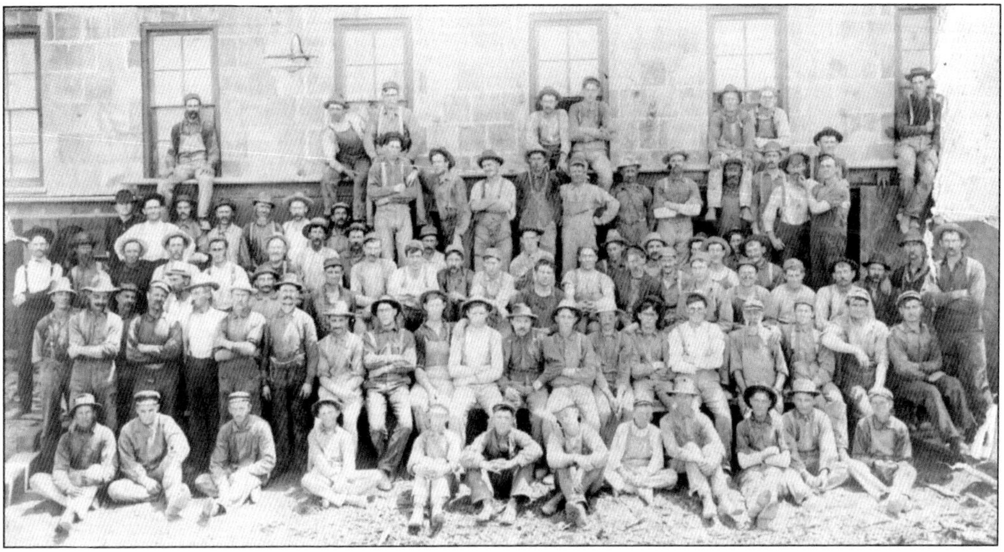

BRICKYARD EMPLOYEES. Between the 1880 and 1900 censuses, Hobart saw nearly 1,000 new residents. The brick companies reported having between 50 and over 125 employees. The men worked 10-hour days, and some gained employment after completing eighth grade. These brickyard employees pose in front of the National Fire Proofing Company around 1900.

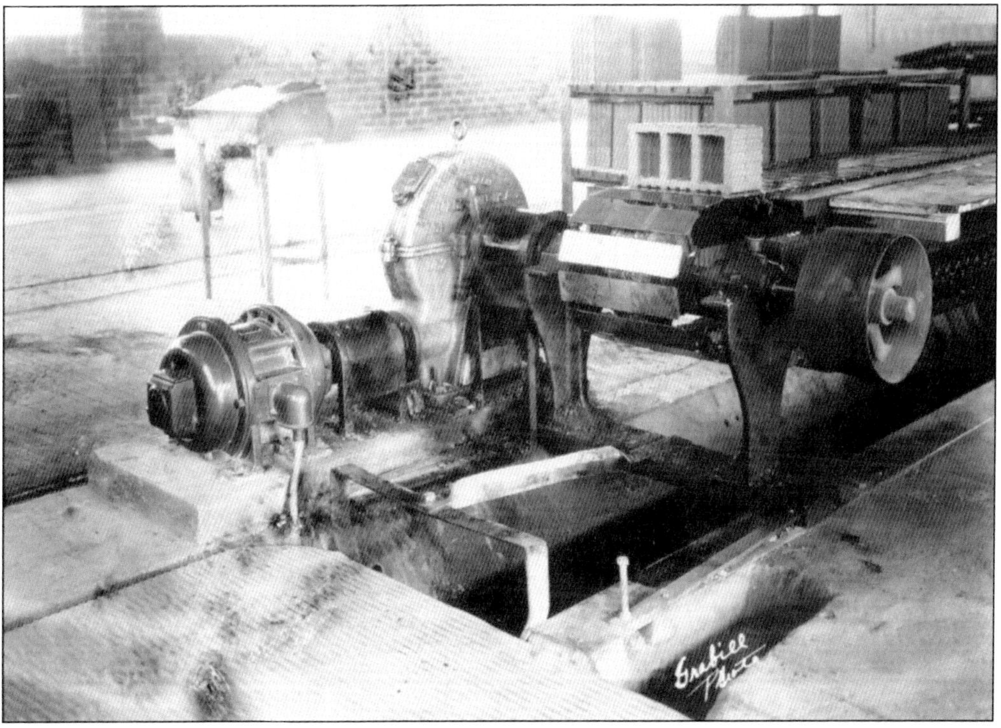

BRICKYARD PRODUCT. The brick industry in Hobart was capable of producing 80 tons of brick products per kiln, which were maintained on the industry's site. Owen Hollow Porous Clay Tile Works had 10 kilns. Loading the bricks on freight cars for shipment was labor intensive, requiring three men. The final product the brickyards produced was "Brickies," a name the high school athletic teams and residents identify with even today.

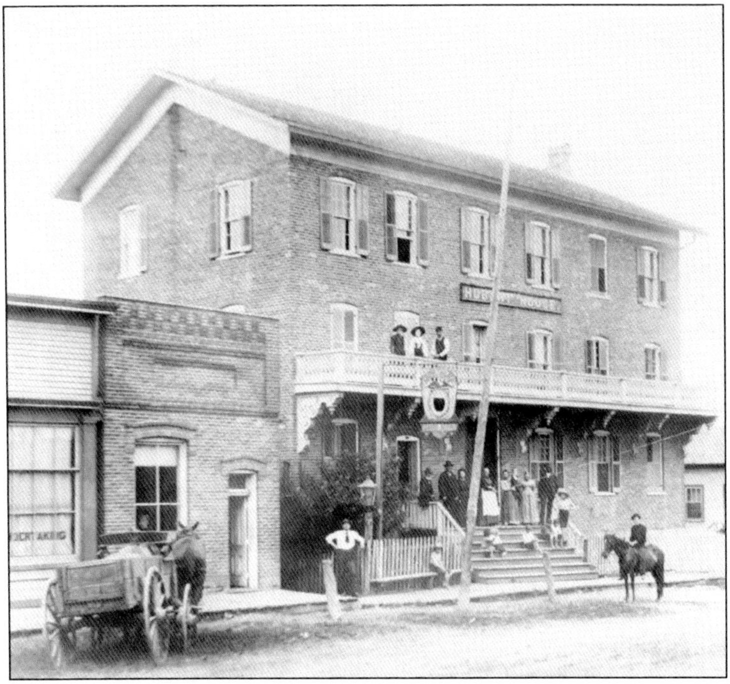

Early Hotel. The Hobart House, built by Edward Roper in 1867, was a three-story structure that rested on a high basement and had a wide staircase leading to a veranda. A kitchen and dining room were located in the basement, and a ballroom was located on the third floor. Early on, the building was said to have towered over what was then a growing village. This photograph was taken sometime before 1884, as the State Bank is not yet in the one-story building immediately to the left of the Hobart House.

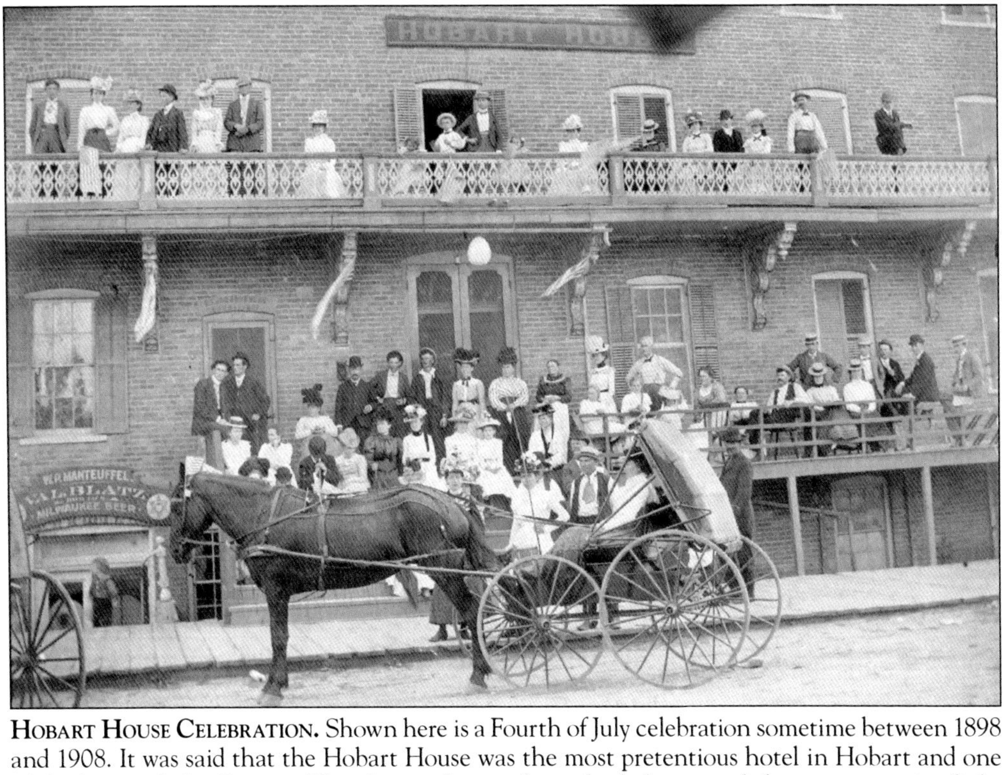

Hobart House Celebration. Shown here is a Fourth of July celebration sometime between 1898 and 1908. It was said that the Hobart House was the most pretentious hotel in Hobart and one of the best in Lake County. The electrical wire along the balcony and the center portico light suggest that the photograph was taken after 1898, when the town had electricity. The American flag shows 45 stars, suggesting it is before 1908.

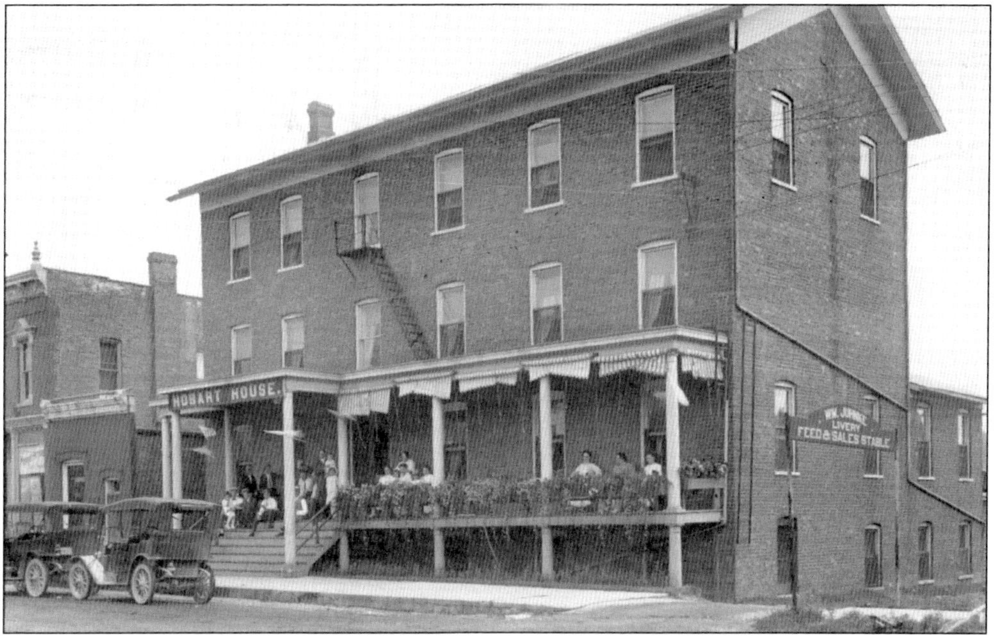

HOBART HOUSE. The concrete sidewalks and unpaved road date this photograph of the Hobart House to between 1913 and 1918. By the 1920s, the Hobart House was being used as a school, and during the Depression, it was used by the township for family government assistance. In November 1939, the building was condemned as a "fire trap." It was purchased by Ignatious Prusiecki and razed in 1940.

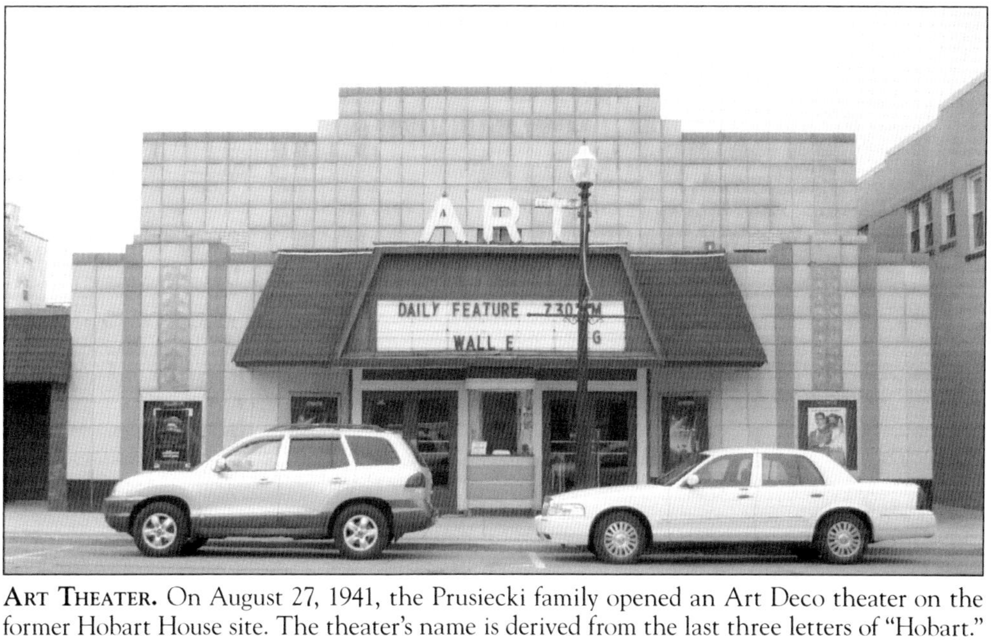

ART THEATER. On August 27, 1941, the Prusiecki family opened an Art Deco theater on the former Hobart House site. The theater's name is derived from the last three letters of "Hobart." The original facade was once covered with glazed terra-cotta tiles, as seen here, but in 2007 an exterior insulation finish system was applied over the tiles. Recent interior remodeling has maintained its 1940s atmosphere. (Courtesy of Tiffany Tolbert.)

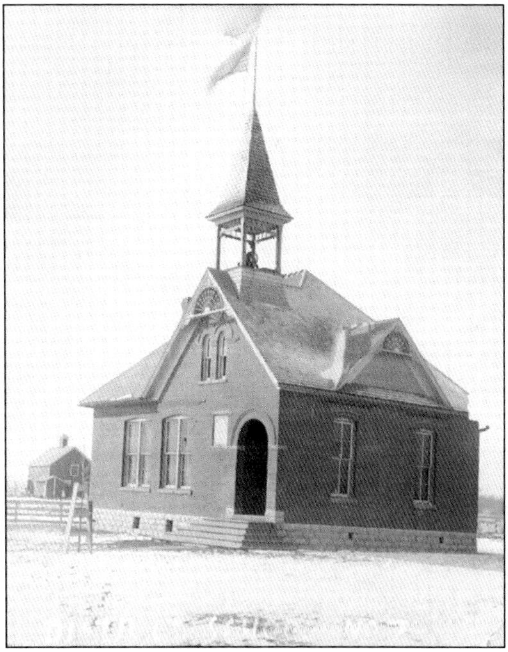

Banks' School. District 7 Township School, built around 1897, was located south of town on the west side of Lake Park Avenue (Highway 51) and was the last Lake County school in Hobart Township to be consolidated. It was said that the trustee was compelled to close the school due to low attendance in October 1911. The former school is currently being used as a private residence.

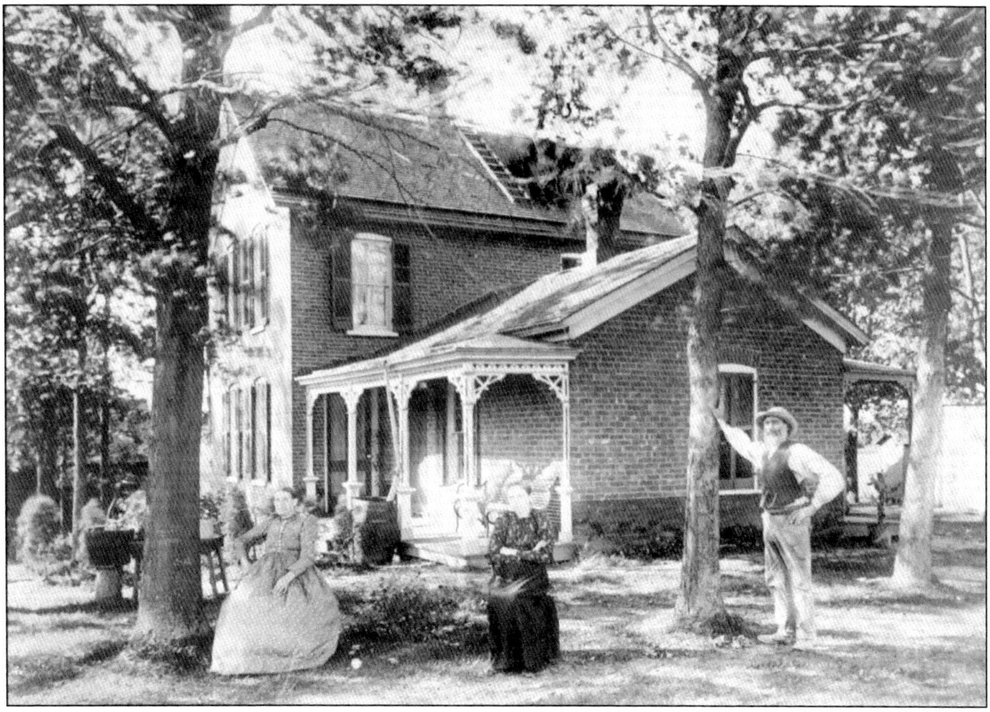

Scriba Homestead. This Italianate upright and wing structure was originally a single-story brick home, built in 1870 by John and Kitty Howe. In 1885, the two-story brick addition was erected by Peter and Sophia Strom, who arrived from Sweden. The home is located at the intersection of Michigan Avenue and South Street and is currently being used as a private residence. Michigan Avenue was also known as "Swede Avenue" because of the Swedish immigrant population living in the area at the turn of the 20th century. (Courtesy of Jay and Mona Scriba.)

Two

FAITH IN A VILLAGE

Hobart, founded by an English gentleman, followed many early British traditions. One tradition in particular includes the growth of a hamlet (settlement) and when it earns the title of a village, which does not occur until the hamlet has a church. Hobart grew from an 1847 settlement/hamlet to a village in 1869 with the construction of its first church, Augustana Lutheran Church. During this time, between 1860 and 1900, it was estimated that 14 million immigrants arrived in America, with nearly half arriving around 1870. The largest wave of European immigrants arrived first from Sweden, then Germany, and eventually immigrants from Ireland and Italy began to arrive. In 1871, the village of Hobart reported 95 different families and a population of over 500. The 19th century ended with over 1,300 Hobart residents when the village incorporated as a town in 1889, and finally a city in 1921.

Some of those who first came to the Hobart area were of British and German descent. Many Germans remained, while some British, having made investments in the area, headed back to the New England states. Between 1850 and 1880, the largest non-English-speaking ethnic group in Indiana was the Germans. The Swedish began settling in Northwest Indiana around 1840 and came to Hobart in the 1860s. Around 1900, Irish and Italians began immigrating to America, with some families coming to the Midwest for farming and manufacturing jobs in the brick and steel industry. Many of the churches were established by these early immigrants, who retained much of their culture and language, until the late 1930s, when pubic schools became predominant and English became the standardized language.

In 1870s America, there was a period of religious revival, a belief that a functioning civilization and the Bible go hand in hand. These adherents also believed that it was the religious institution's role to provide education as part of its service to society. During this time, there was increasing competition among various religious organizations; however, Protestants remained the largest affiliation, with an increasing number of Catholics and Jews immigrating to America. Hobart was no exception during this period. The town saw eight churches established before 1900: Swedish Lutheran (1862), Methodist Episcopal (1871), Roman Catholic (1873), Unitarian (1874), German Methodist Episcopal (1875), German Lutheran (1876), Congregational (1876), and Swedish Methodist (1885). The creation of Sunday schools was part of the religious revival that had started in the late 1860s and went well into the 1880s. Sunday schools began in Hobart around 1864 and were supported by various Methodist congregations. A Christian Sunday school was formed in 1883.

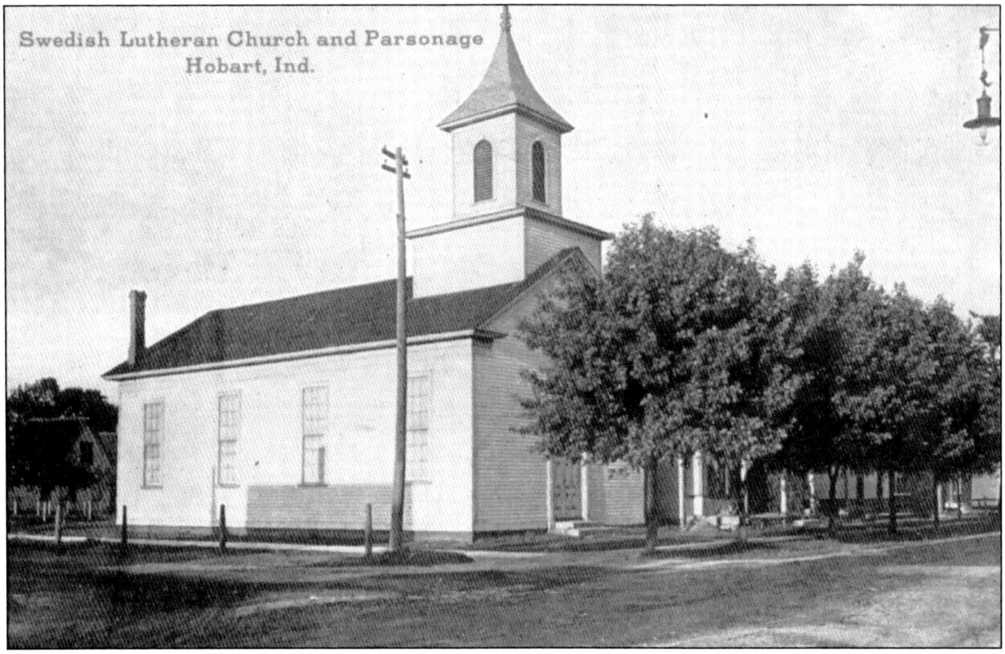

FORMER AUGUSTANA LUTHERAN CHURCH. Construction began on this gable-front building in 1869 and was completed in 1873 on property bought for $1 from George Earle. The church bell, added in 1874, is claimed to be the first church bell in Hobart. The bell has been relocated to the current Augustana Lutheran Church site. The congregation, founded by Swedish immigrants, has the distinction of being the oldest, and it was the first to build a church structure in Hobart.

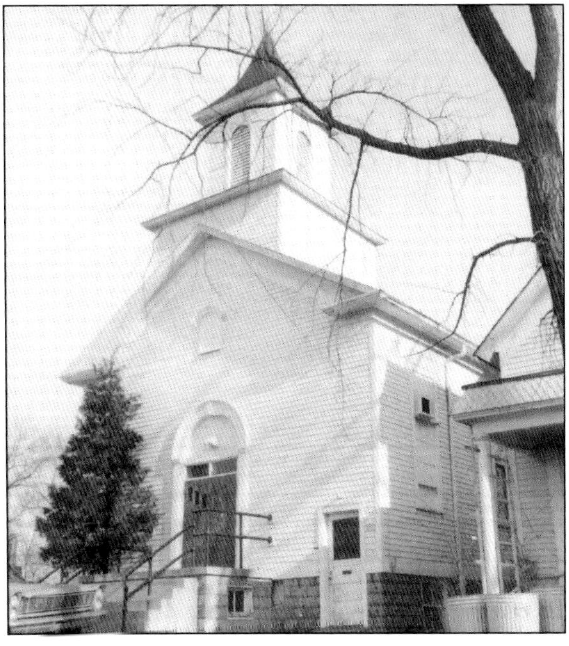

RAISED AUGUSTANA LUTHERAN CHURCH. In 1921, the church added a basement, giving the congregation much-needed space. Controversy arose among the members regarding the stability of raising the church onto a basement foundation. Parishioners in support of a new foundation vowed to climb the roof during the raising of the church to testify to its structural integrity. In 1977, a tornado swept through Hobart, damaging the steeple and completely removing the second floor of an 1869 home at the northeast corner of Third and Linda Streets. The church and home still stand today, the church without its tall steeple, and the home now a business, The Glass Pane, at 804 East Third Street, without its second floor.

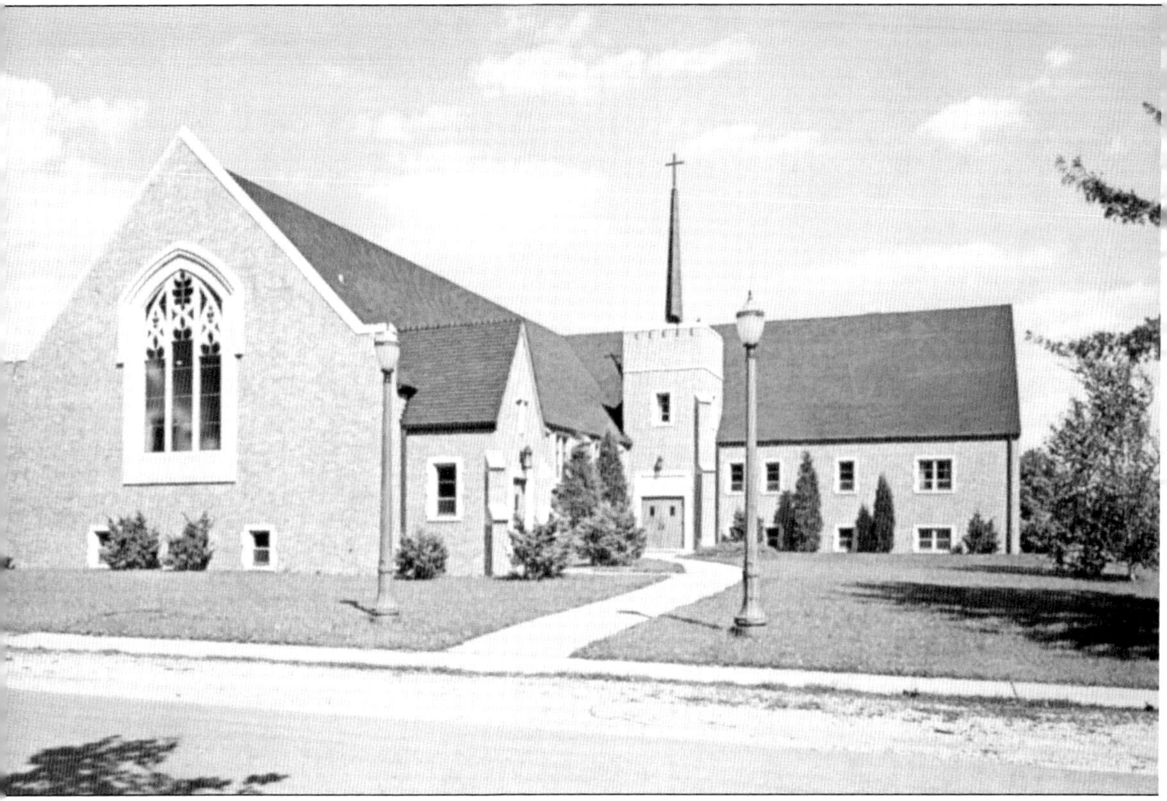

CURRENT AUGUSTANA LUTHERAN CHURCH. Swedish immigrants were drawn to Hobart for its rich farmland and for work prospects in the brickyards. In February 1862, an organizational meeting was held, and a charter group of 18 adults and 2 children was recorded under the church's original name, Swedish Evangelical Lutheran Church. One of the deacons elected was Gustaf Isakson, who has descendants in the church today. The church, which began primarily to serve the Swedish community, today has over 800 members of many ethnicities. In 1952, the congregation purchased property at the northeast corner of Kelly and Hickey Streets for a new building. During a congregation meeting, Clarence Isakson stood up and declared that his grandfather, a founding member, would not have approved of a new building. After this, his brother, Walter Isakson, stood up and declared that his grandfather was also a founding member and that he would definitely have approved a new building. Construction of the new Augustana Lutheran Church began on May 27, 1956, and the structure was dedicated on February 16, 1958.

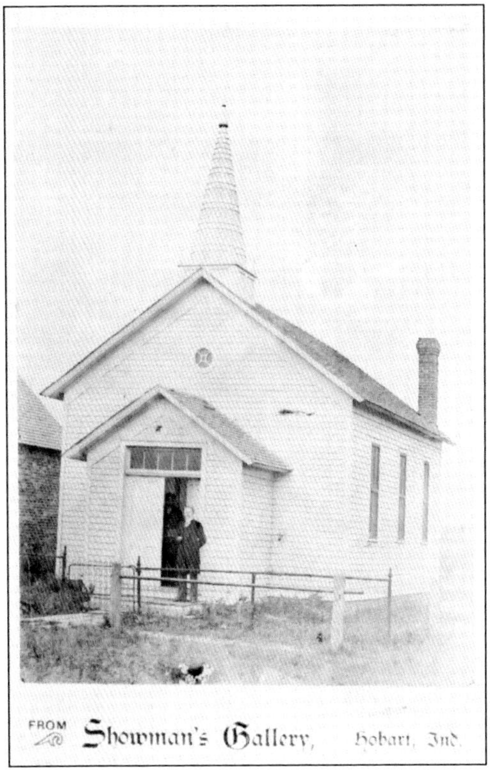

SWEDISH METHODIST EPISCOPAL CHURCH. The congregation formed in 1885 and, in 1889, built a simple white gable-front building with an elaborate conical steeple. The founding congregation still occupies this building, making it Hobart's second-oldest congregation in its original church. The founding congregation was formed by Swedish Methodist immigrants who came to work in the brickyards. John Earle initially offered the congregation a triangular piece of land bounded by Front, Main, and Center Streets, but they preferred to build closer to their parishioners' homes on Michigan Avenue. The church is seen here around 1895.

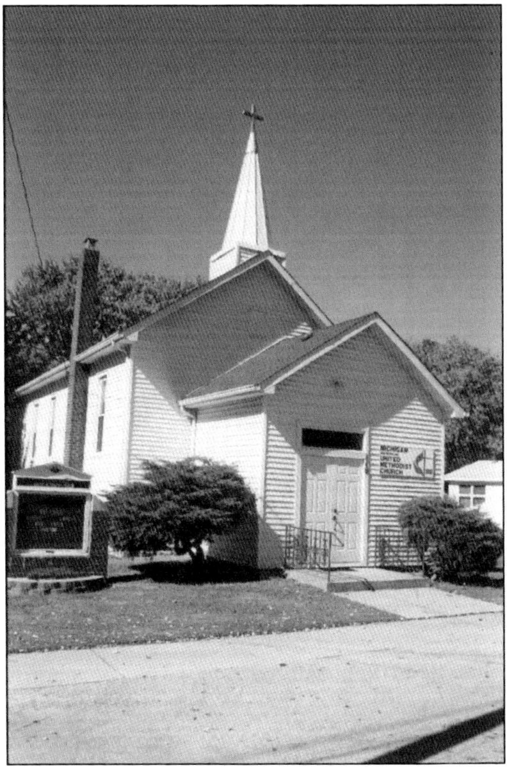

CURRENT SWEDISH M.E. CHURCH. In 1902, the Swedish Methodist Episcopal Church expanded and added space for a pulpit and organ. In 1922, the structure was raised and a basement was added to provide needed space for a furnace and a social room. In 1968, the church was renamed to Michigan Avenue United Methodist Church. A six-and-a-half-foot-by-ten-foot mural, *If Thou Hadst, O Jerusalem*, hangs in the church. The artwork depicts Christ looking out onto a great city. It was restored in 1986 as part of the church's 100th anniversary.

First Methodist Episcopal Church. The congregation organized in 1870, and in 1871 constructed a brick church at the northwest corner of Fourth and East Streets. It has been said that the Methodist Church's bell was hung on February 22, 1872, and rang for the first time that day announcing the death of an infant girl. In the early 1880s the steeple was struck by lightning, causing the bell to crash through the floor of the church and cracking the bell.

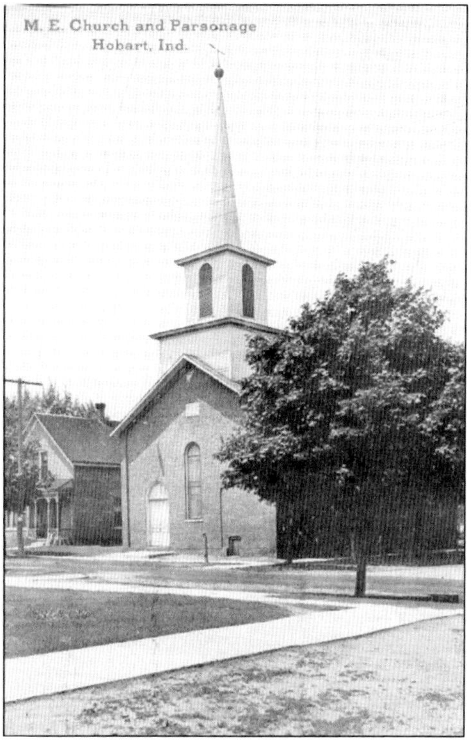

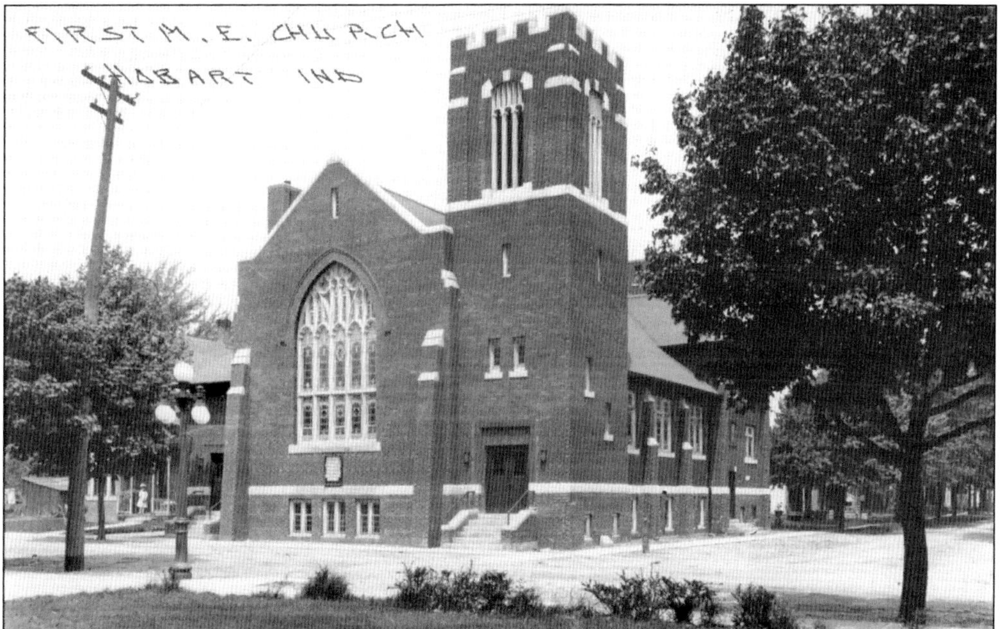

Current First United Methodist Church. This church was constructed in 1916 and dedicated on March 18, 1917. It is an outstanding example of Gothic Revival architecture, with distinctive pointed arch front windows, a castellated parapet, and projecting buttresses. Additions were made in 1955, and then again in 1969 to expand on its educational interests. The congregation has maintained its presence at the northwest corner of Fourth and East Streets since 1871.

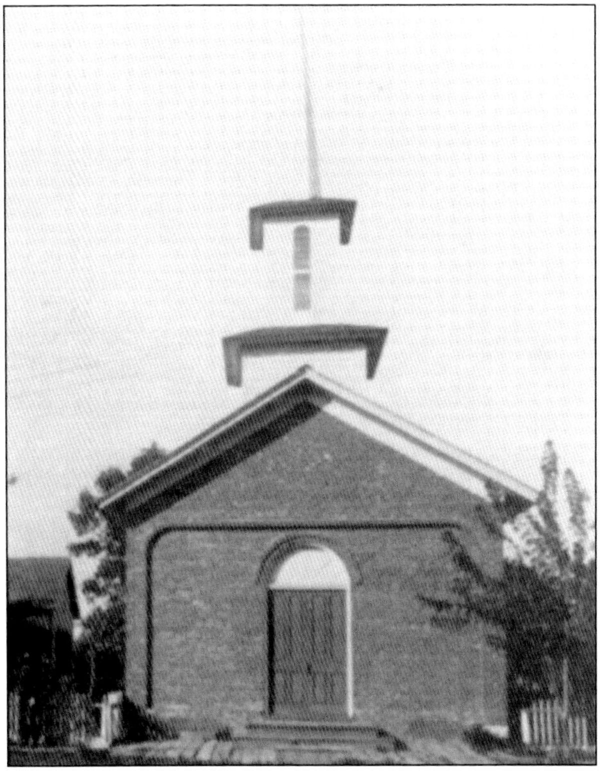

German Trinity Evangelical Lutheran Church. The congregation organized in 1873, and in 1876 it constructed a gable-front Italianate building on land donated by the Earle family. The site is on the northwest corner of the intersection of Center Street and the Nickel Plate Railroad. In 1900, the congregation outgrew its facility and relocated to Main Street. (Courtesy of Trinity Lutheran Church.)

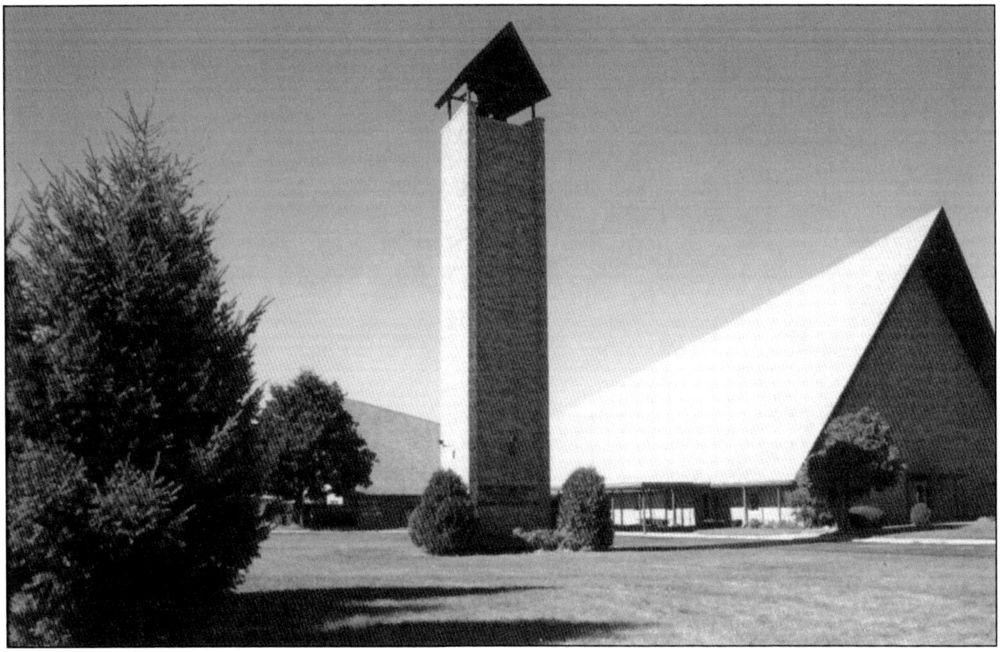

Trinity Lutheran Church and School. The current and third location of the original German Evangelical Lutheran Trinity Church, now identified as Trinity Lutheran Church and School, is at the 800 block of Linda Street and the 900 block of Luther Drive. The Trinity Lutheran Church continues its quality Christian education, which it has offered since its Center Street location.

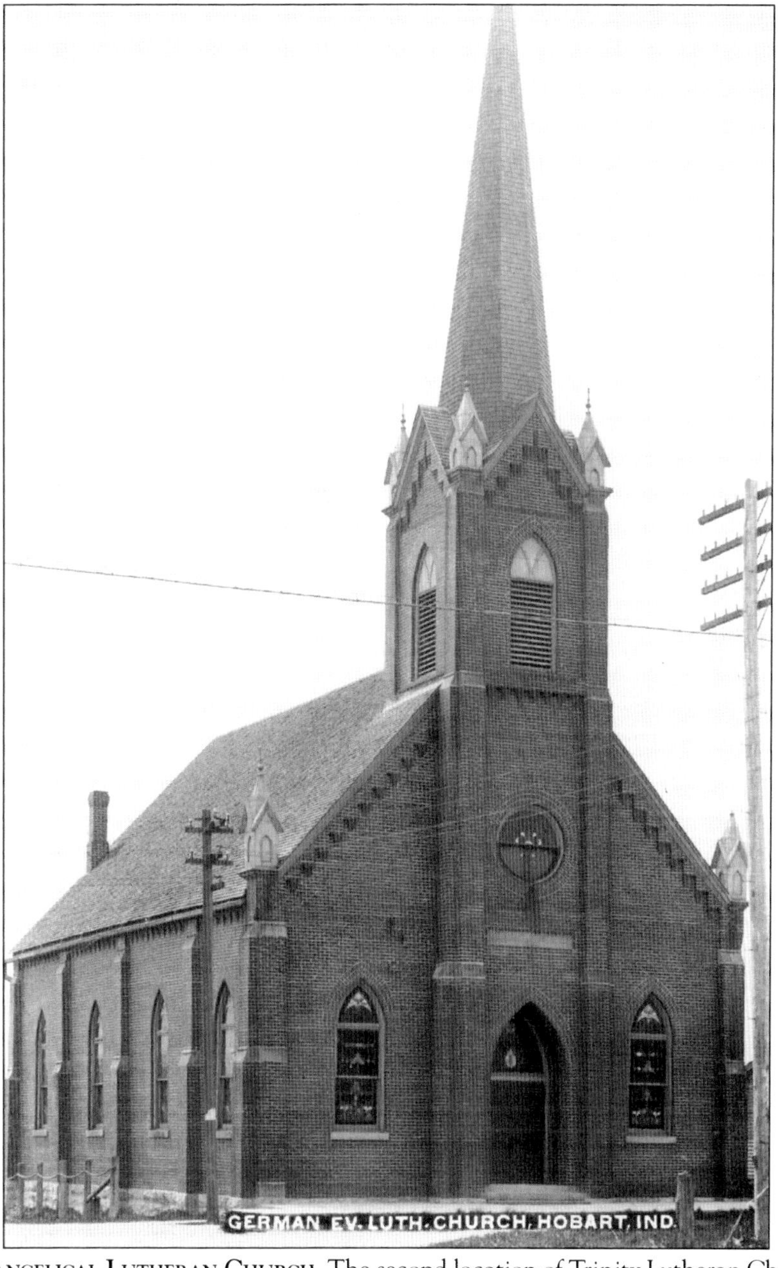

Trinity Evangelical Lutheran Church. The second location of Trinity Lutheran Church was at the northwest corner of Second and Main Streets. The Gothic Revival structure, built in 1900, is shown here around 1910. The architectural features of this church once included pointed arch windows, projecting buttresses, and a Gothic steeple. The nearly 700-member congregation remained at this location until 1963, when the church was razed and the current multi-unit residential complex was built on this site. While the church was on Main Street, the congregation maintained its original Center Street building as a school. Maintaining the Lutheran School at the end of the World War I era proved somewhat of a challenge due to public misunderstanding of the school, which was often referred to as the "German School." An extensive article was published in the *Hobart Gazette* in March 1919 clarifying the misnomers.

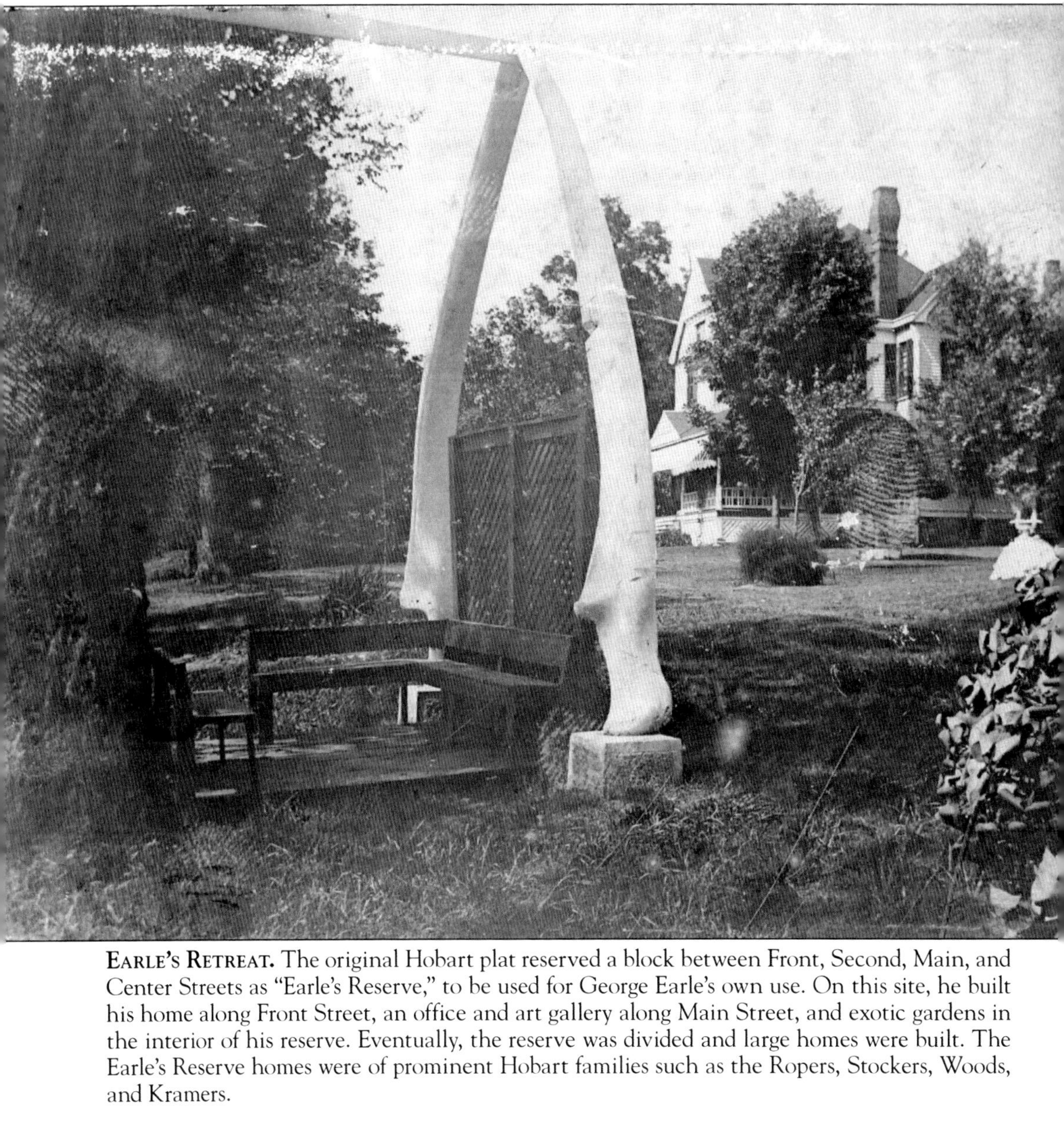

EARLE'S RETREAT. The original Hobart plat reserved a block between Front, Second, Main, and Center Streets as "Earle's Reserve," to be used for George Earle's own use. On this site, he built his home along Front Street, an office and art gallery along Main Street, and exotic gardens in the interior of his reserve. Eventually, the reserve was divided and large homes were built. The Earle's Reserve homes were of prominent Hobart families such as the Ropers, Stockers, Woods, and Kramers.

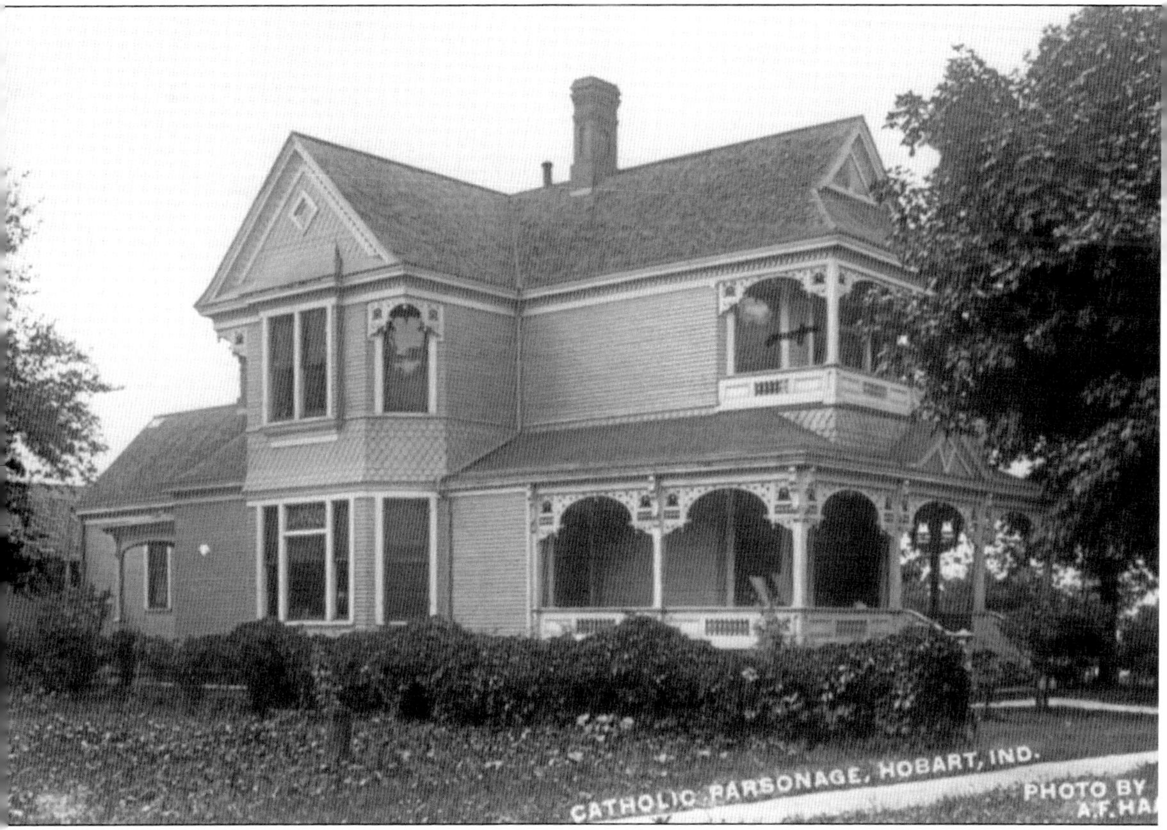

Wood's Home. The 1895 Sanborn map indicates that this Queen Anne–style home of Augustus Wood was "being built." A 1910 Sanborn map identifies the detached structure in back of Wood's home. The concrete sidewalk in the foreground dates this photograph to sometime after 1912, around the time that the home was being used as a parsonage. During the 1950s, Saint Bridget stood immediately north of Wood's home. Eventually, the home was razed for parking.

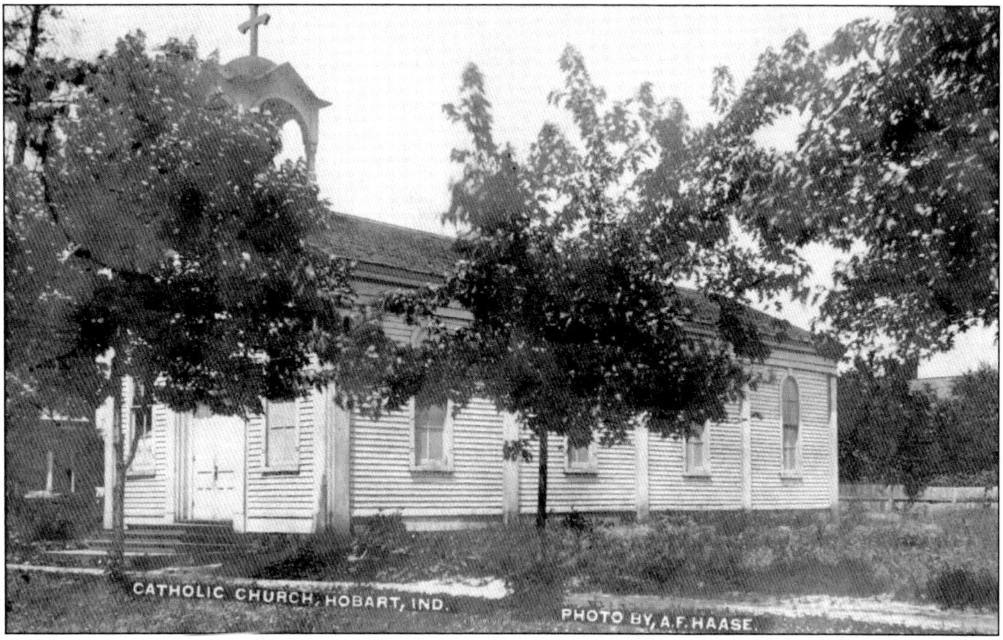

EARLE ART GALLERY. The frame structure was built in 1858 as the Hobart Art Gallery, which displayed over 300 of George Earle's paintings and collections. The gallery was said to attract the interests of many visitors and to bring culture to the area. In 1873, the art gallery and three lots on the east side of Main Street between Front and Second Streets were purchased. The gallery was used as Saint Bridget's first Catholic Church.

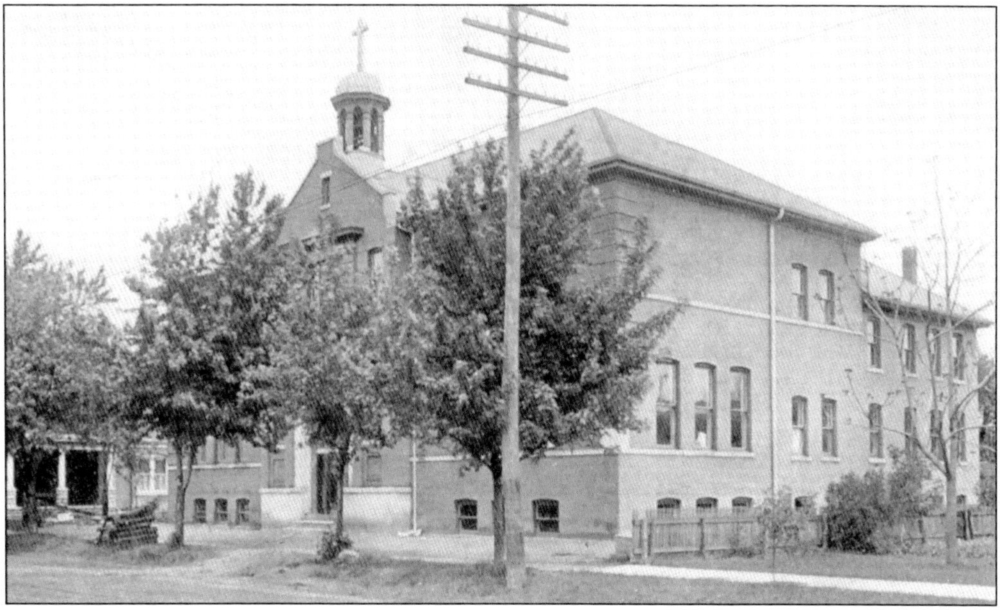

ST. BRIDGET ROMAN CATHOLIC CHURCH. Employment in the Hobart brickyards and railroads generated an influx of Irish and German immigrant families, which created a local demand for Catholic institutions. Mass was held in the former Hobart Art Gallery until August 7, 1911, when the converted church was razed and a new church with a school was dedicated on May 30, 1912, by Bishop J.F. Noll.

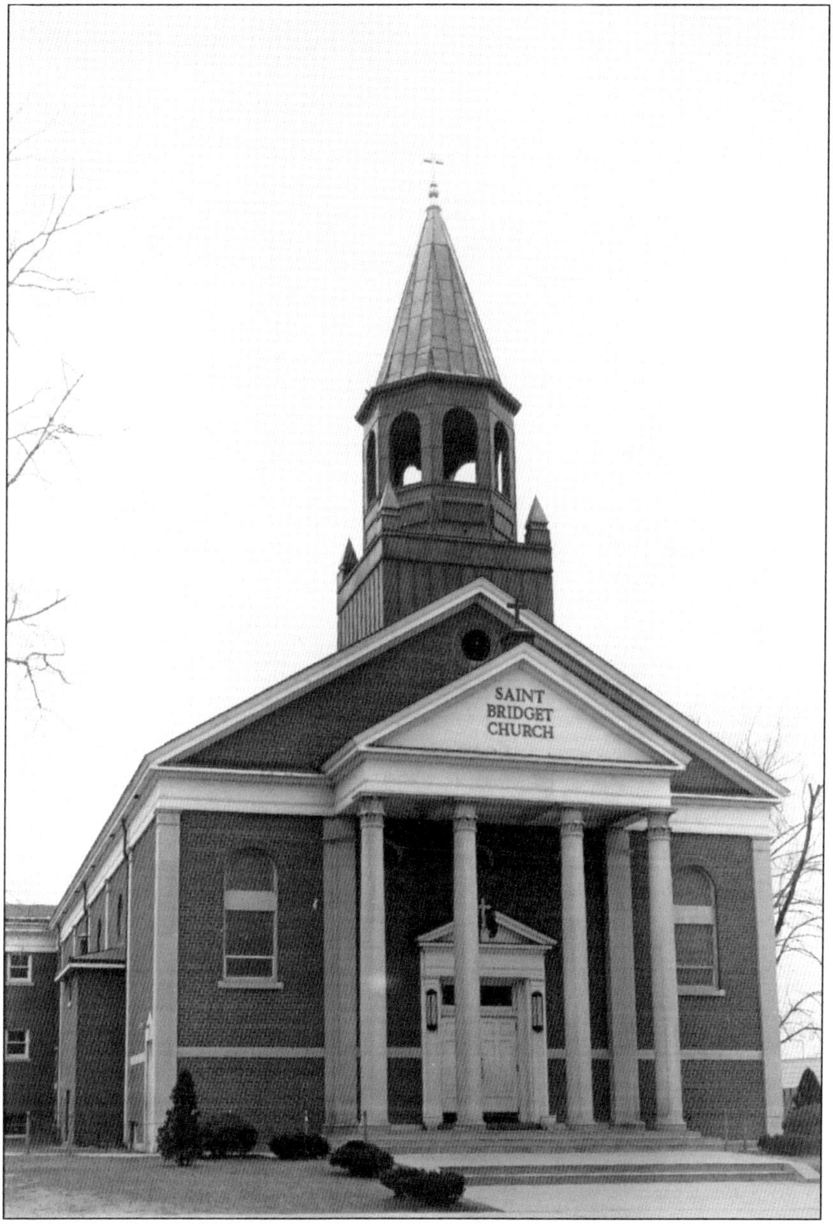

CURRENT ST. BRIDGET CATHOLIC CHURCH. Around 1912, the congregation consisted of 350 parishioners, and it grew steadily until the school opened in 1927. In 1950, the parish's growth required plans to be drawn up for a new Colonial Revival building. The proposed building was constructed on a post-free basement that seated over 500 parishioners. On April 12, 1953, ground was broken, and on September 13, 1953, the cornerstone ceremony was held. The new church was dedicated on June 27, 1954. The old church was renovated and used for school purposes until the summer of 1964, when work began on a new school on the southeast corner of Main and Front Streets. The school, completed in 1966, held 16 classrooms, a library, a cafeteria, offices, and meeting rooms. In 1968, the convent was built at the northwest corner of Second and Main Streets, and in 1987, a gymnasium was added near the northeast corner of Second and Main Streets. By the 1990s, what was once Earle's Reserve had become the St. Bridget complex.

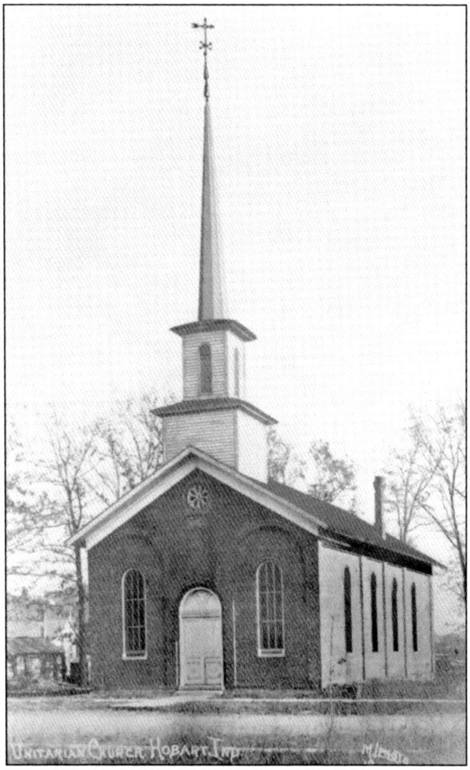

First Unitarian Church. The Unitarian congregation formed in 1874 in Hobart. On January 27, 1876, the church bell rang, announcing the church's completion on land purchased from the Earle family for $1, at the northeast corner of Main and Fifth Streets. When the church was dedicated, it was considered to be at the edge of the village. The Unitarian Church was the first church in Indiana constructed by a Unitarian congregation. The First Unitarian Church also has the distinction of being the oldest Hobart congregation still occupying its first church. The parish house along Fifth Street was added in 1953.

Current Unitarian Church. The church, which still has its original front doors, was listed in the National Register of Historic Places on September 9, 1999. The gable-front Italianate design was done by Pollard, O.D. & Co.

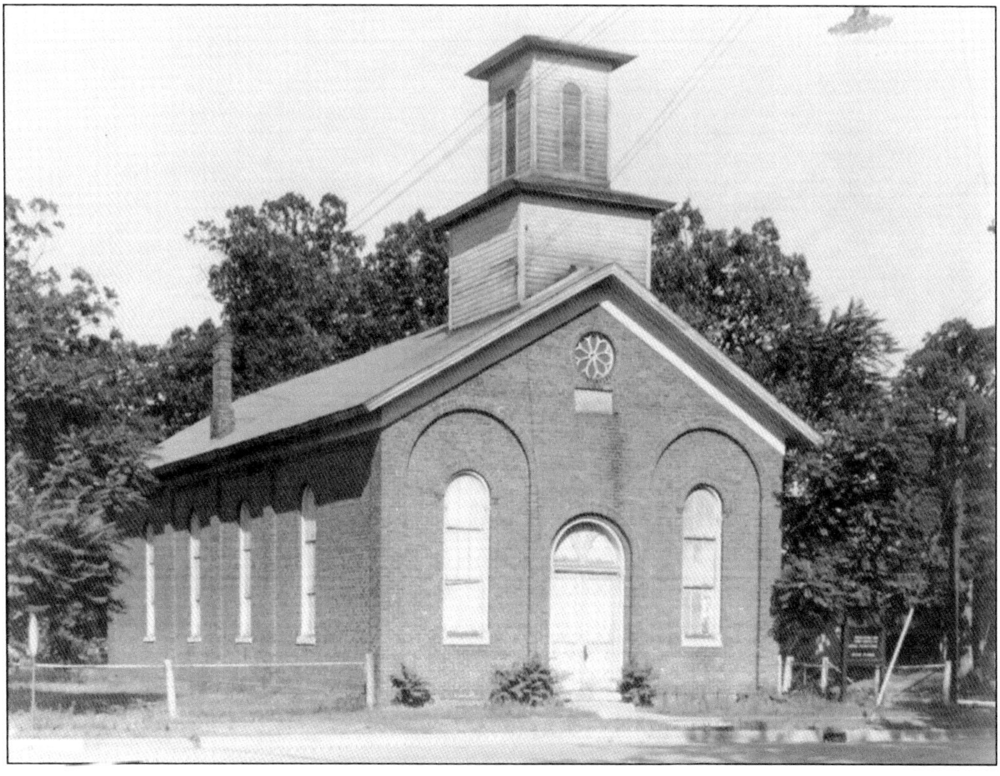

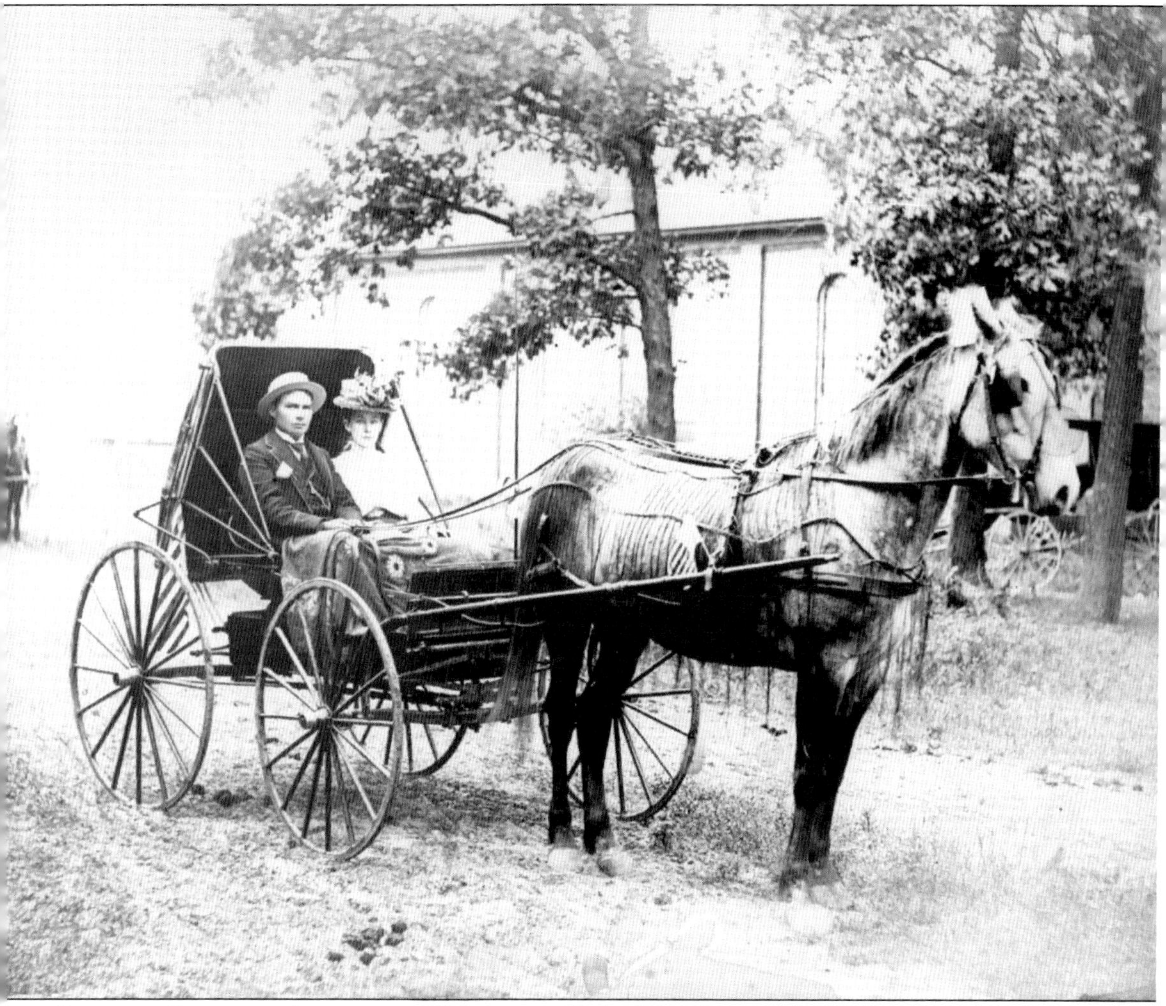

Carriage Ceremony. It was reported that some Hobart couples would celebrate their wedding ceremony on the Fourth of July, and that the festivities would occur at the "grove," also known as the "commons" or "lover's lane," which was located between Fifth and Sixth Streets on the east side of Main Street. Here, Robert Rossow is on a date in a horse-drawn carriage on Fifth Street. This scene took place in the early 1900s during a Fourth of July celebration. The Unitarian church is seen in the background.

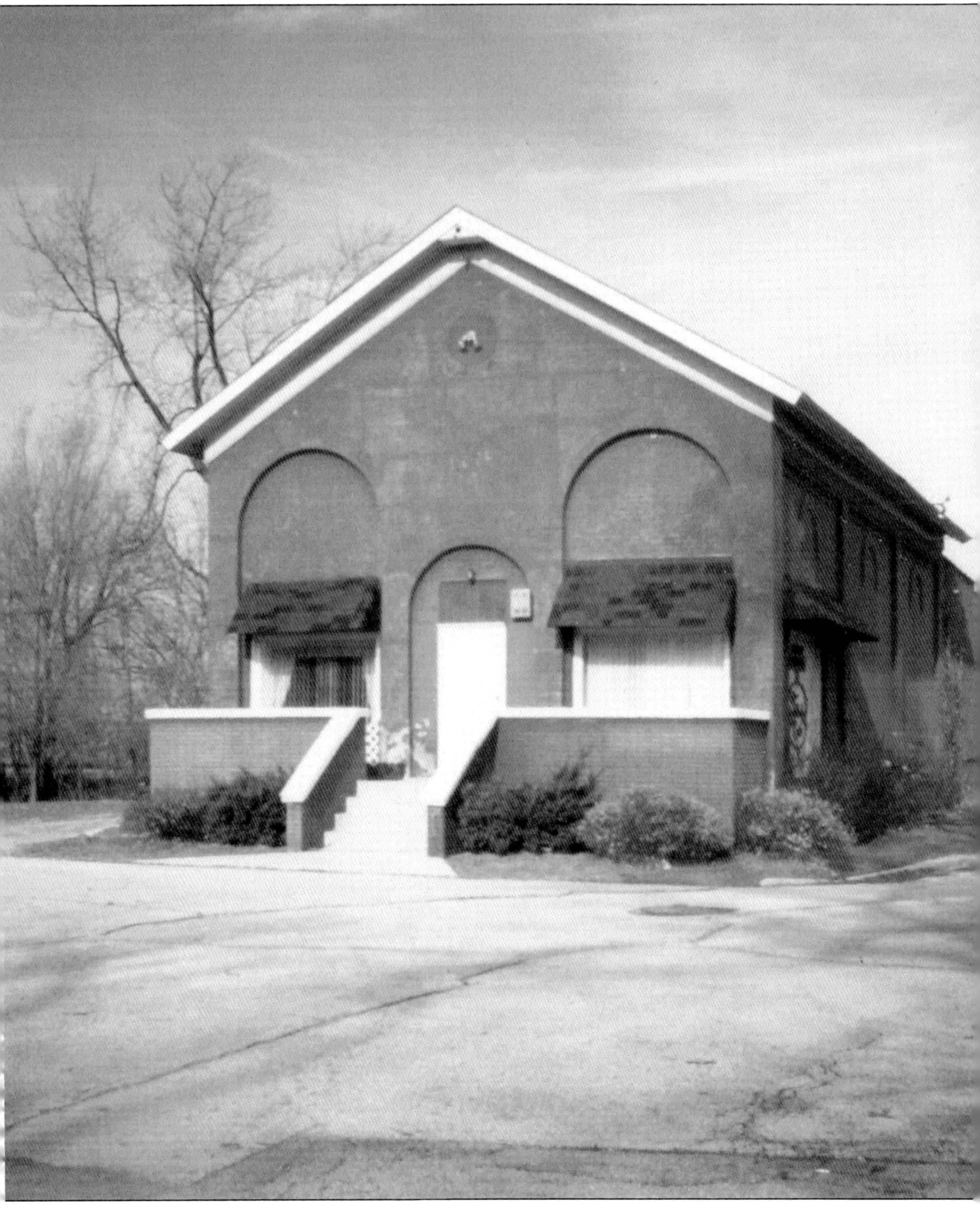

GERMAN ZION SOCIETY, METHODIST EPISCOPAL CHURCH. Located on the north side of Fifth Street at the intersection of Lake and Fifth Streets is an 1875 gable-front Italianate building. The congregation remained small, and in 1914, the church closed. In 1916, a 30-foot addition was built at the rear of the original structure.

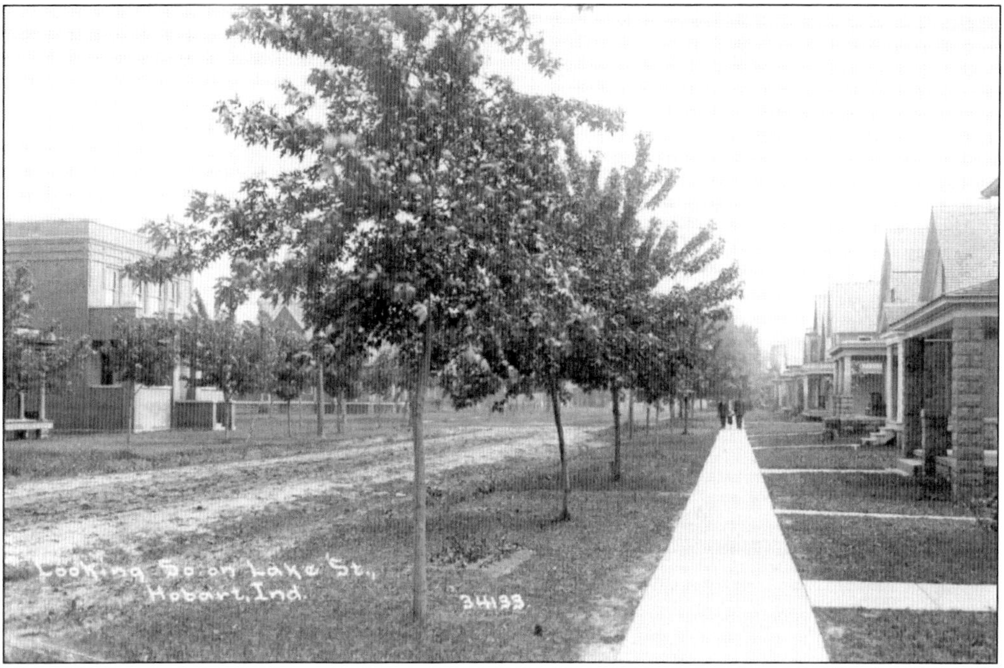

LAKE STREET. The above photograph, facing south from the intersection of Lake and Fifth Streets, shows an intact turn-of-the-19th-century residential neighborhood. Above, brick gable homes line the right side of the 500 block of Lake Street, with a Vernacular apartment building on the left. At the southeast corner of Lake and Sixth Streets is a Queen Anne home. An American Four Square home is at 615 Lake Street, and just south of that is the Union Mission Church site. The first home on the right, at the southwest corner of Lake and Sixth Streets, still stands today but its wraparound porch has been enclosed.

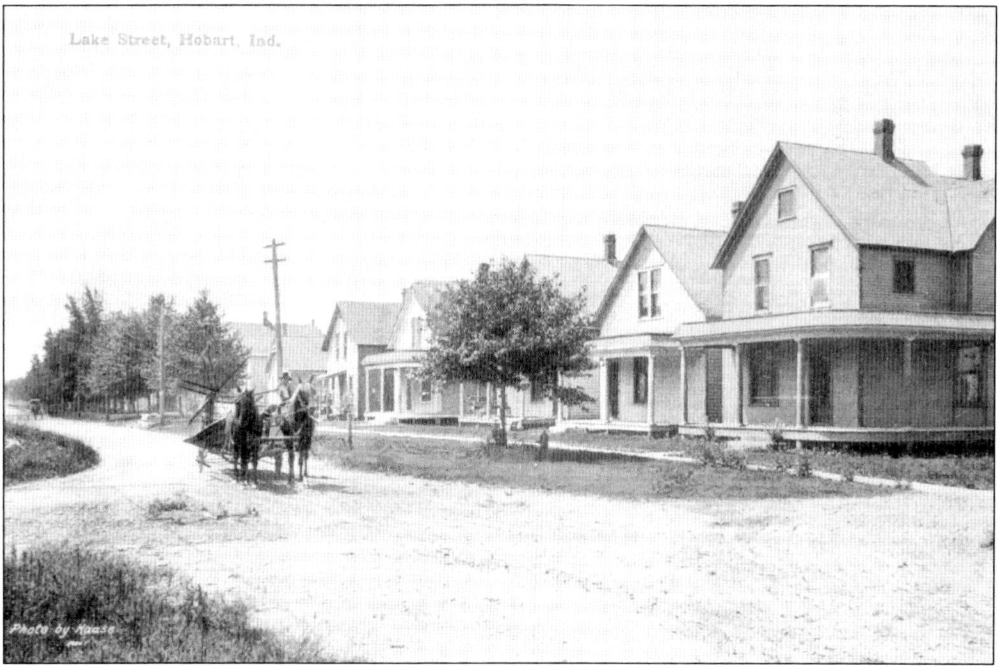

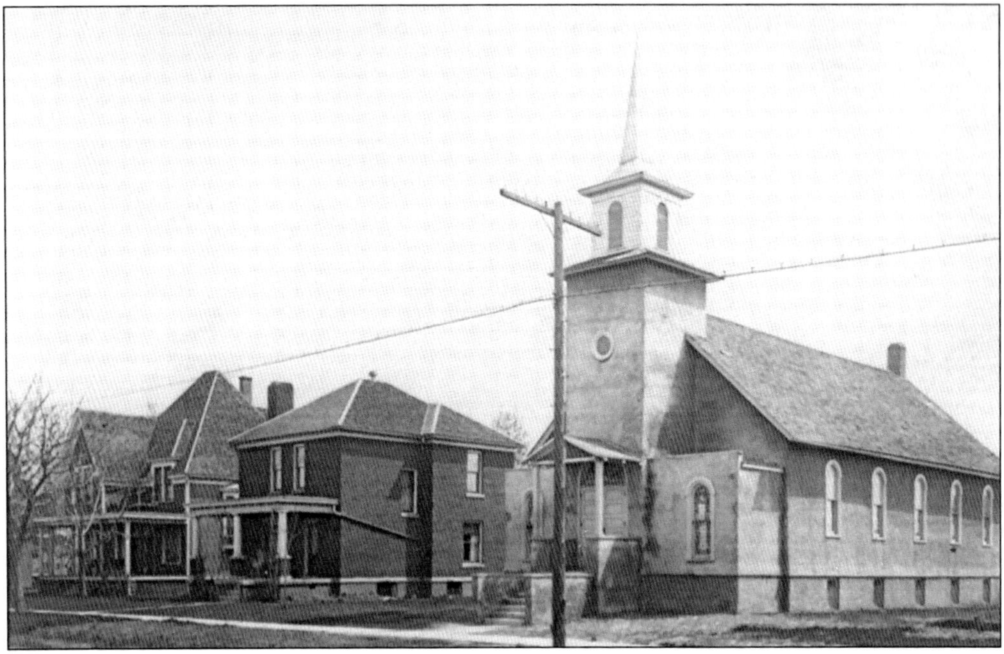

UNION MISSION CHURCH. In 1876, a nondenominational congregation formed in Hobart and created the Union Mission Church. The congregation built an edifice on the east side of Lake Street, south of Sixth Street, in 1877. In 1948, the church burned down and was rebuilt on the same site.

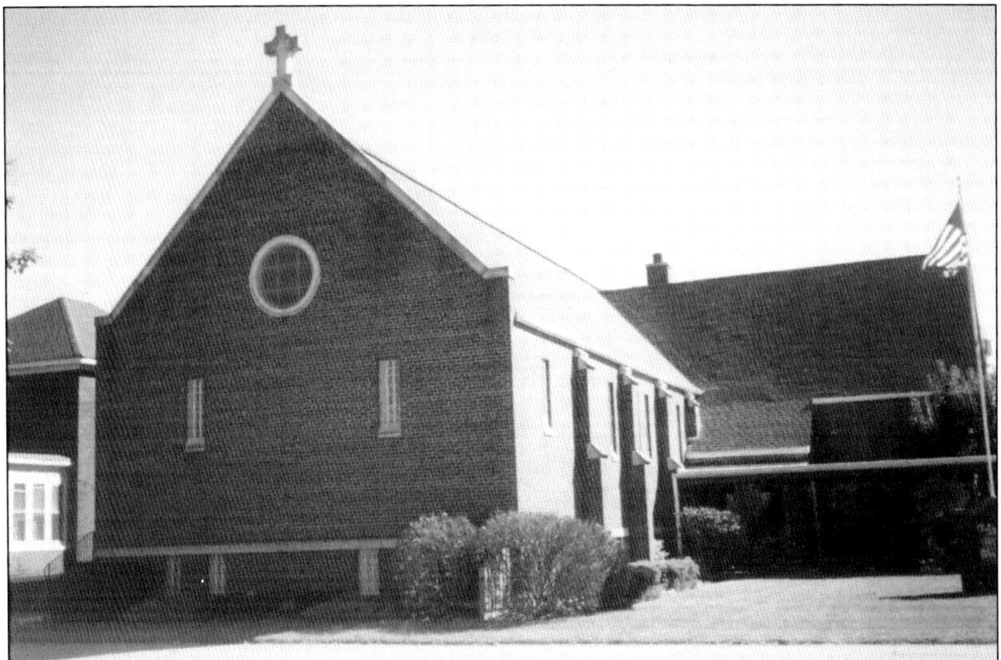

CHRISTIAN UNION CHURCH. The Union Mission Church reformed and became the Congregational Church, and the building was known as the "Tabernacle." The Christian Union Church, or Tabernacle Society, was eventually purchased and used by the First Christian Church. Currently, the church is home to Suncrest Christian Church.

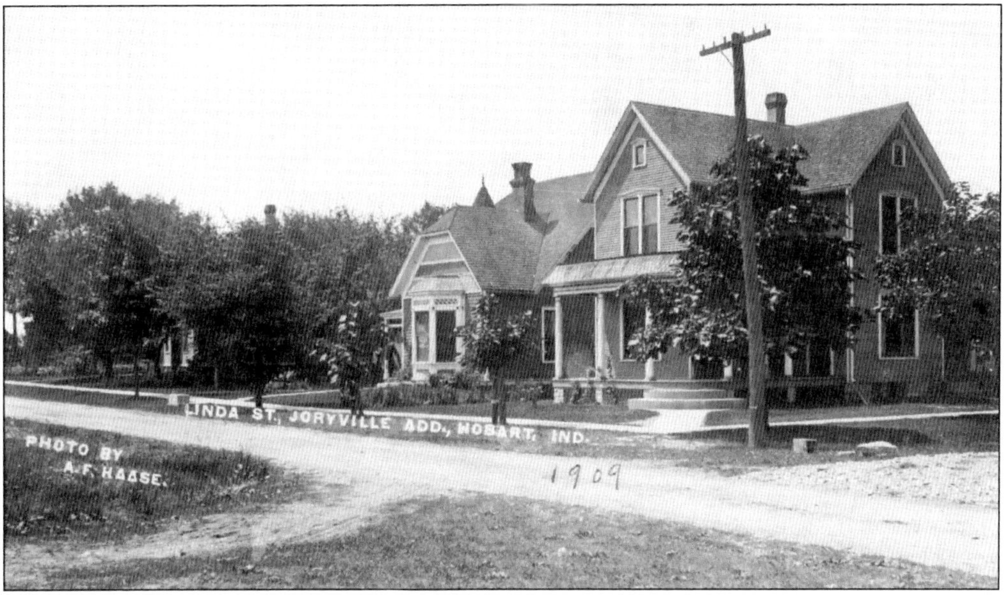

JORYVILLE. An area of approximately five acres, south of the former EJ&E right-of-way along Linda Street, east of Lincoln Street, and north of Eighth Street, was referred to as a Hobart suburb in the 1890s. It eventually became a neighborhood subdivision. The neighborhood was created by Thomas Jory, who was the town's undertaker and a furniture retailer. The home shown here, on the southwest corner of Linda and Eighth Streets, still stands. The home to the left, the Jory family home, no longer stands.

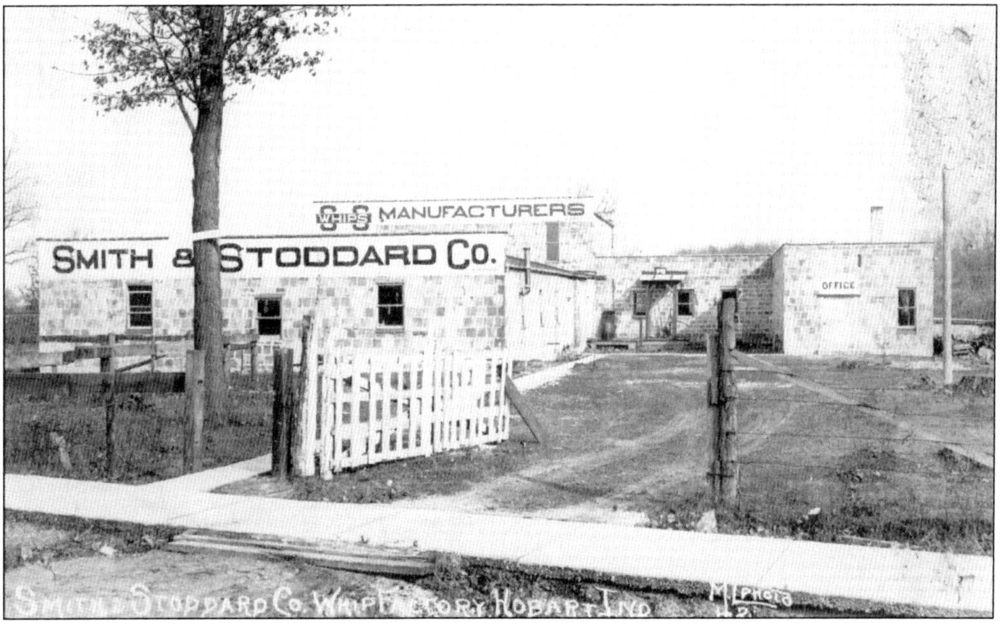

SMITH & STODDARD WHIP COMPANY. At the turn of the 20th century, Smith & Stoddard was one of Hobart's largest employers. This northeast-facing photograph was taken just south of the EJ&E tracks. Seen here is the back of the Smith & Stoddard building, on the east side of Main Street. Today, the site is occupied by a True Value store owned by Hobart Lumber, which has served Hobart since 1915.

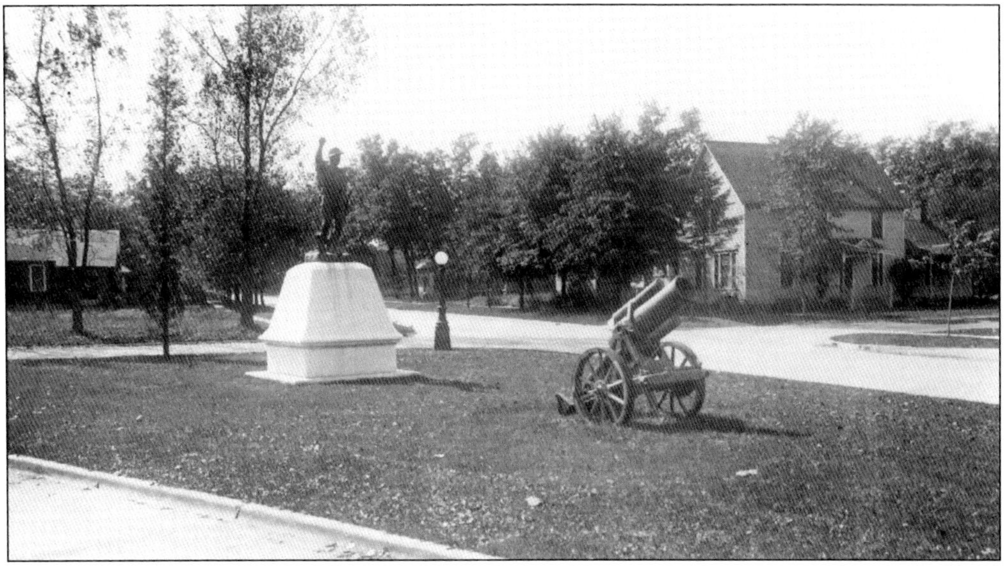

DOUGHBOY. Hobart's doughboy was dedicated on November 11, 1925, on a triangular piece of land donated by the Earle family in 1922. It is a reproduction of a life-sized sculpture titled *Spirit of the American Doughboy* by Ernest More "Dick" Visquesney. The sculpture was installed by American Legion Post No. 54. A cannon was once located on the site, but it was probably scrapped for metal during World War II. Plaques on the statue identify nearly 100 Hobart lives lost in war. The grass has been replaced with brick pavers that identify Hobart veterans.

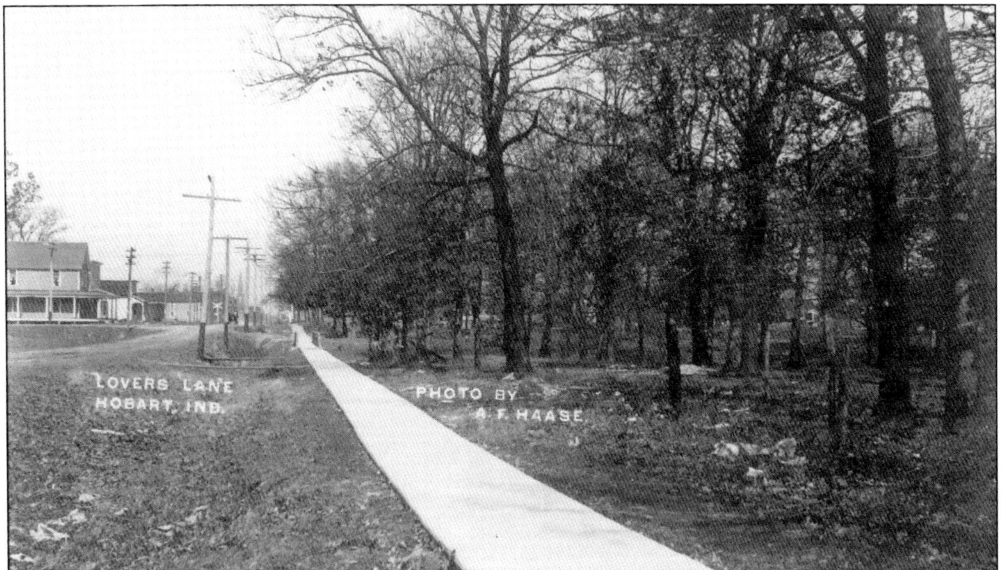

MAIN STREET. This north-facing photograph looks into downtown Hobart from Main Street, just north of the EJ&E line and south of Sixth Street. Seen here are the Trinity Lutheran Church steeple and the Strattan Building screening tower in the distance. The photograph was taken along the east side of Main Street near an area once identified as the "town commons." The two-story frame house on the left is the current site of the Dairy Queen. The Frey family opened the Dairy Queen in 1951. At the time, it was the second Dairy Queen in Indiana. In the 1970s, a new building was constructed. A dining room was added in 1991.

Three

Heart of a Community

In 1893, it was written that, "some think Hobart looks tough but if they visit some towns, they will be convinced that our streets are kept remarkably clean." The following year, it was reported that Hobart's aggregate for 1893 was "a phenomenally prosperous growth during a season of financial depression. . . . Hobart is one of the most enterprising and pushing towns of which we have any knowledge." These statements testify to what lies at the heart of the community, including the many transportation opportunities that have helped keep downtown Hobart viable.

Transportation opportunities affect the development of a community. Among transportation options are roads, rail lines, waterways, and even streetcars, all of which have helped the exchange of various goods and services. In Hobart, some of the earliest goods were products of local sawmills and gristmills. The goods were transported via waterways. The attractiveness of these types of mill structures was based on function and reliability. As advancements in goods and services continued to evolve and facilitate the development of villages, consumers' interests changed, and the presentation of the products did as well. Product competition forced merchants to change American business by incorporating product display (marketing) of their goods and services.

Downtown Hobart's commercial and public buildings of the late 19th and early 20th century represent American optimism and growth. In the late 1800s, new building materials and transportation advancements gave downtown proprietors the opportunity to make their investments more attractive through affordable pressed metal and cast-iron molding and cornice details. Also, advancements in structural engineering allowed business owners to widen window displays and upgrade facades to make their buildings more attractive. Decorative wood panels and transoms also were incorporated. It was common for two-story buildings to use decorative pressed metal window hoods with complementary cornice. Also, an apex, steeple, or merchant's name became part of the building's architectural integrity.

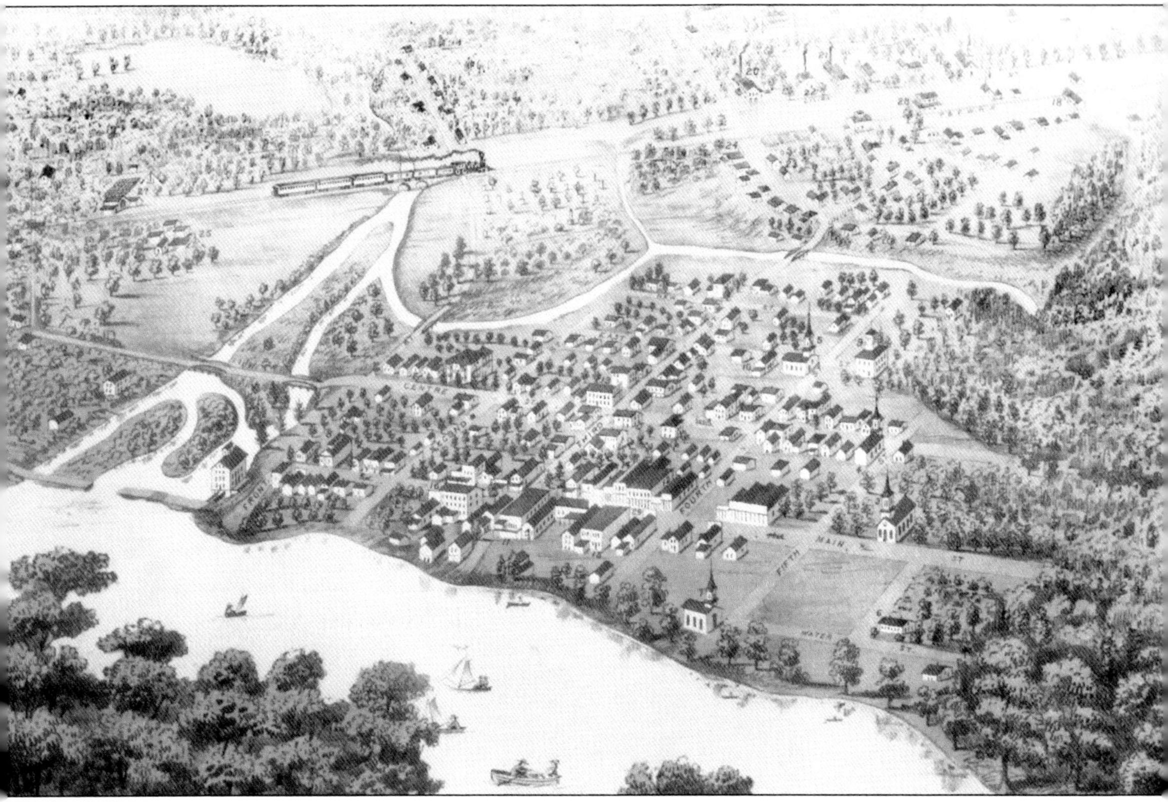

BIRD'S-EYE VIEW. In 1877, Hobart was fast approaching a population of 600. It was said that Hobart, still a village, had the "air of a city." This 1877 rendering accurately reflects village life in Hobart, with the Pittsburgh, Fort Wayne & Chicago Railway train rolling by in the background and boaters on Lake George in the foreground. In the upper left are the early brickyards of Nash, Guyer, Holmes, and Waterbury, as well as a pottery yard. In the upper right are the planing mills, lumberyards, foundry, and the Scholl hay press. During this time, Hobart had secured itself as a manufacturing community, while the Pennsy Depot kept busy exporting nearby agricultural goods and brickyard and lumberyard products. Shown here are seven of the first eight churches in town, as well as the Hobart School. The Rifenburg Home, Earle's Mills, Hobart House, and the Stocker Building are also represented in this bird's-eye view. One notable missing structure is the Third Street Bridge over Lake George. Since 1847 the growth of the Hobart settlement has been gradual, but substantial enough to attract many in the service industry, such as bakers, lawyers, doctors, furniture makers and retailers, drugstore and dry-goods storekeepers, undertakers, dress- and shoemakers, and restaurateurs, as well as many social and fraternal organizations.

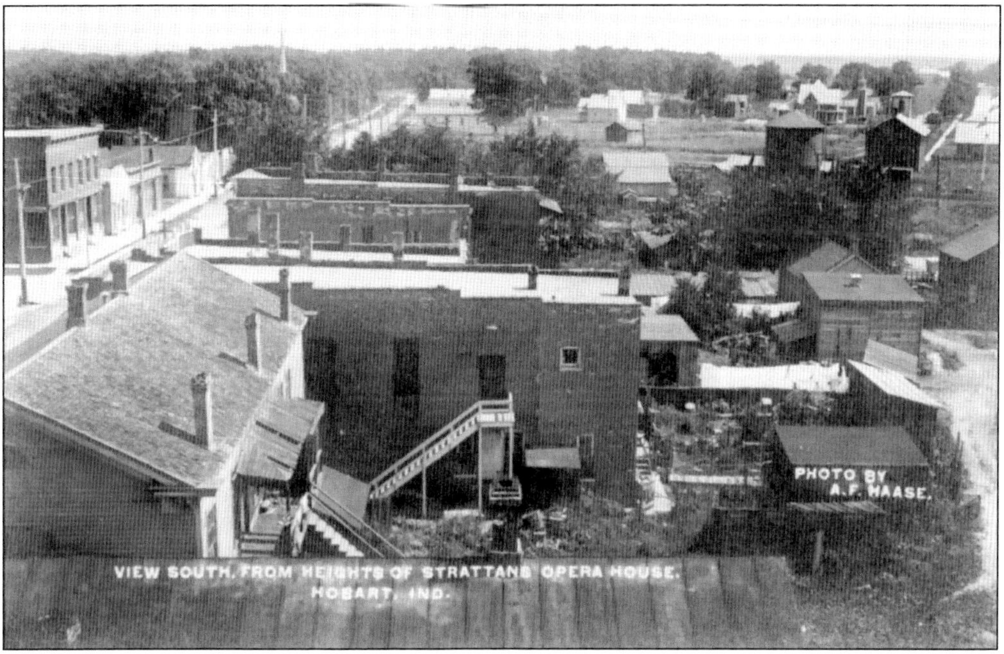

400 BLOCK OF MAIN STREET, C. 1912. This south-facing photograph predates the construction of the Carstensen Building at 411–413 Main Street. In the upper right is the German Methodist Church on Fifth Street. In the upper left, on the southeast corner of Main and Second Streets, is the Odd Fellows Hall, constructed in 1885 on land donated by the Earle family. In the mid-1900s, the building was used as the Liechty Hatchery, later known as the Hobart Hatchery. Over the years, this structure has undergone several facade changes and is now home to Ginter Realty, a long-time business in the city.

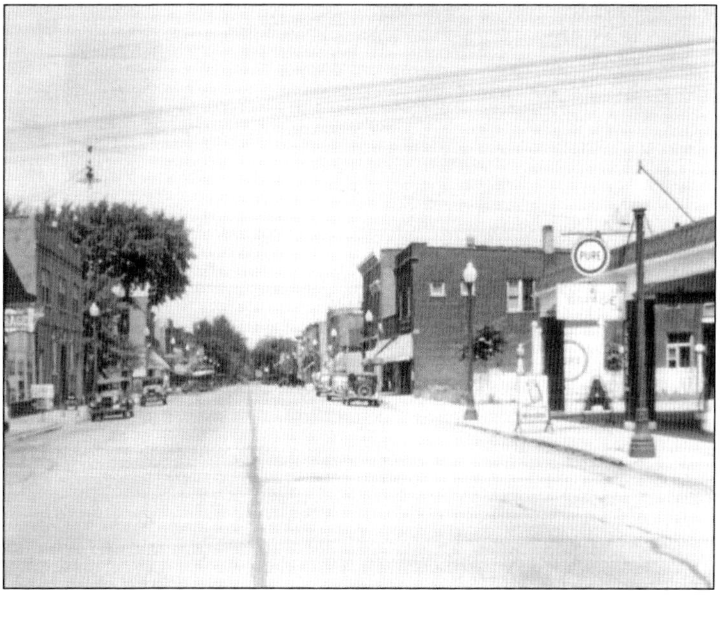

400 BLOCK OF MAIN STREET. This is a north-facing photograph of Main Street, taken from the Nickel Plate Railroad. At right of center is the two-story brick Carstensen Building. It was constructed around 1915 by Anna Carstensen for her meat market. Eventually, George Sauter bought it for a grocery store. The second floor was used as a residence, and the structure still stands at 411–413 Main Street.

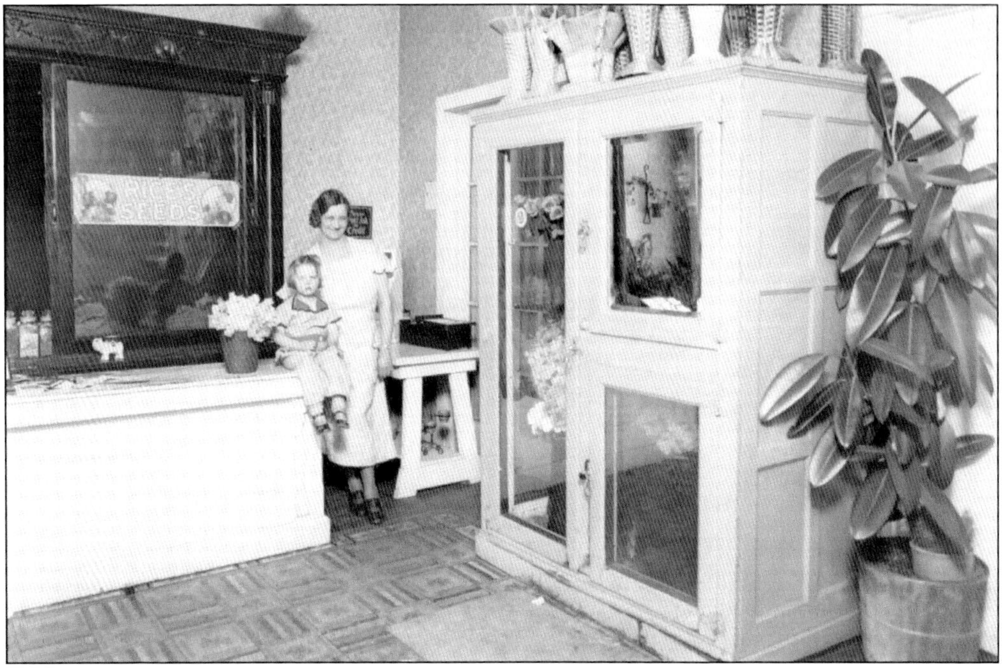

Kellen's Interior. Hobart's oldest florist was established in 1928 by Neil and Marie Kellen. It was originally located north of the Carstensen Building at 409 Main Street. In 1970, the business relocated to its current location at 342 Main Street. (Courtesy of Nic Holzmer.)

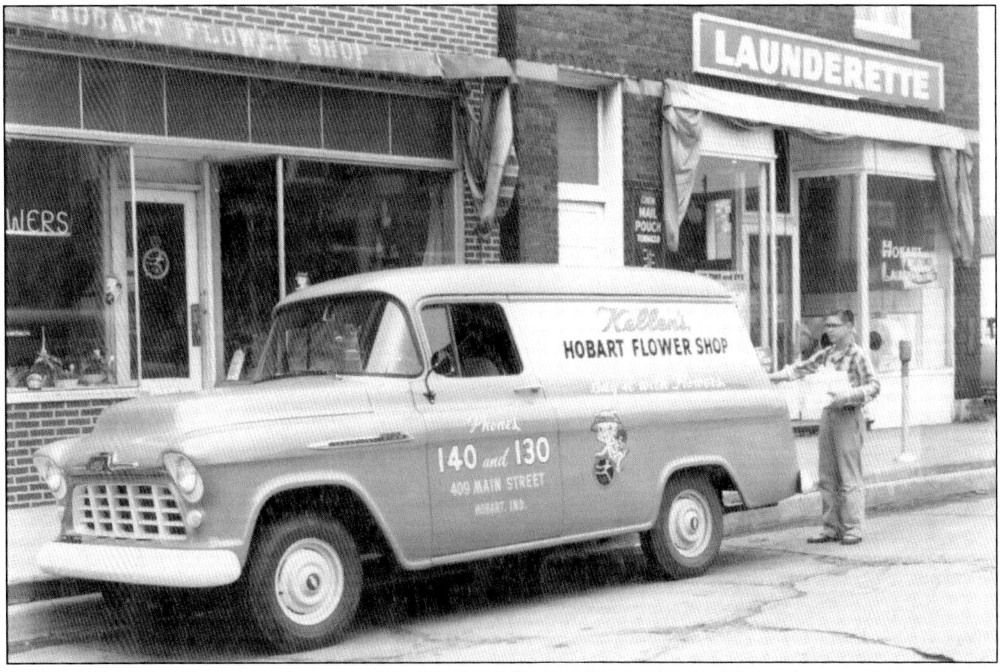

409–413 Main Street. Seen on the left is Kellen's Flower Shop. Next door to it is Hobart Launderette, which was formerly Sauter Grocery. The building was then sold to Ed Gernsey, who sold it to Mr. Harkins. Eventually, this space became the office of the *Hobart Gazette* from 1989 to 1998. (Courtesy of Nic Holzmer.)

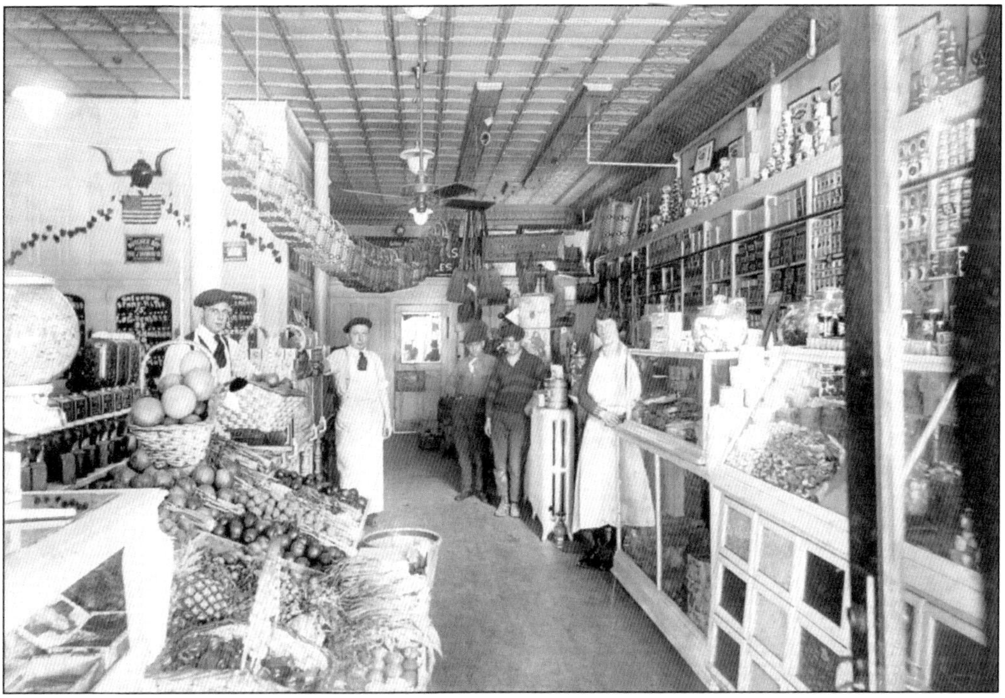

SAUTER GROCERY. George Sauter went into business operating a combination grocery store and meat market. Anna Carstensen had owned a meat market at this location, 413 Main Street. Sauter had gained experience years before clerking at Stommel & Co. at the Union Block on Third Street. The grocery is seen here around 1920.

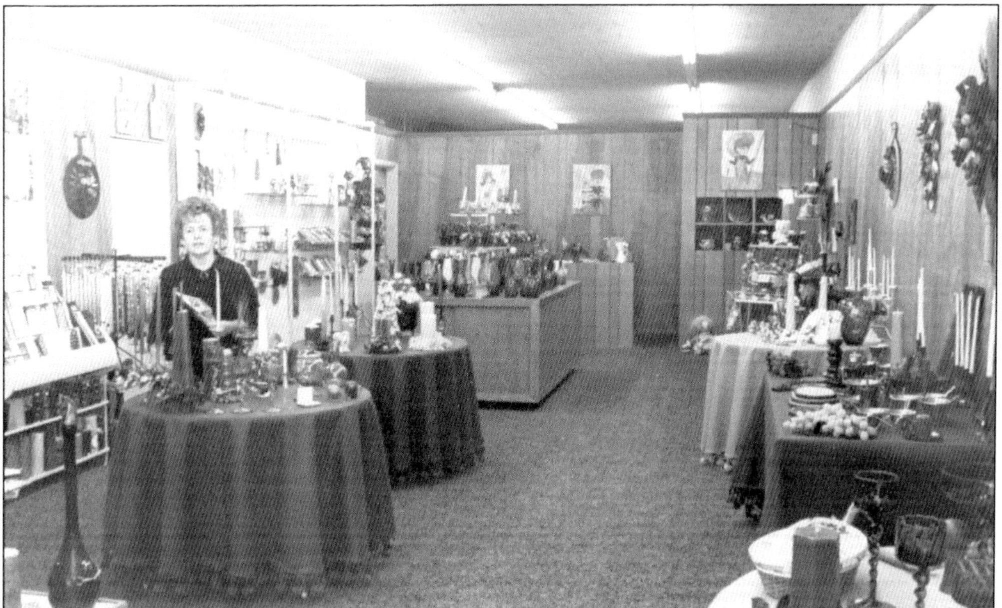

CANDLE GLOW SHOPPE. In the 1970s, this was a popular shop for gift-giving and home-decor items for Hobart residents. It was located at 325 Main Street. Seen here is the shop's proprietor, Dorris Mayer.

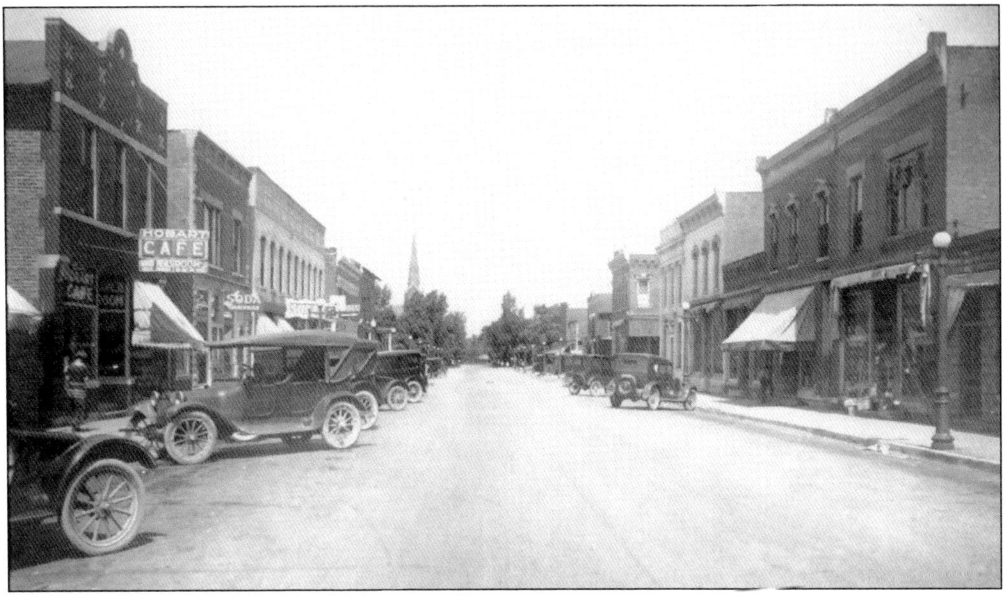

300 Block of Main Street. This c. 1929 photograph, looking north from Fourth Street, shows the George Stocker buildings on the right, constructed between 1888 and 1909. On the left, from near to far, are the Orcutt building; the Morton building, constructed in 1907 and once the location of Walgreens; and the Strattan Opera house, later Hobart Hardware.

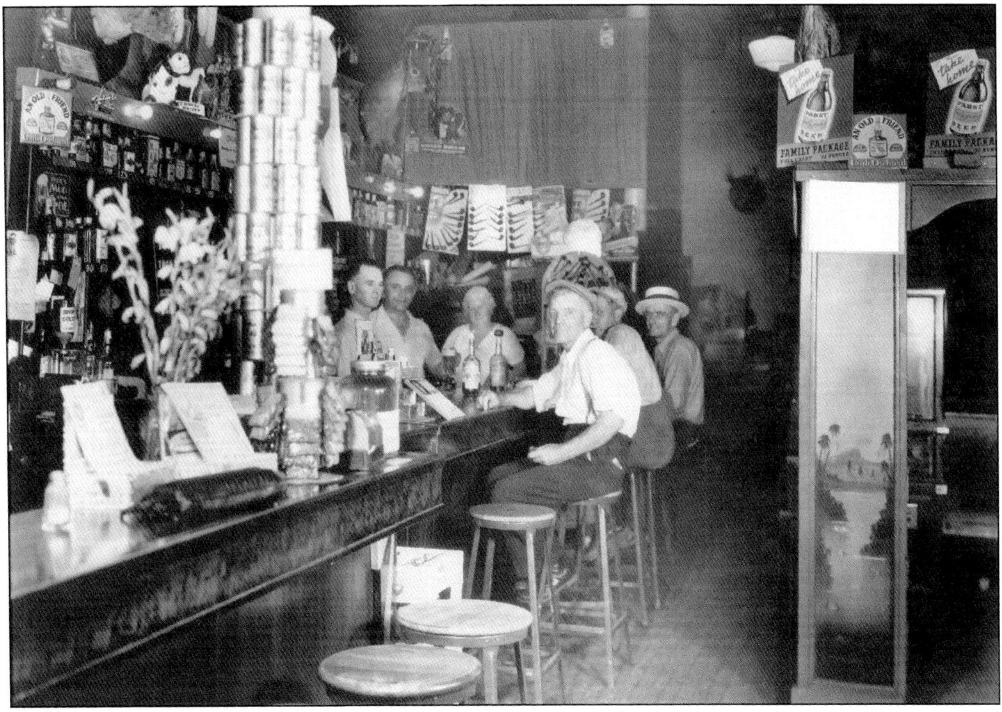

Bates Tavern. In 1921, the Mander Building, at 314 Main Street, operated as a variety store and post office until it was reconstructed in brick by John Mander's son-in-law, Albert Orcutt. After the reconstruction, this building opened as a restaurant and hotel, and then became the popular Pete Bates Tavern, as seen here. It is the current home of the End Zone.

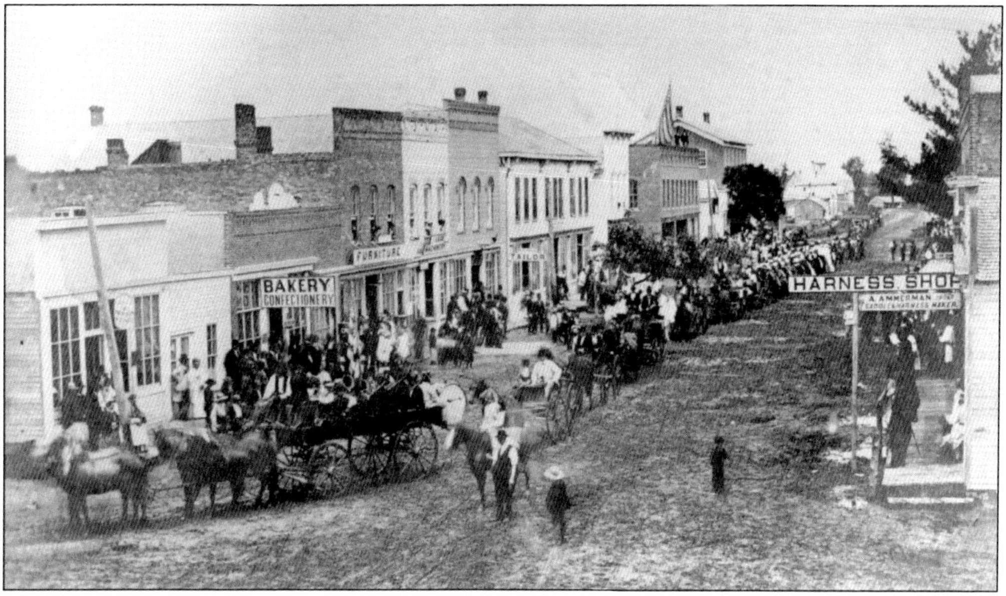

300 Block of Main Street, West View. This photograph was taken in 1876, when Hobart celebrated the American centennial on dirt roads and wooden sidewalks. In the distance is the "Old Mill," followed by the nine-year-old Hobart House and the newly constructed Strattan Building at the southeast corner of Third and Main Streets. The harness shop at right is the site of Odell-Smith Jeweler, which has been in business on Main Street since 1866. Odell-Smith rebuilt the northeast corner of Fourth and Main Streets in 1934.

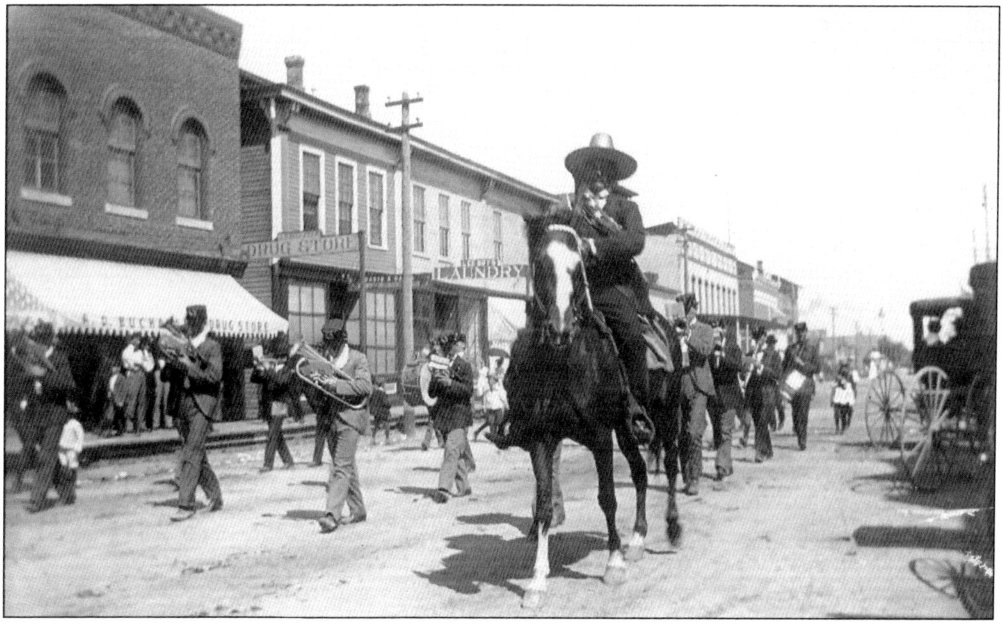

300 Block of Main Street, North View. In October 1897, Buchanan Drug Store began business on the west side of the 300 block of Main Street. Mid-block is a two-story, three-unit frame structure that was replaced in 1928 by Albert Verplank with a four-unit, single-story commercial edifice. The Verplank Building, still standing, was constructed of gold-colored pressed brick, decorative terra-cotta tiles, and prism glass on the facade.

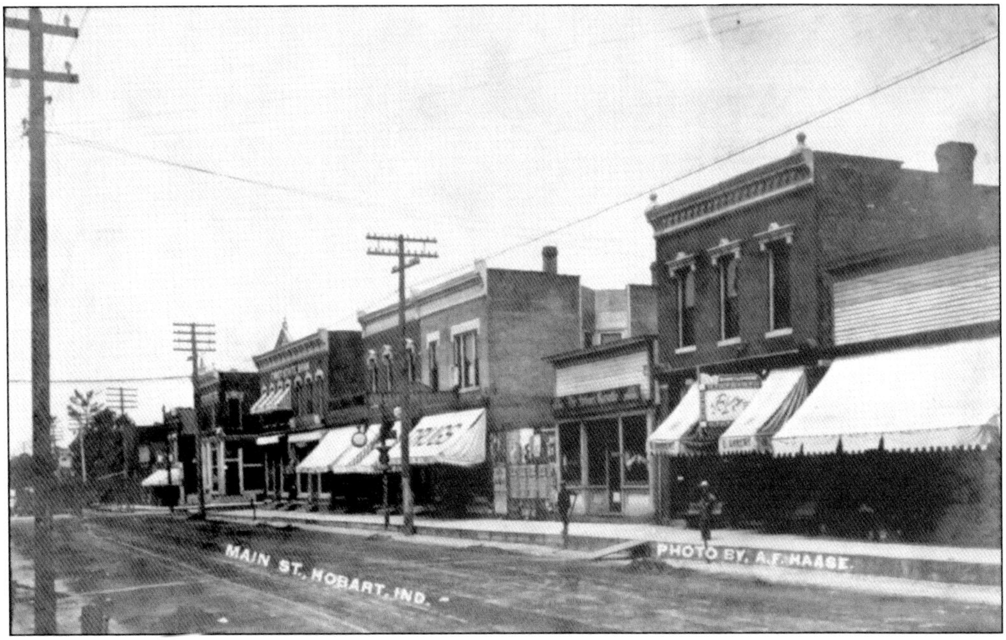

300 Block of Main Street, North View. In this c. 1911 photograph, the Ittel Building is the single-story building to the right. Adjacent to it is a two-story Italianate Revival–style brick building constructed in 1895. The remaining three two-story buildings are also of Italianate Revival style. The two-story brick building in the center housed Hobart City Hall on the second floor in 1922.

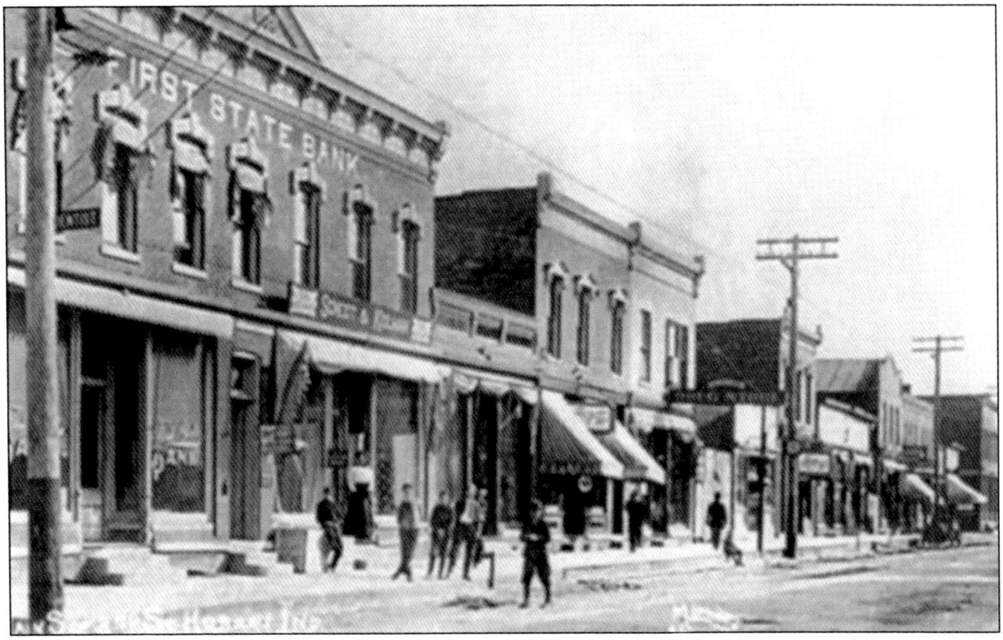

300 Block of Main Street, South View. The First State Bank building is on the left, on the southeast corner of Main and Third Streets. Built in 1888 by George Stocker, it was occupied by the First State Bank in 1899 and remained a bank institution until 1945. The single-story building at center was built by Stocker around 1870. From this building, Stocker operated a shoe shop when he first arrived in Hobart. This photograph was taken around 1911.

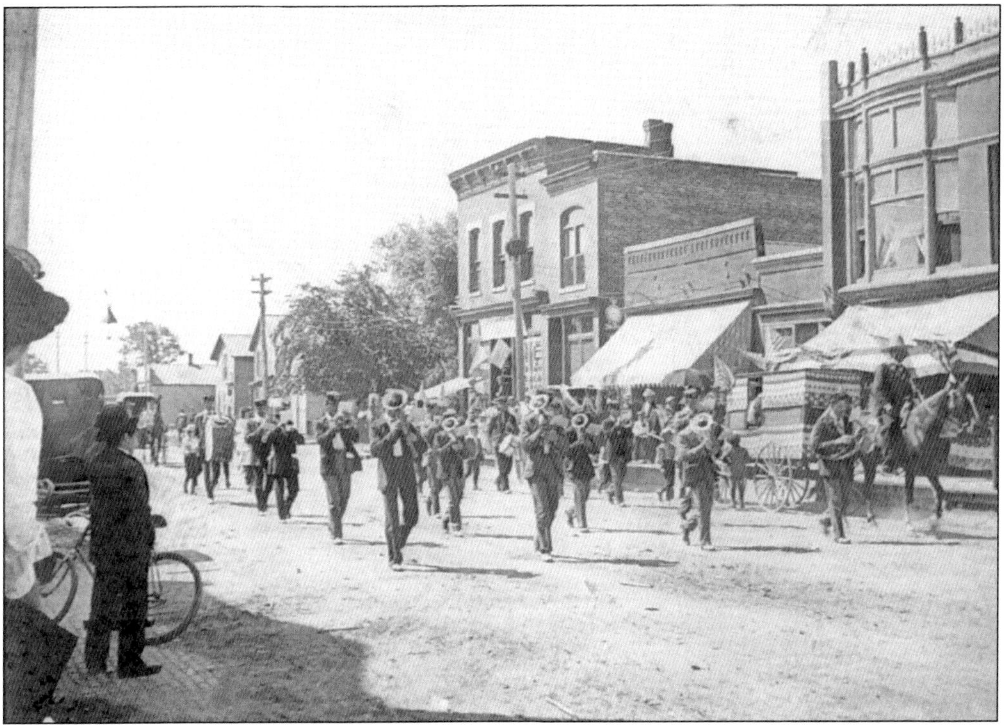

300 Block of Main Street, West Views. In the above photograph, taken around 1900, the two-story brick, Italianate building on the northwest corner of Fourth and Main Streets was home to Thomas Jory's furniture store and undertaking establishment in 1898. Years later, in 1961, the same structure was being used as Corey Brothers Bakery (below). Today, this building has had facade changes and is now a body art and tattoo shop. The two-story brick building with the bowed window on the second story, seen at right in the above photograph, was constructed by Seward Lightner. It is the white building at center below. Lightner was on the town board and served as a township trustee. He was described as a prominent and progressive citizen and merchant. Jory was described as a useful and esteemed citizen who worked for progress in business and municipal life.

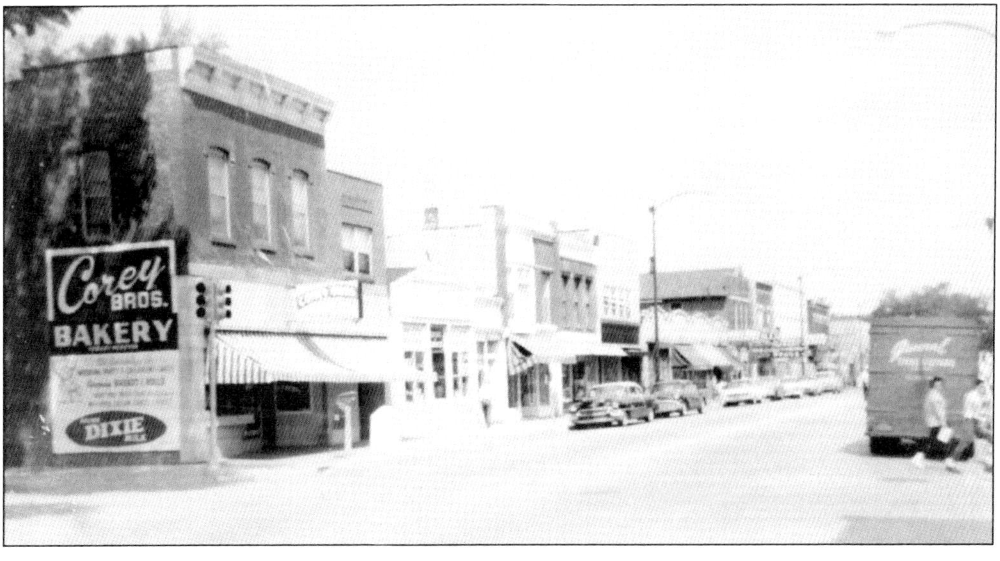

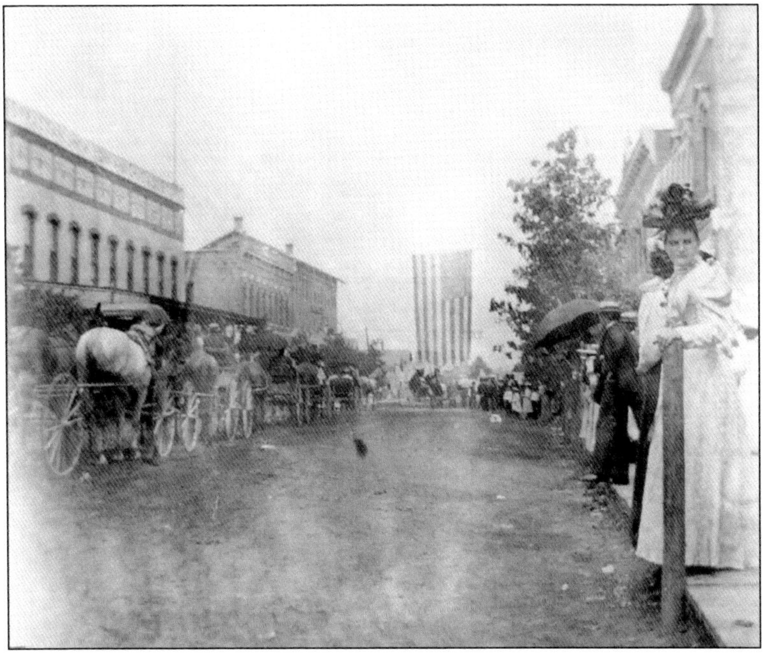

1895 CELEBRATION. Hobart's Fourth of July celebrations were held under the auspices of the Hobart Women's Reading Club. At the turn of the 20th century, Jennie McClaren served as president of the club. On the left, beginning with the nearest, are three of Hobart's most notable buildings, the Strattan Building, Fiester Building, and the Hobart House.

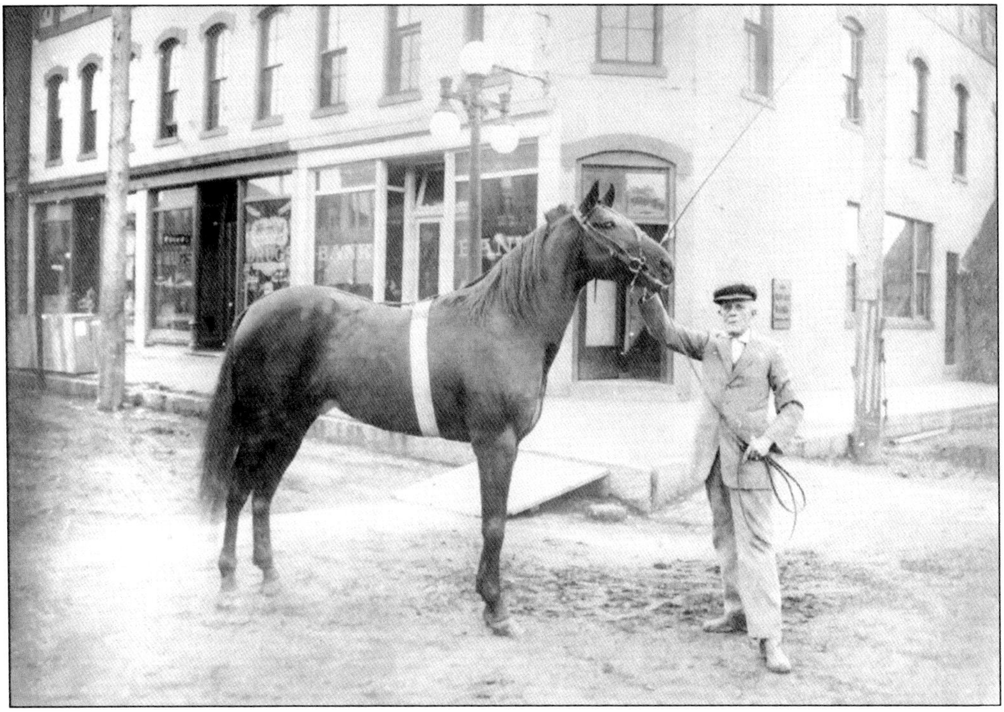

B.W. STRATTAN. Benjamin W. Strattan poses with his horse, Gloria, on the southwest corner of Main and Third Streets in front of his building. The concrete sidewalks and unpaved road date this photograph between 1913 and 1918. Strattan was said to have been born in Richmond, Indiana, around 1835, making him between 78 and 83 years of age at the time of this photograph. In 1862, he managed a mercantile business in New York before settling in Hobart for over 20 years. He was said to be a practical, substantial, and spirited man who revolutionized commerce in Hobart.

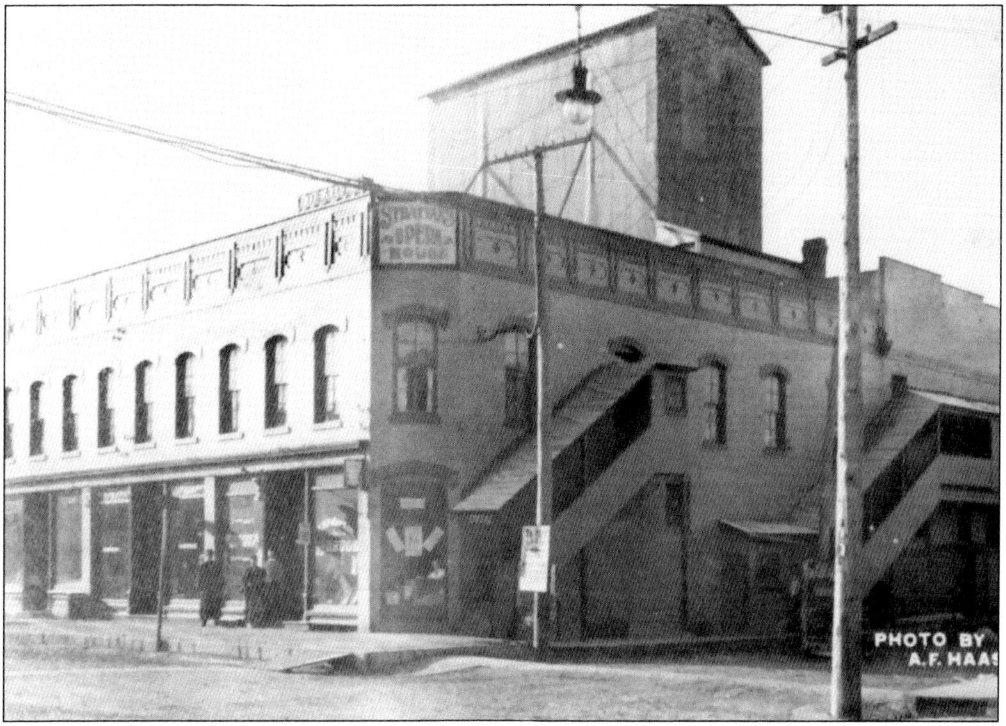

Strattan Opera House. This Italianate structure was built in 1876 by George Stocker. It was sold to Benjamin Strattan, who managed opera house operations in 1887. In 1894, he converted the second floor into a theater. In 1907, a 25-foot superstructure screen tower was added above the roof, which allowed for backdrop screen changes. The opera house closed in 1916. In 2007, the structure was deemed unsafe and was razed. The site was converted into downtown parking.

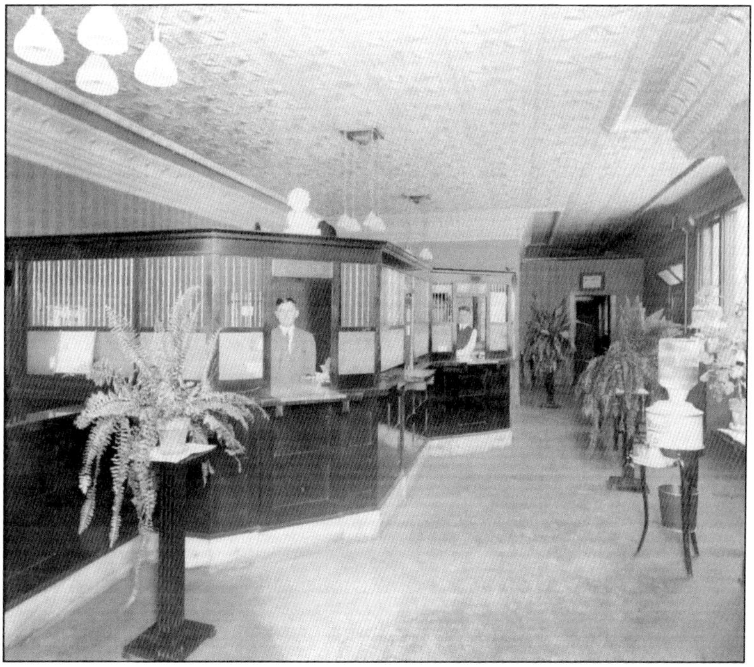

Strattan Building Interior. First State Bank moved into the Strattan Building in 1913 and closed in 1925. It was the first bank in Hobart and the second in the county. The Strattan Building had also been used for musical performances, community dances, high school basketball games, and wedding ceremonies.

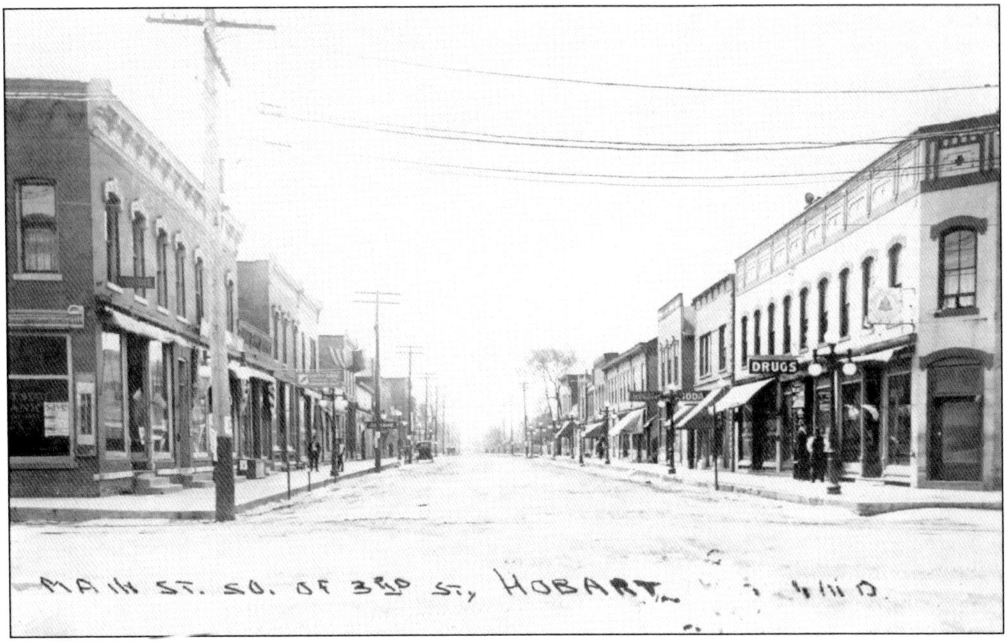

300 Block of Main Street, South Views. The concrete sidewalk, streetlight style, and gravel road date the above photograph to between 1913 and 1918. The below photograph, showing the same view, was taken 10 years later, between 1923 and 1928. The image below depicts the Neoclassical facade on the First State Bank (left). The four-unit Verplank Building, constructed in 1928, predates both these images. Unity Shoe Store still operates from its 1870 single-story construction, seen at the center left in both images. Adjacent to Unity Shoes are two brick buildings that were also constructed in Italianate style. In 1951, the second floors of the two building in the bottom image (center left, with awnings) were removed, and the building facades were remodeled.

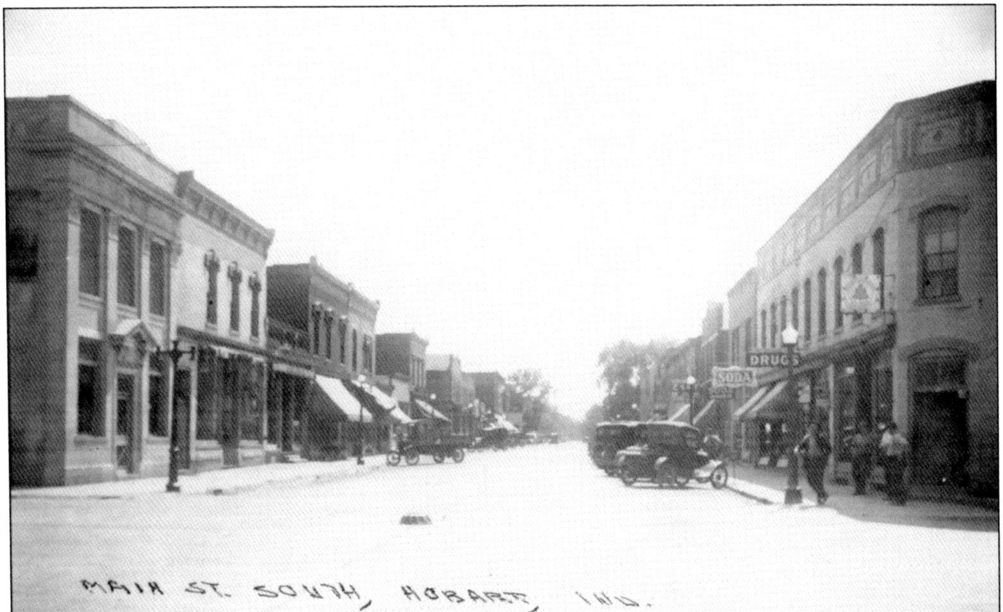

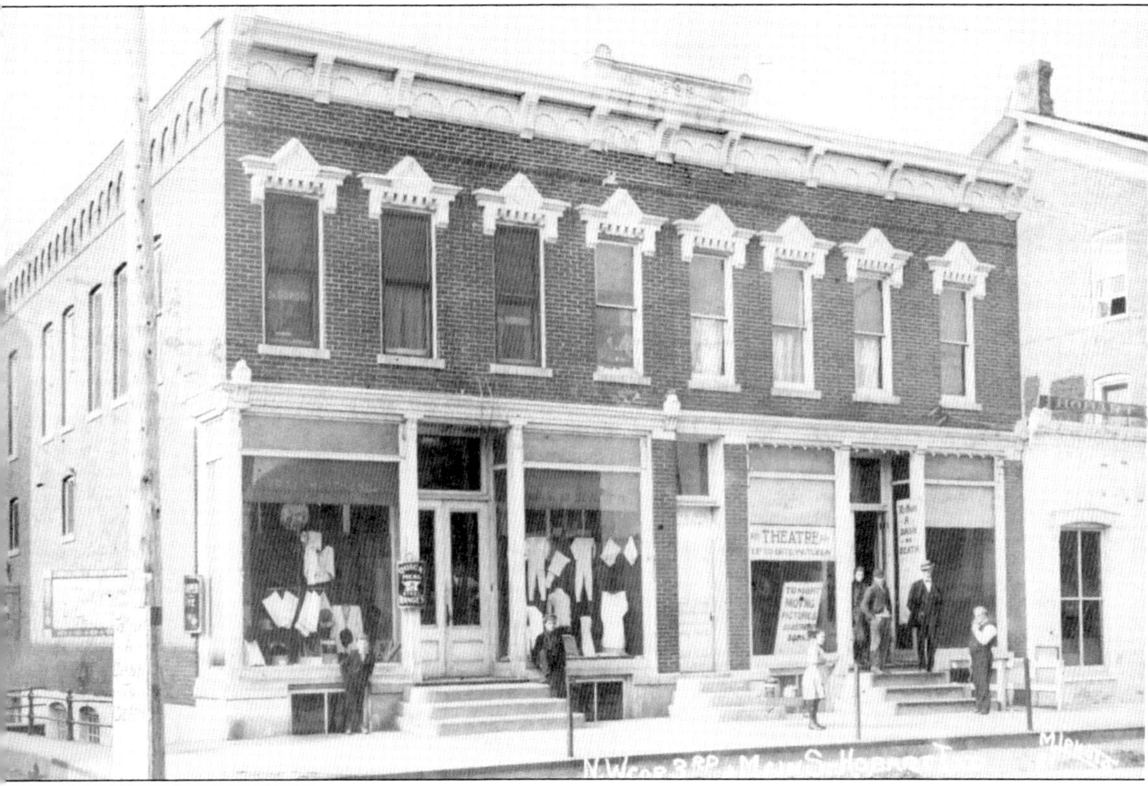

Fiester Building. Built in 1893 at the northwest corner of the 200 block of Main Street is a double-occupancy, two-story brick building constructed in the Italianate architecture style. The building's owners, John Fiester and Jerry Killigrew, conducted a very large general merchandise business from this chief corner of the town. Over the years building owners have modified its entrances, but much of the Italianate architectural details have remained intact. A succession of general stores and drugstores have conducted business from this location, including Dyche Drug Co. in the 1940s. The basement was used as a bowling alley and pool parlor. It was said that J.L. Fiester was a longtime Hobart resident who was trained as a businessman and that his liberal treatment of customers and competitive prices made him a success. On the second floor, windows identify the office of Dr. Gordon, who made Hobart his home in 1865. Dr. Gordon graduated from Buffalo Medical College and was said to be a noteworthy citizen who devoted his time to advancing the town. He also served two terms as Lake County coroner and was the chief examining physician for a number of insurance companies.

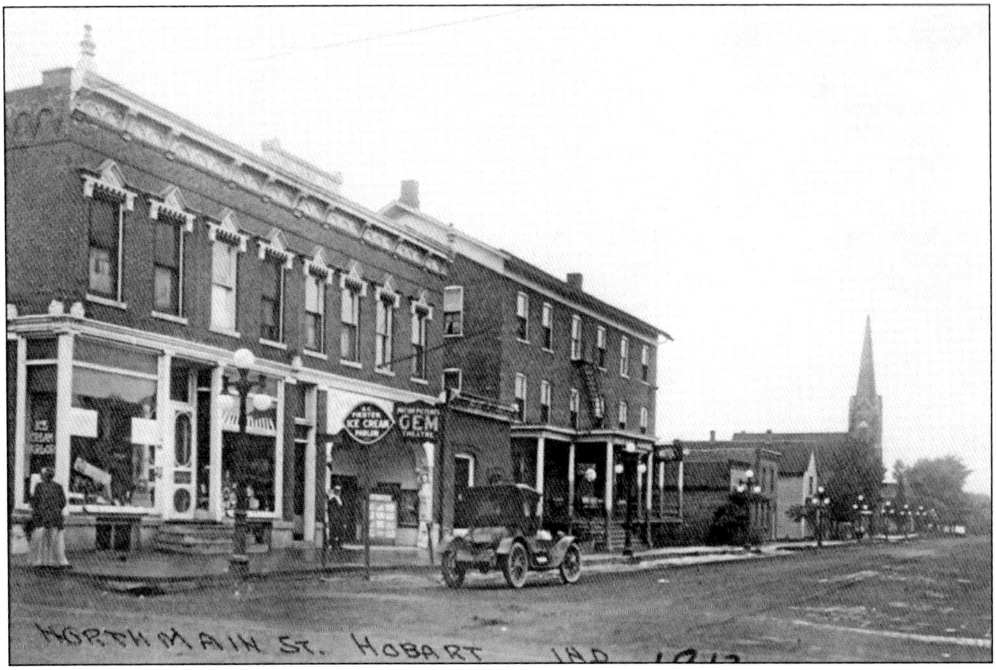

FIESTER BUILDING THEATERS. The north unit of the Fiester Building housed movie theaters from 1912 to 1939. The first theater was called The Colonial, followed by The Gem. Renamed The Strand, it was managed by the Prusiecki family until they purchased the condemned Hobart House and razed it to construct the Art Theater.

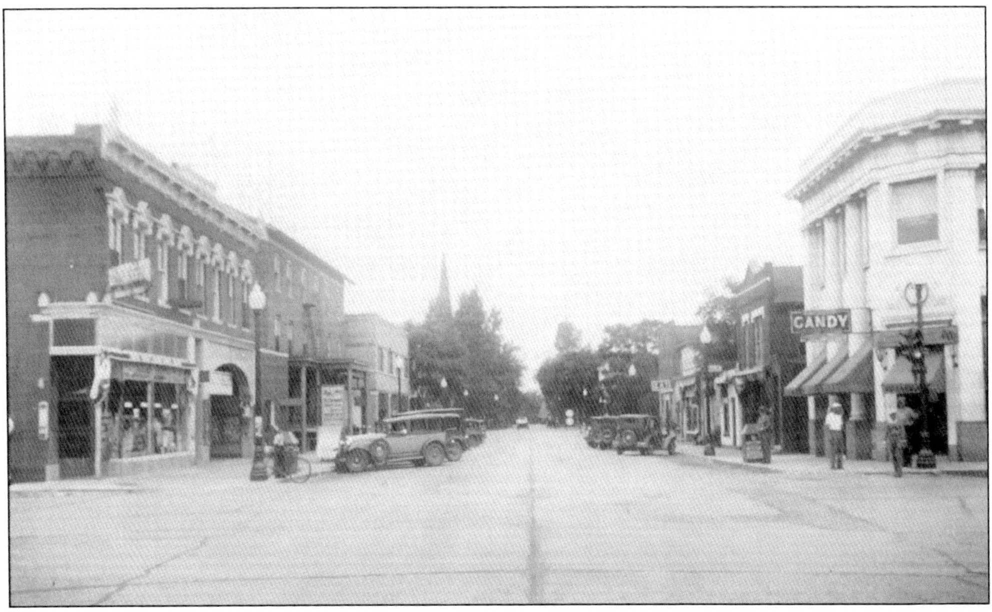

200 BLOCK OF MAIN STREET, NORTH VIEW. The building on the right was constructed in 1890 by James Roper as a red brick structure. It was home to the American Trust & Savings Bank in 1912. In 1926, the Neoclassical granite and stone facade was added, as seen here. Near the left center is the Ben Ack Building, which was erected in 1926 and named after the Potawatomi chief who was once the owner of the land that is now downtown Hobart.

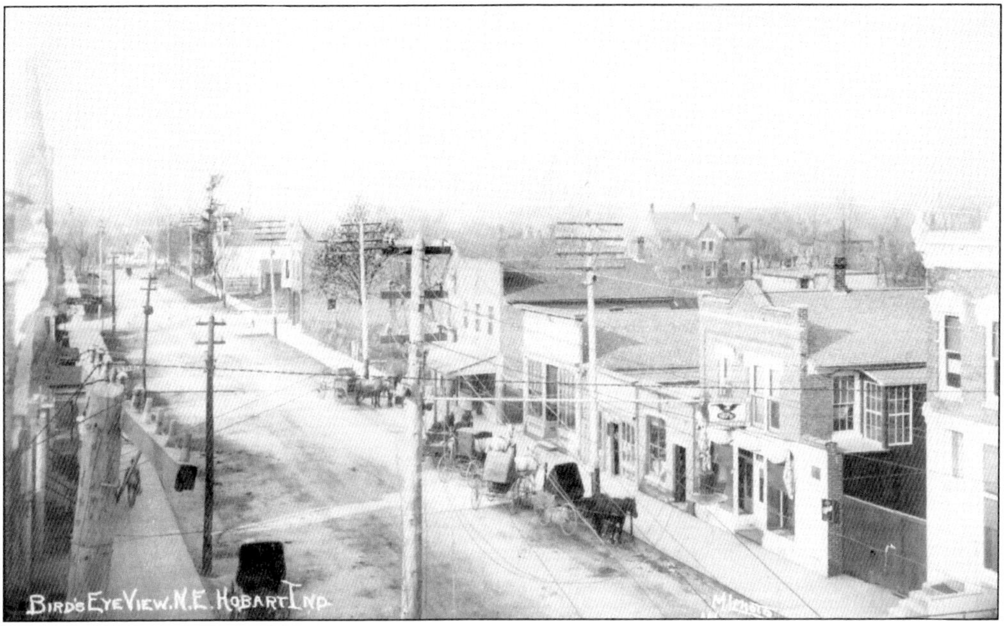

Killigrew and Black Property. In this north-facing photograph, taken around 1911, the Killigrew and Black property is seen on the east side of Main Street. The brick, two-story Joseph Black Building is adjacent to the undeveloped Killigrew family parcel, which is the future site of the Hobart Federal Post Office. At the end of the block, the Pedersen Building turret is seen, followed by Earle's former art gallery operating as St. Bridget's first church.

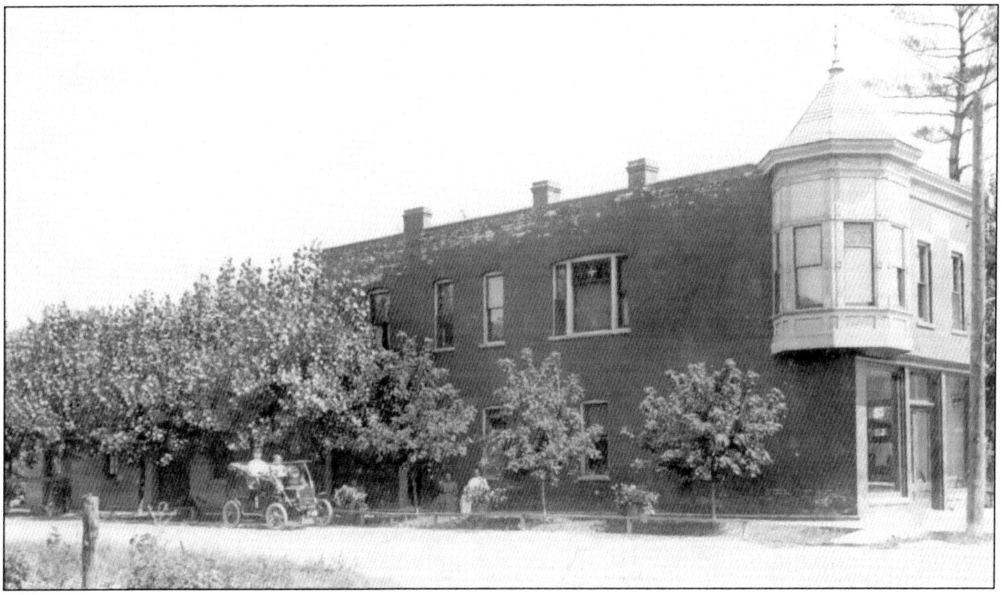

Pedersen Building. George Pedersen constructed a two-story brick building at the southeast corner of Main and Second Streets around 1900. Pedersen had living quarters on the second floor and operated a wagon shop on the first floor. A blacksmith shop was located in the rear. Eventually, Northern Indiana Public Service Company (NIPSCO) offices were located here until it built a facility across the street, at the southwest corner of Second and Main Streets. Also, the Hobart License Bureau was located here at one time.

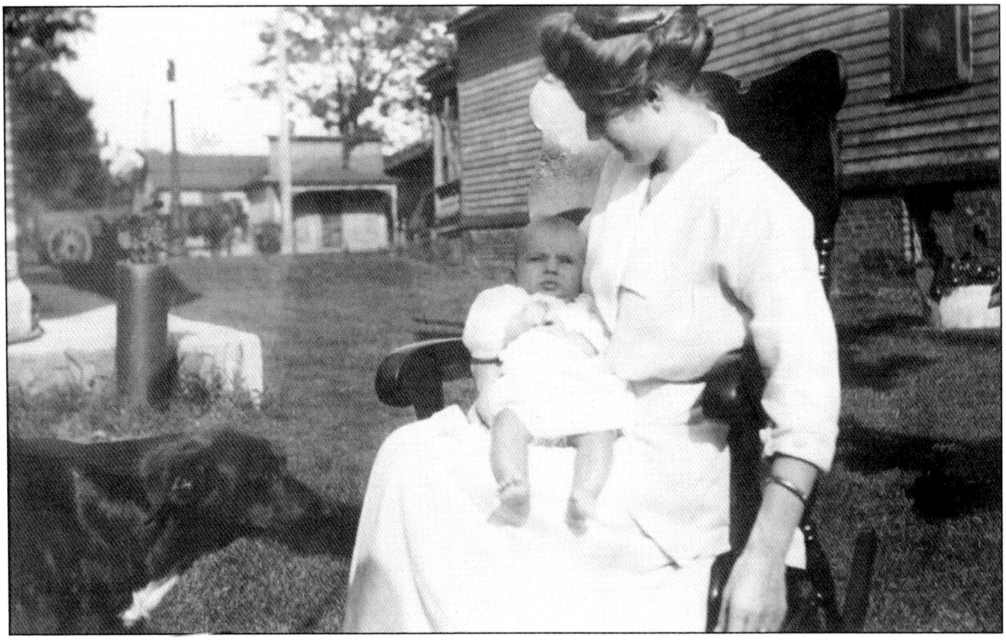

Clare Fleck. Clare Fleck, seen here tending to an infant relative, was born in a Hobart log cabin in 1887. In the background of this photograph is the 200 block of Main Street, the future site of the Hobart Federal Post Office. Fleck never married, but was dedicated to community activities and served as the national director of the Izaak Walton League for over seven years.

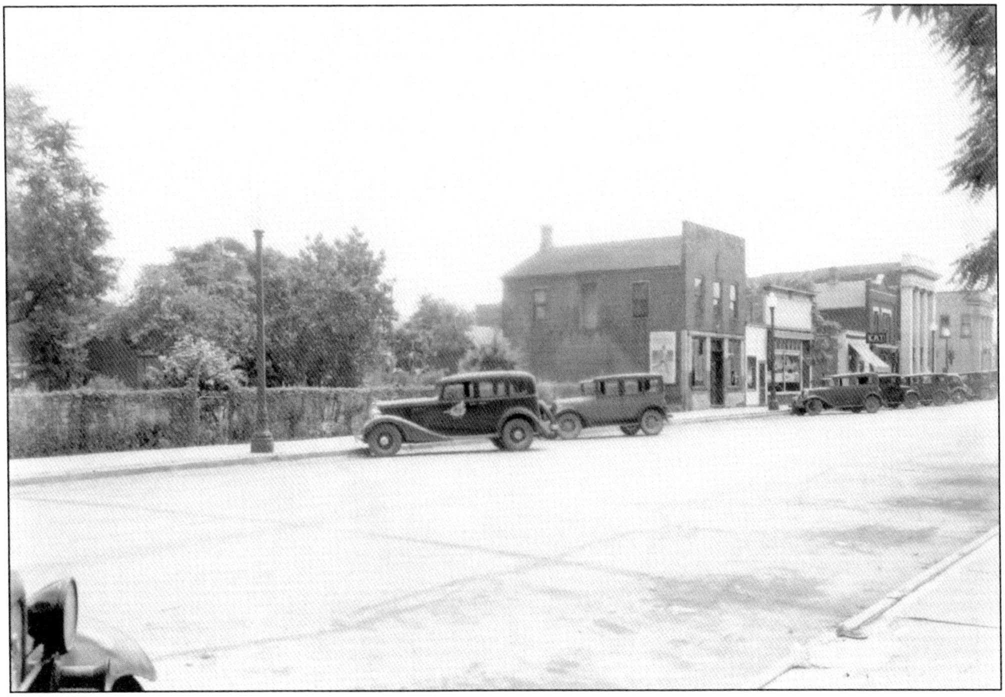

Post Office Site. Joseph Black operated a trading post and post office from 1861 to 1869 in the two-story brick building adjacent to the vacant lot. Black's building was razed in 1935, and excavation began for the Hobart Federal Post Office on August 18, 1936.

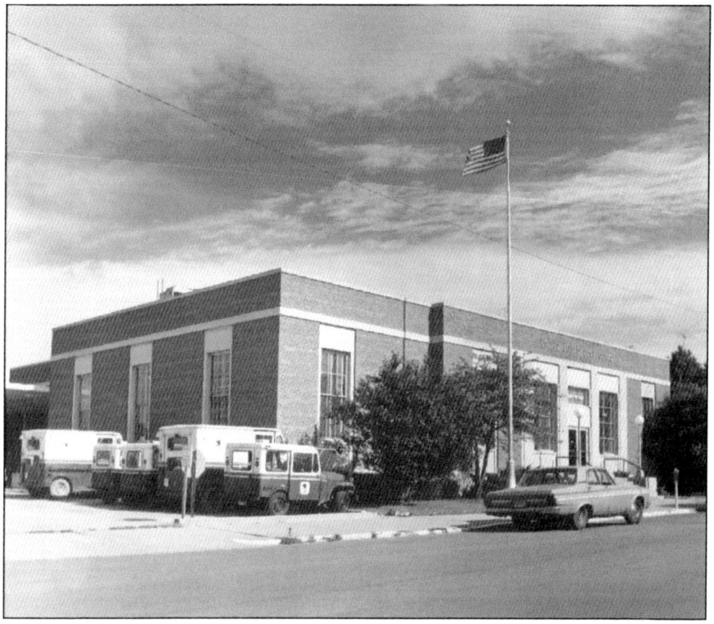

Post Office. This 1937 Colonial Revival structure was Hobart's first government owned post office. On May 23, 1937, a dedication ceremony was held on Main Street, with a speakers' platform and a performance by the high school band. The federally owned Hobart Post Office became a first-class facility on July 1, 1950. In 1963, the US Post Office Department implemented the Zoning Improvement Plan (ZIP). Hobart received the code 46342.

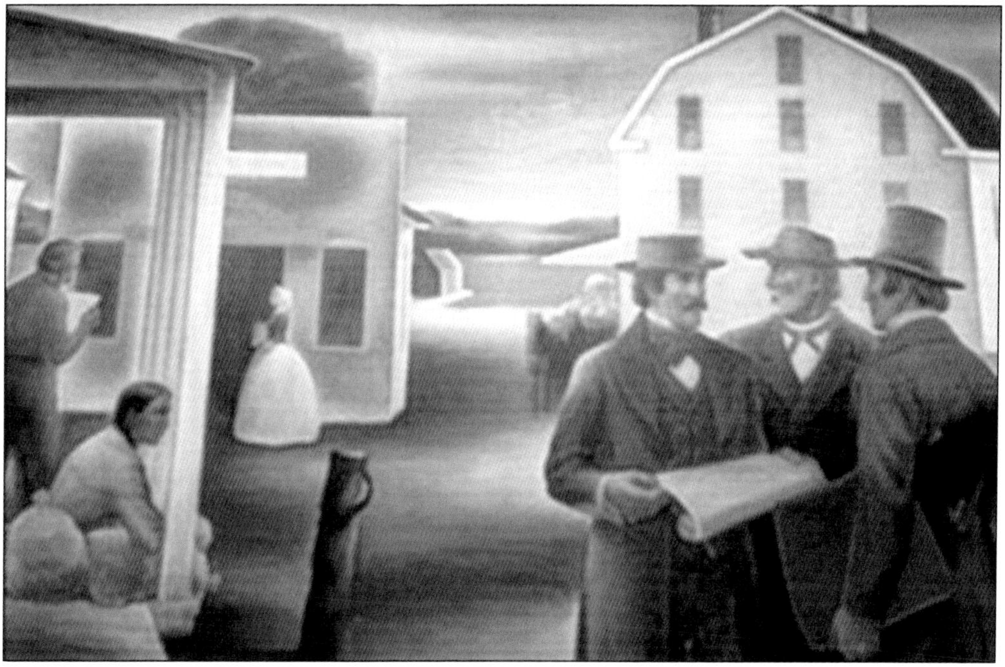

Post Office Mural. The US Treasury Procurement Division authorized the painting of a mural for the lobby of Hobart's new post office in January 1938. The mural, *Early Hobart*, has been registered with the Office of Fine Arts and Historic Preservation in Washington, DC. An example of WPA-sponsored art, it was painted by William Dolwick. The painting is a west perspective of Hobart, near the corner of Front and Center Streets. This portion of the mural depicts founding settlers and Native Americans. (Courtesy of Sergio Mendoza.)

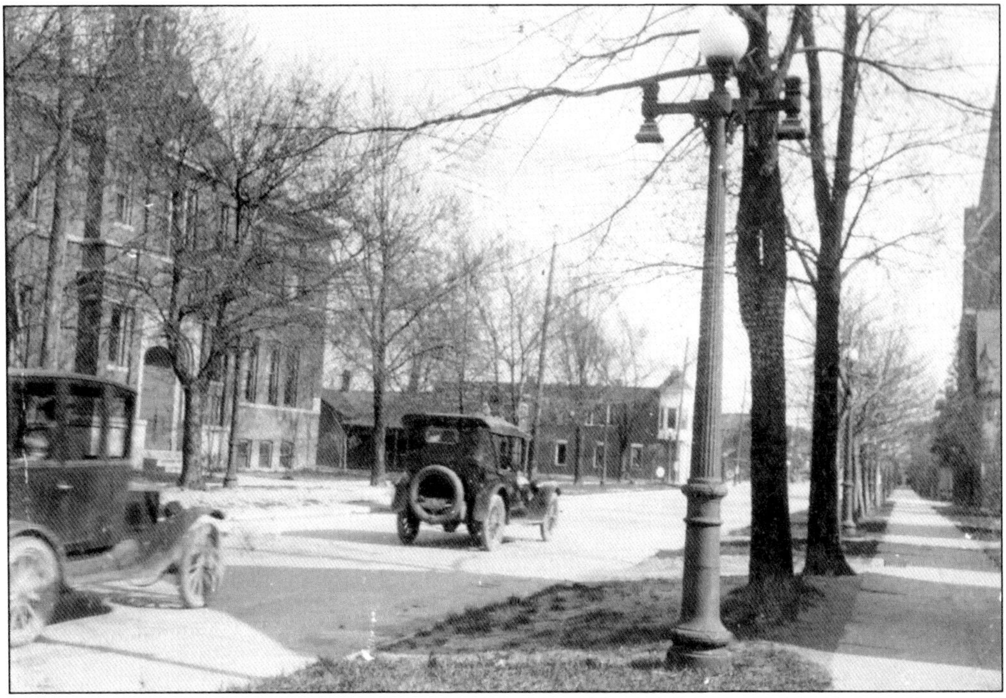

100 Block of Main Street, South Views. The above photograph shows Saint Bridget's second church, on the east side of Main Street. At the 200 block, the Pedersen Building is visible in the distance at center, with the turret. On the west (right) side of Main Street, Trinity Lutheran Church's steeple can be seen. Above, the second St. Bridget Church is partially visible on the left. The sidewalks and missing streetlights on Main Street date this image to around 1912. Both of these photographs were taken at a point near the intersection of Main and Front Streets, where Lew Hammond's Tavern and stagecoach stop once stood. The structure later burned down, and four homes were built, as seen below, but only one still stands today at 128 Main Street.

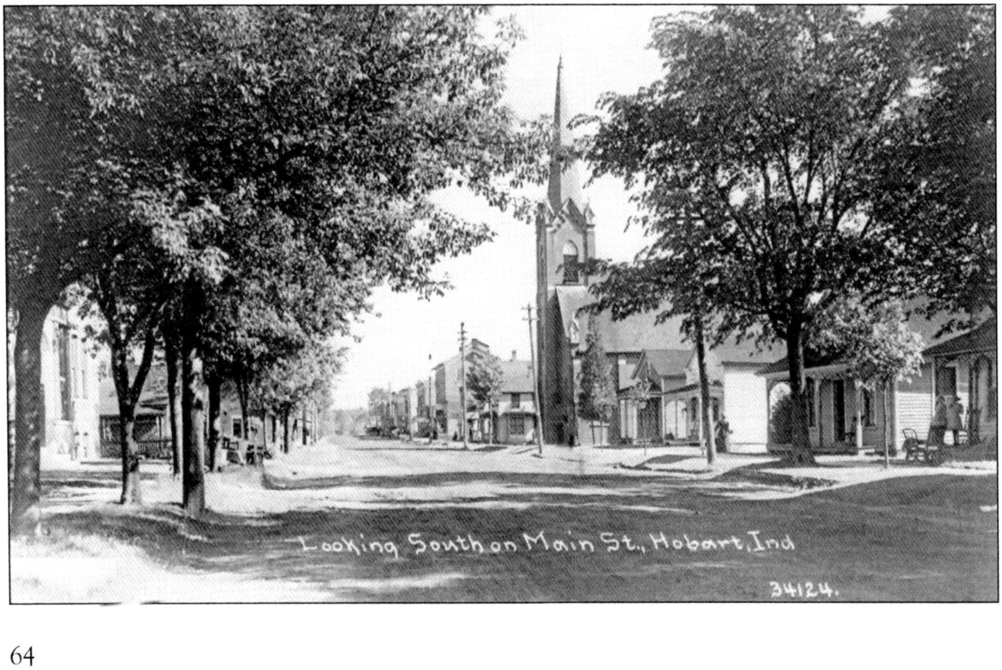

Four

The Elusive Roads

Hobart was platted in a grid pattern, but the natural features led many first-time visitors to question the street pattern, with merging roads and right-angle, dead-end roads abutting the natural waterways. The streets of downtown Hobart are filled with various forms of architecture, one of the earliest of which is Gothic Revival, seen in some of Hobart's first churches, which had strong vertical patterns and pointed arches, steep-pitched gable roofs, eared drip moldings around openings, and medieval or castellated parapets. However, during the Economic Panic of 1873, less expensive frame construction structures were built.

Italianate architecture appeared in Lake County a few years after the Gothic Revival period, and it lasted until the 1890s. This style can be found in both commercial and residential structures. Italianate, the most popular style in downtown Hobart, can be identified through its details in the elaborate wood, brick, and iron cornices and moldings around upper-story windows, which can be seen on both brick and frame construction. In Hobart, several of the brick buildings still standing today exhibit this popular Italianate Architectural feature of that era.

Shortly after the turn of the 20th century, the Neoclassical style emerged as a dominant force in American architecture, and that style prevailed into the 1930s, mostly in large public and commercial buildings. Characteristics of the style include the use of Classical elements, such as columned porticoes, pilasters, keystones, pediment openings, and cornice dentils. The Neoclassical style is known for the historical correctness of meticulous detail and for its exaggerated scale. The final architectural style used in downtown Hobart buildings is Art Deco, which flourished between World War I and World War II. Art Deco is a French-influenced, highly stylized, modern design consisting of sharp right angles on chevron patterns.

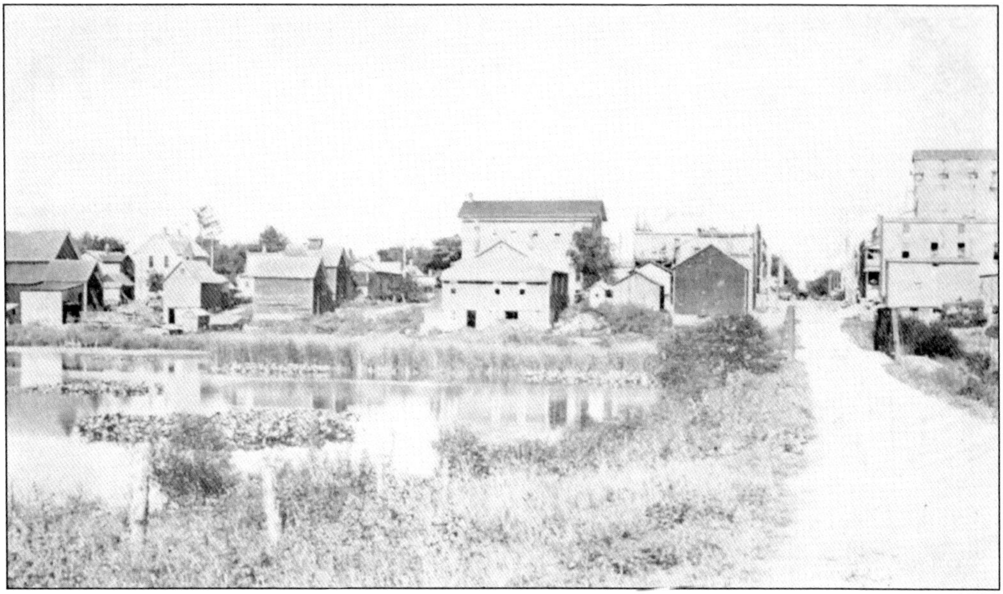

400 Block of Third Street. These two east-facing photographs, taken about eight years apart, reflect the progress made in the Town of Hobart between 1908 and 1916. The Strattan Opera House screen superstructure, seen above (right) and below (near center right), was constructed around 1907 and removed around 1917. The above photograph shows the Third Street Bridge prior to the 1912 streetcar rail line construction and the town's decision that year to accept the Lake County Council's proposal to have a substantial and modern bridge built over Lake George. It was reported that both the town and county council discussed a new bridge during dinner at the Hobart House, seen above, center. The substantial and modern bridge (below) was reconstructed in 1916 by Boyd Construction Company.

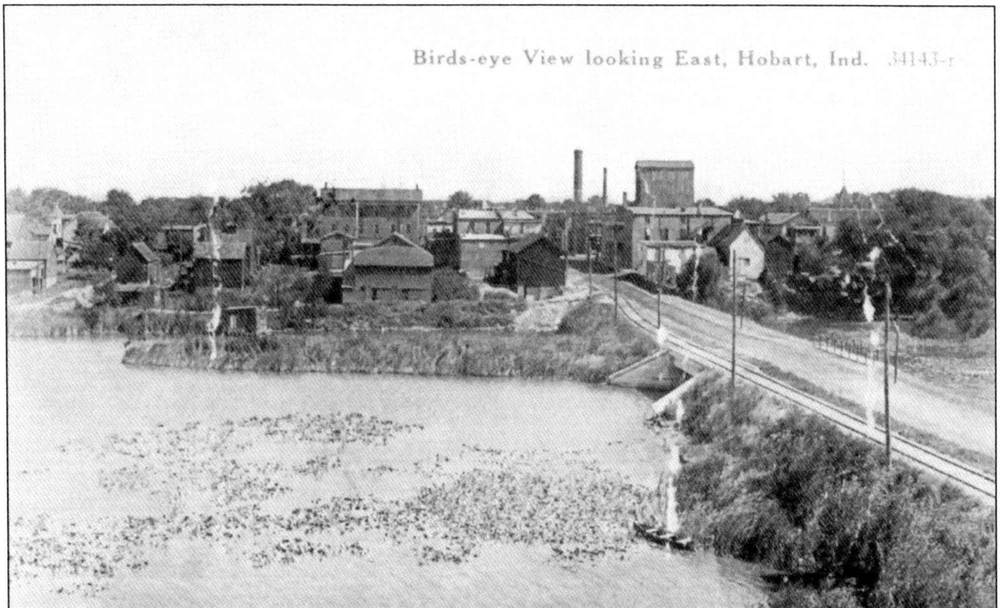

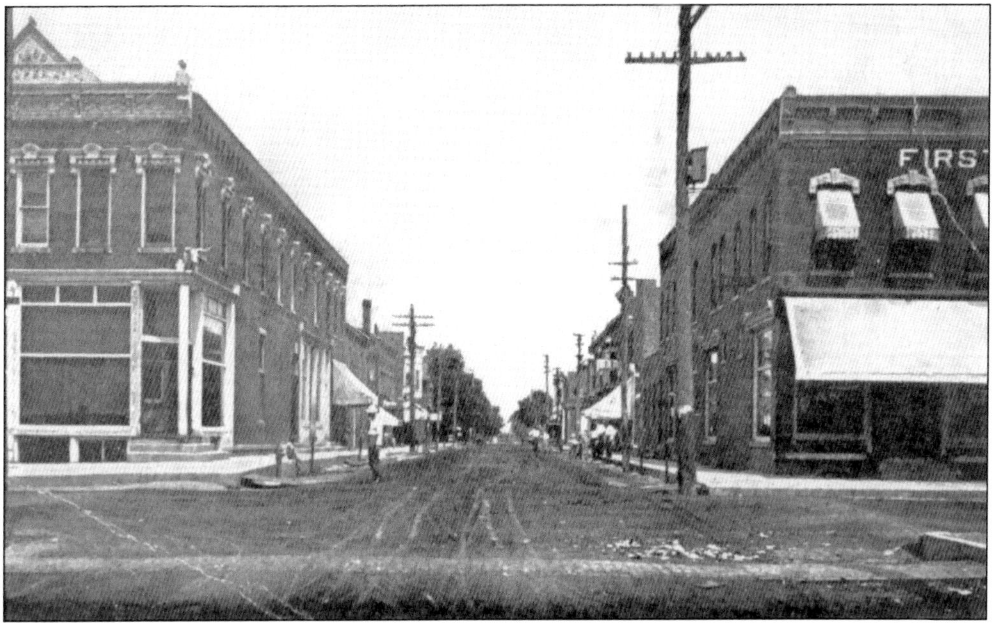

Roper and Stocker Buildings. The building at the northeast corner of Main and Third Streets (left) is the Roper Building, named after James Roper Jr. The building on the southeast corner (right) is the Stocker Building, named after George Stocker. Both men were described as active in the public and commercial life of Hobart. Roper served as a township trustee, and Stocker held various town, township, and county seats, including postmaster from 1884 to 1888. This photograph was taken around 1911.

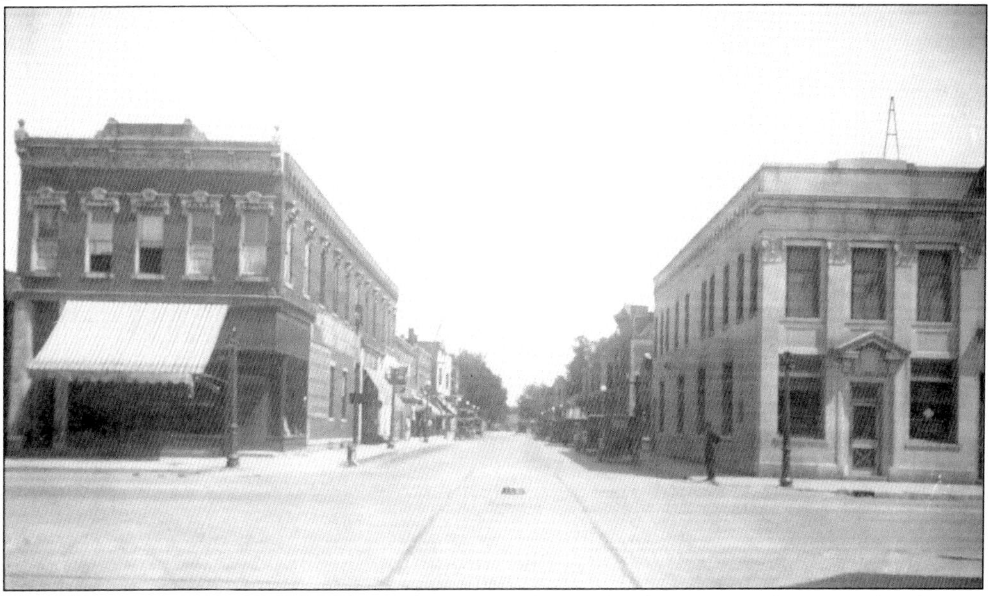

Third Street, East View. The two buildings flanking Third Street, on the east side of Main Street, are the Stocker Building (right), constructed in 1888, and the Roper Building (left), constructed in 1890. Both structures were originally designed in the Italianate style. They both later received new facades in the Neoclassical style; the Stocker Building in 1922, and the Roper Building in 1926. This photograph was taken sometime between 1923 and 1925.

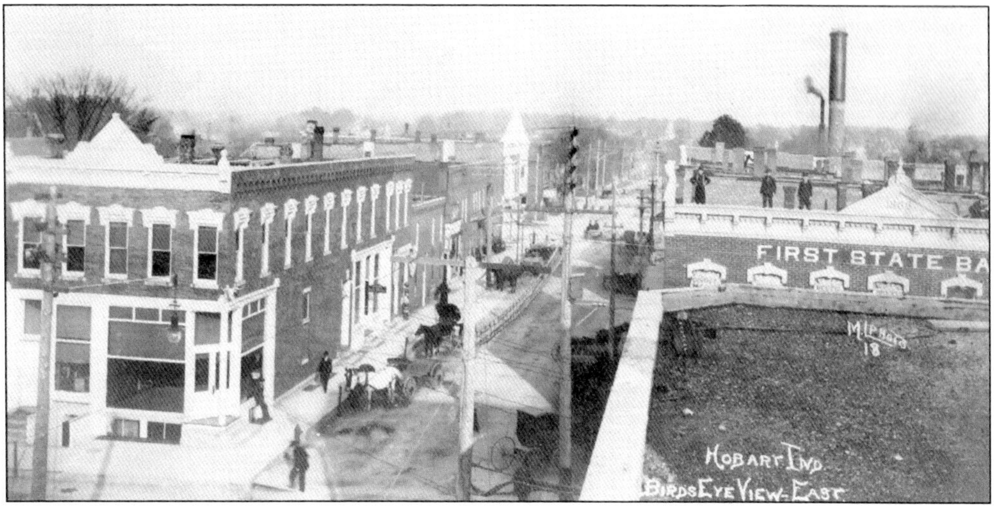

Roper Block. Shown in this northeast-facing photograph is the Roper Building, which was home to the American Trust & Savings Bank for many years until it closed during the Depression. The rear of the Roper Building housed the post office from 1889 to 1910, as seen in this image. In the distance, near the center, the Guyer Building turret is visible, as is the Elgin, Joliet & Eastern rail line spur crossing on Third Street.

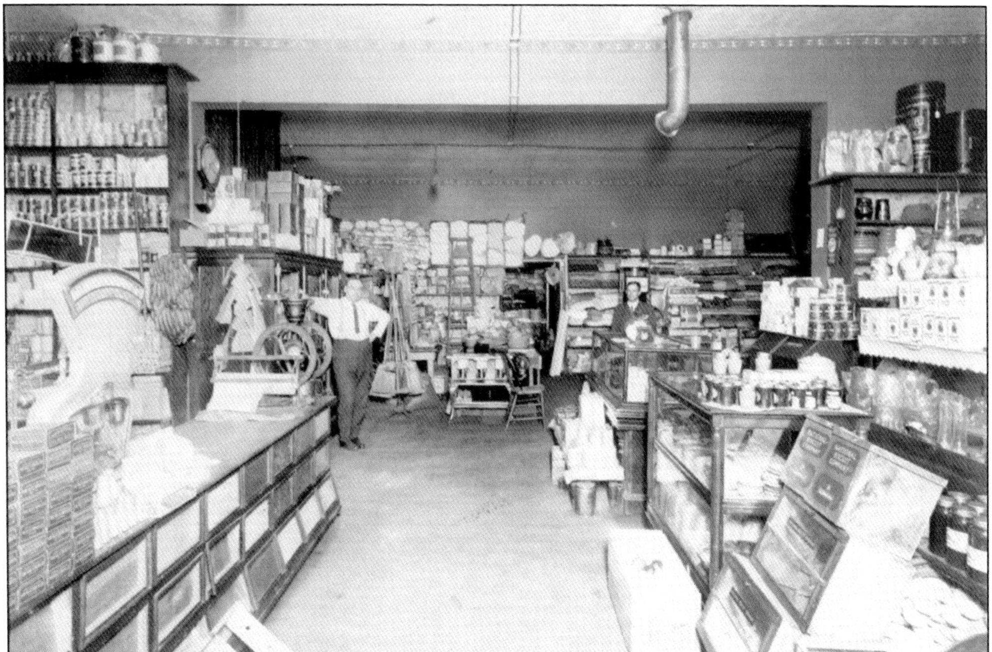

Bee Hive Store. The proprietors of the Bee Hive Store were Edward Scheidt and Henry Keilman. Their store shared the south half of George Stocker's block building, in the rear of the First State Bank. The Bee Hive, seen here around 1920, had access on both Main and Third Streets and was said to have been well organized. In the foreground on the left are dry-goods compartments and boxes of golden dates. On the right are storage boxes of the National Biscuit Company (Nabisco) and fresh baked goods alongside kitchenware. At the rear of the store is the fabric section, and to the left is G.L. Stocker.

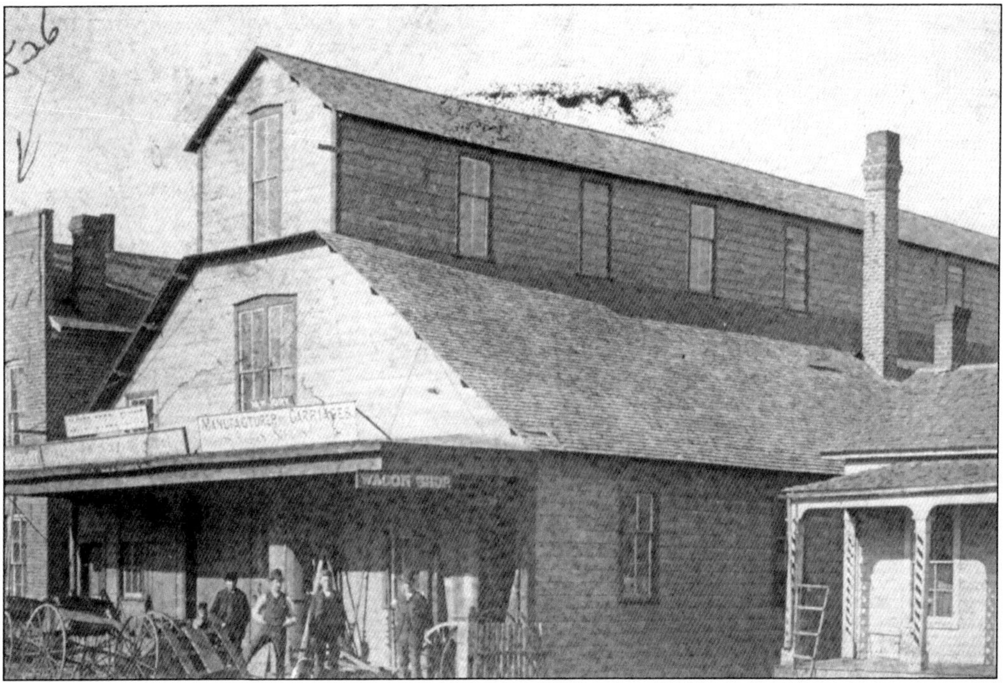

Jory Wagon Shop. In the late 1800s, this structure stood on the north side of the 500 block of Third Street. Eventually, it was rebuilt into a two-story brick building housing the Batterman Machine Shop, a wagon and blacksmith shop that also did machine repair work. The second floor was used for entertainment purposes. This and a subsequent structure were eventually razed due to fire.

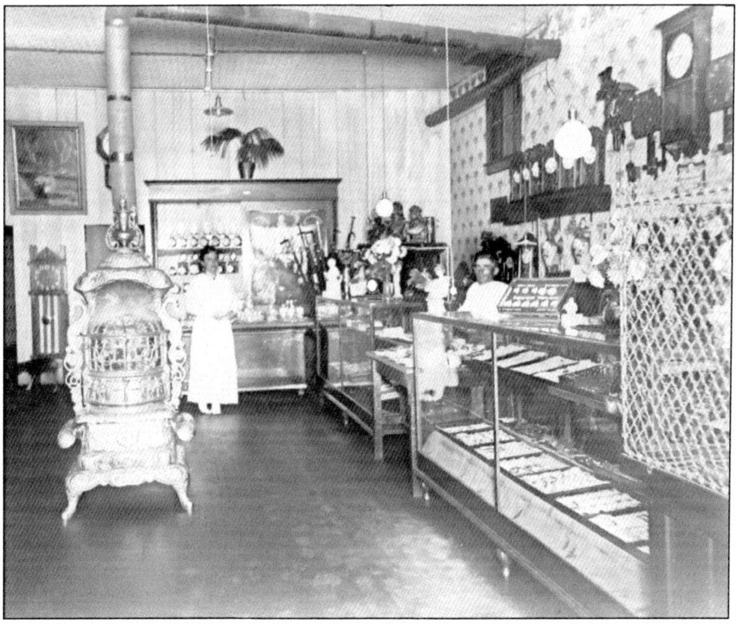

Dell Beach Jewelry. F. Dell Beach's jewelry shop was once located on the north side of the 500 block of Third Street in a commercial building that was erected after the Jory Wagon Shop burned down. The new two-story brick building had a roller rink and hosted dances on the second floor. The building burned down in the 1950s and was replaced with a single-story structure for commercial and banquet use.

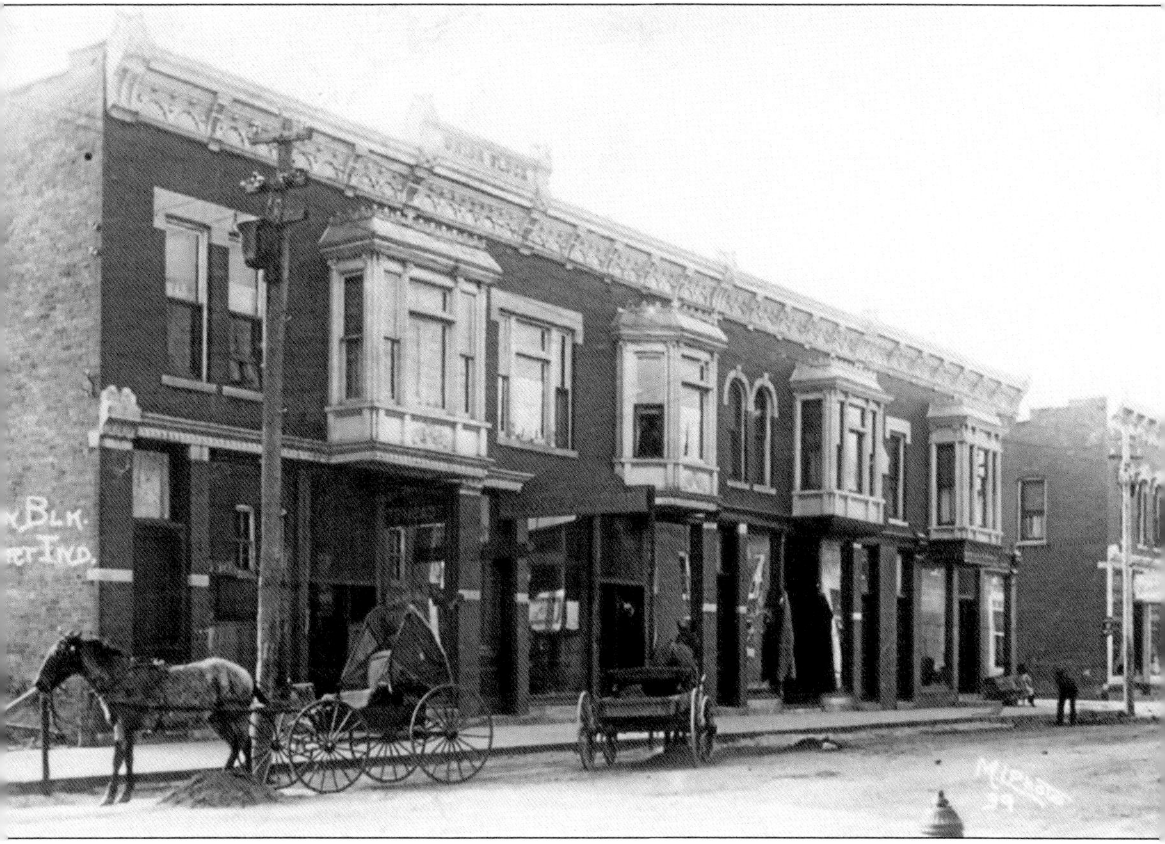

UNION BLOCK. This Italianate building, constructed by George Stocker, had residences on the second floor and commercial space on the first floor. The four-unit building was located on the south side of the 500 block of Third Street. In 1896, William Stommel and Ed Scheidt, identified as skilled retailers, began operation of the Stommel & Co. store in one of the units. The establishment was praised for its low prices and outstanding customer service. It expanded its retail space by connecting two units with an internal arch opening. In 1959, the Union Block was razed and replaced by a Post Modern architectural style building. An incident is said to have occurred in the winter of 1920 in front of the Union Block involving a world-famous opera singer, Madam Ernestine Shumann-Heink. The story goes that Shumann-Heink was traveling through Hobart in the middle of the night when her chauffeur-driven car became stuck in the road. The commotion brought out many of the town's residents, who came to see and help Shumann-Heink as she yelled to her chauffeur in German. As her car became free, she thanked the residents in English, unaware that Hobart had a large German immigrant population. They responded to her in German. Research shows that Shumann-Heink owned property in Chicago until late 1919 or early 1920 and that she had a son enrolled at the military academy at Culver, Indiana, located 60 miles southeast of Hobart.

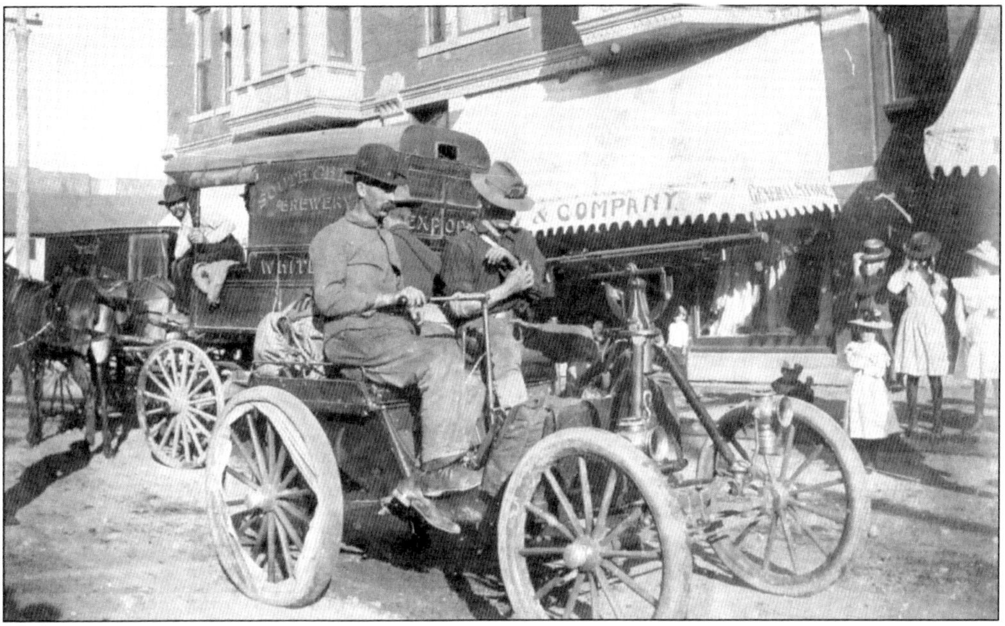

Davidson-Duryea Armored Vehicle. In 1899, Royal P. Davidson of Northwestern Military Academy in Highland Park, Illinois, created a four-wheeled gun carriage after years of experimenting with automobile chassis and a Colt .30-caliber automatic machine gun. He used Charles Duryea's patent to have it produced at his Peoria Rubber and Manufacturing Company. The Davidson-Duryea Armored Vehicle, one of the first of a series of military vehicles that passed through Hobart, is seen here with a flat rear tire in front of the Union Block Building on Third Street.

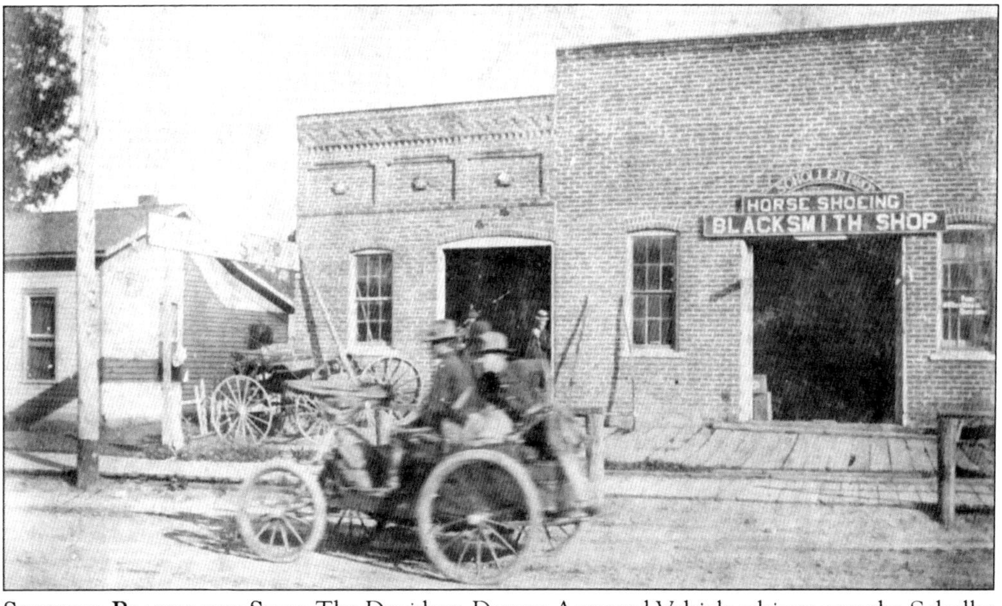

Scholler Blacksmith Shop. The Davidson-Duryea Armored Vehicle whizzes past the Scholler Blacksmith Shop, which was once located at the southeast corner of the alley intersection of the 600 block of Third Street. German-born William Scholler was one of Hobart's longest-serving blacksmiths. The Scholler family operated the blacksmith establishment until the 1950s. The Scholler family home was across the street from the shop.

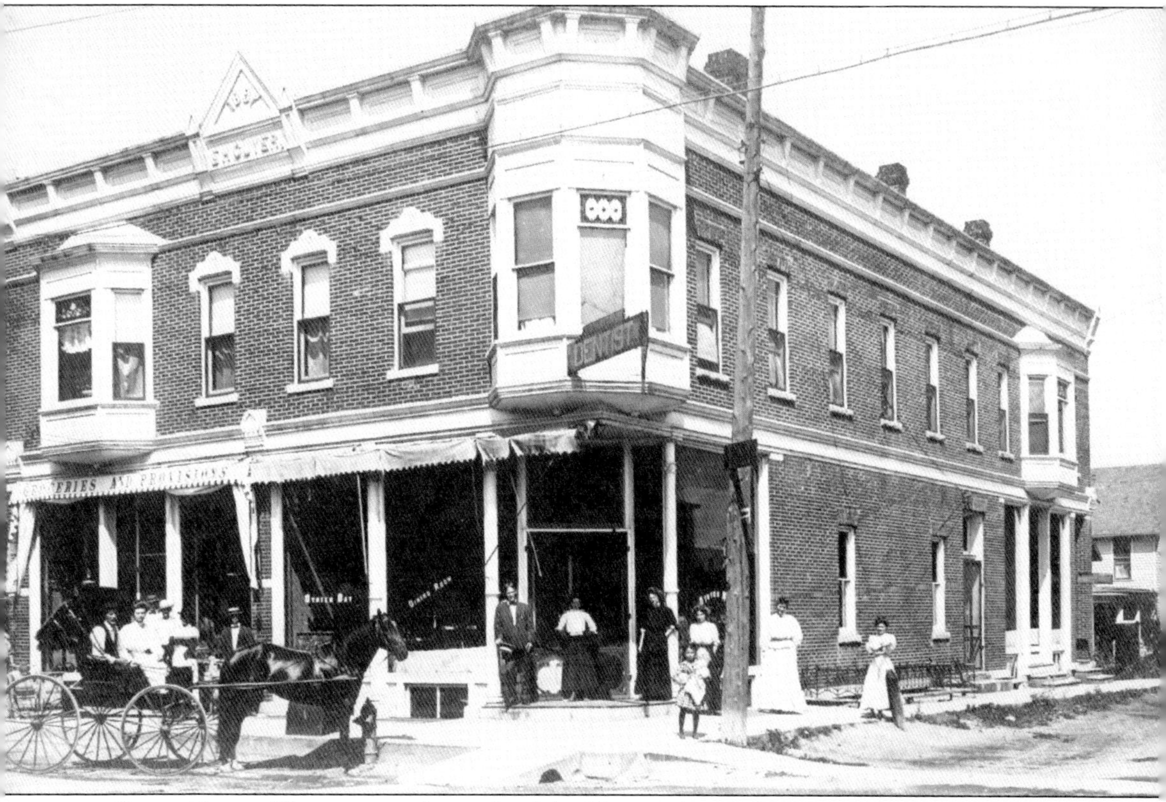

Guyer Block. The two-story brown brick building at the northwest corner of Center and Third Streets was constructed in 1897 by Elijah H. Guyer. The Italianate structure had white trimmed bay windows and a corner steeple and was heavily corniced. The building, which served a variety of uses over the years, had living space on the second floor and housed a dentist's office and a chiropractor's office. However, one of its most distinguished uses was when it served as the Hobart Post Office from 1910 to 1923. In 1972, the Hobart Development Corporation expanded the building and added three apartments in the upper level, with commercial space in the lower level. Guyer, a native of Michigan, was born in 1854. He lived in Hobart for almost 25 years, and his constant business activity and high personal integrity made him a notable character in town. Guyer was known as a successful stock buyer and was thought of as a true representative of the town's citizenry. He always worked for its betterment, never mixing politics and business.

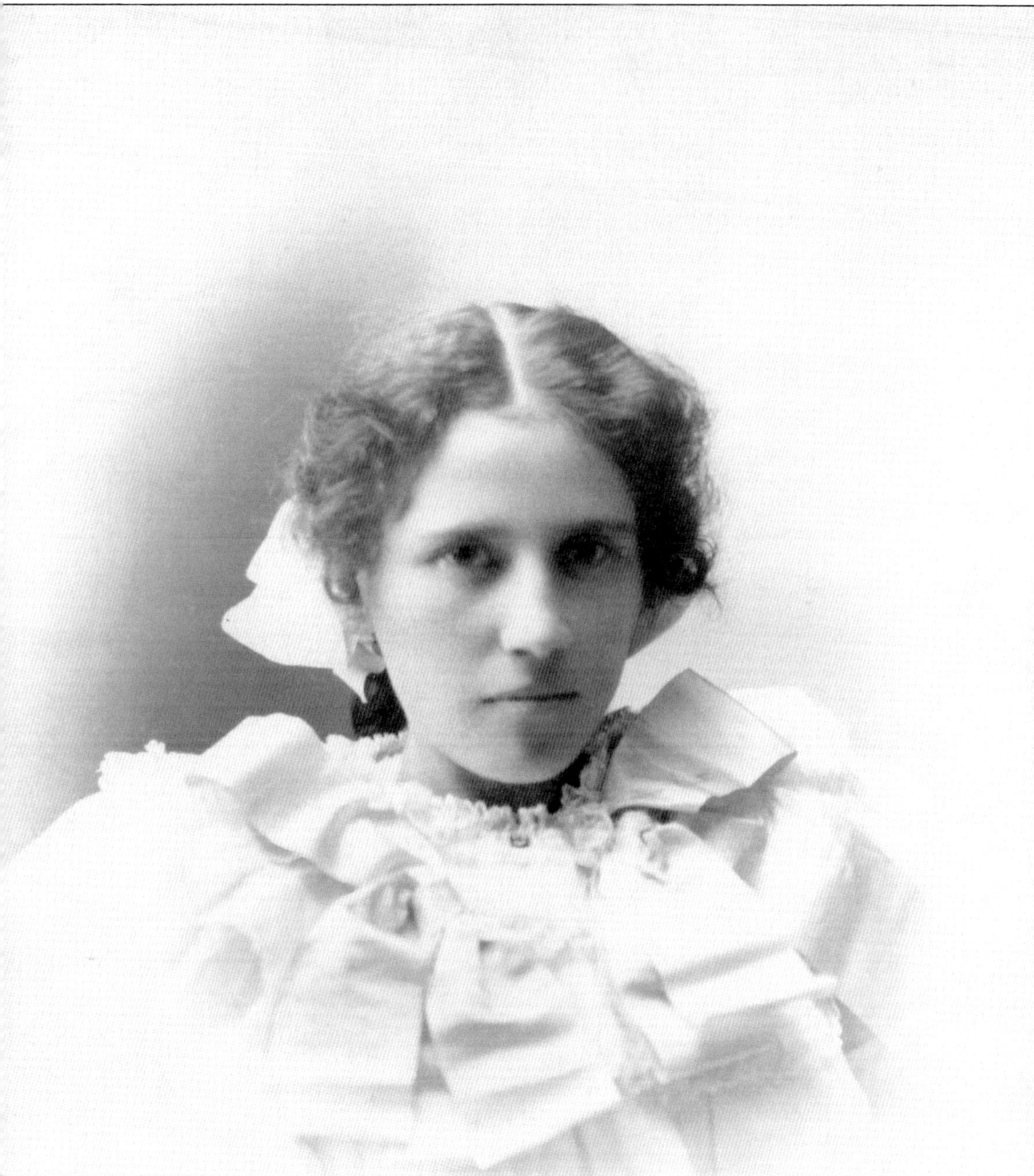

JANE SPRAY. Hobart's first female postmaster, and the longest-serving postmaster before the 20th century, was Jane "Jennie" Spray. She served the public for nearly a quarter of a century, beginning in 1885 as a clerk for the Hobart Post Office under Postmaster Stocker. In February 1889, the same year Hobart incorporated as a town, Spray was assigned by Pres. Grover Cleveland as the Hobart postmistress until December 1902. She then served as the post office deputy under Postmaster Johnston until she retired in 1908. Jennie never married and was said to have kyphosis. She was identified as a very cheerful, efficient, and popular young lady who was an active member of the community until a few years before her death in October 1918.

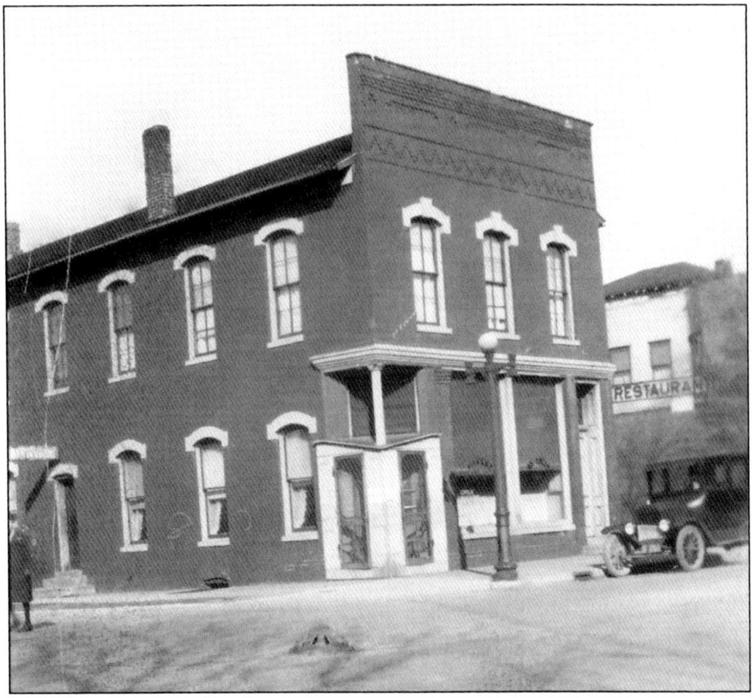

The Amazon. The northeast corner of Third and Center Streets was once occupied by a two-story wood frame building that served as an inn and saloon. The frame structure was later razed, and a two-story brick building was constructed in its place. The building became the home of a popular restaurant and café until it was razed in the early 1950s.

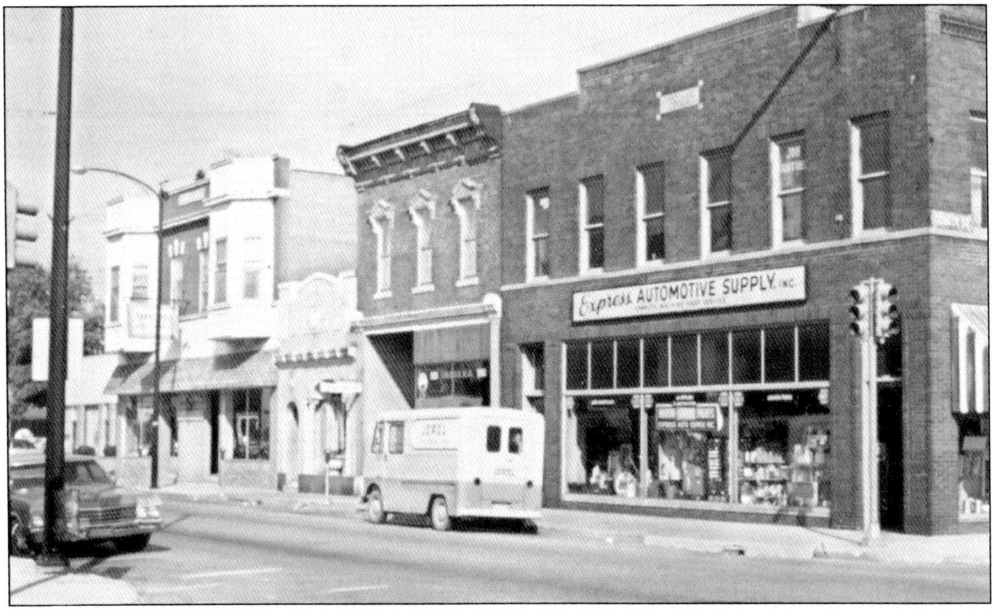

Newman Building. The southeast corner of Third and Center Streets was once the site of a long, wood frame building that was later rebuilt into a two-story brick building by Paul Newman and his son Mickey. The building, at right, still stands today along with Alwin Wild's three Italianate structures east of the Newman building. The two-story brick building next to the Newman building was constructed in 1893 with a shell-pattern cornice and was once the office of William Krull, town engineer. Next is a single-story yellow buff brick and terra-cotta building, followed by a two-story building carrying the "Wild" name with a pair of second-floor symmetrical bowed windows, which was once Alwin's funeral parlors.

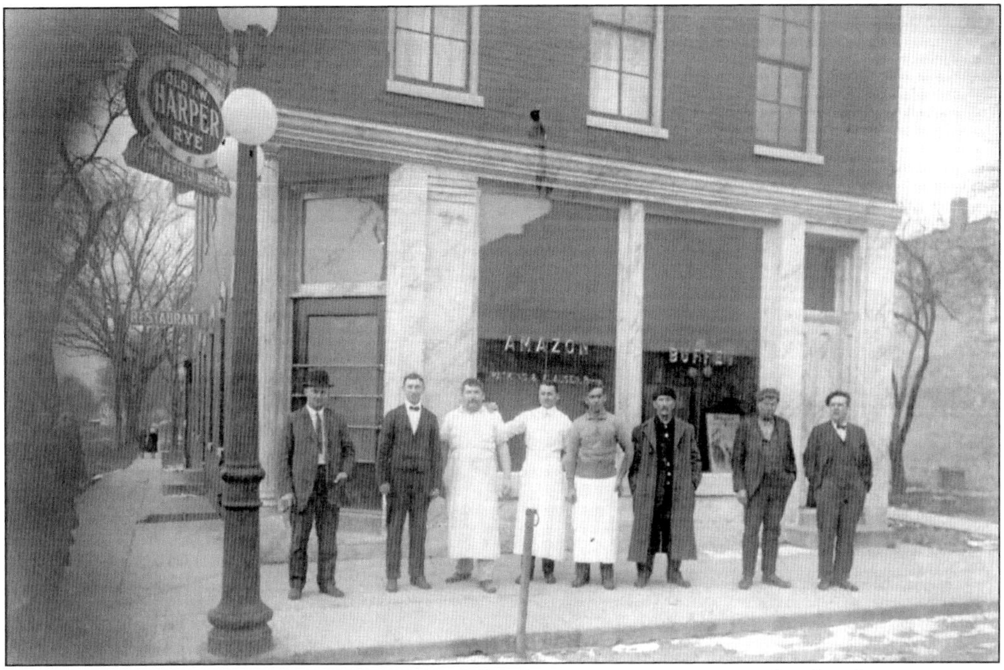

AMAZON RESTAURANT. This photograph of the Amazon restaurant can be dated to sometime between 1913 and 1918, due to the presence of streetlights, the gravel road, concrete sidewalk, and open corner entrance. The Amazon restaurant was reported to be one of the few eating establishments in downtown at this time. In 1918, the proprietor, George Watkins, announced the closing of the Amazon and conducted a sale of its items. However, later that same year, he reopened the restaurant as a short-order lunchroom that, in the late 1920s, was identified as the Amazon Café.

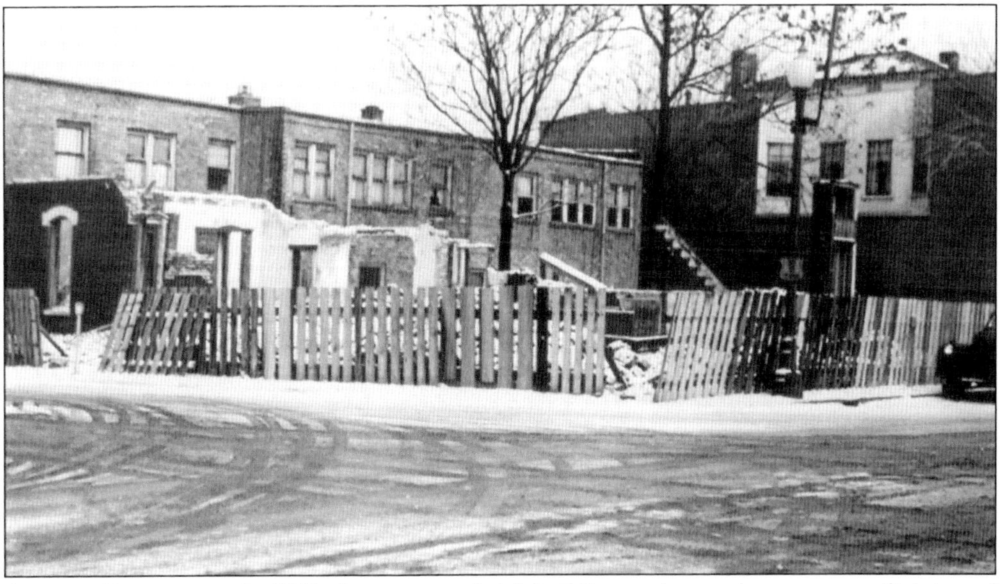

AMAZON DEMOLITION. In 1951, the two-story brick building at the northeast corner of Main and Center Streets was demolished by W.B. Mitchell. On this site, the north side of the 600 block of Third Street, he constructed the current single-story, five-storefront unit.

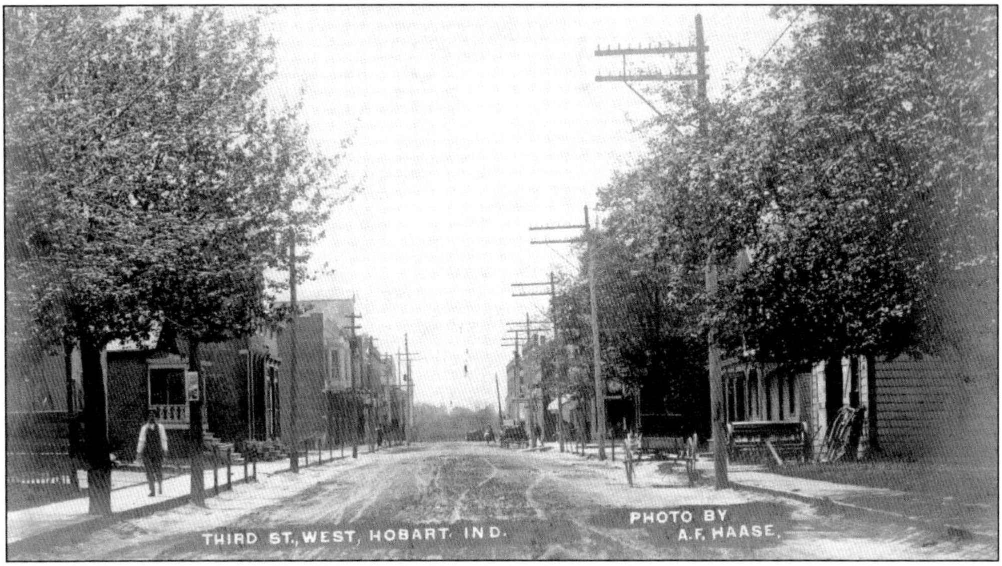

600 Block of Third Street, West View. The Strattan Opera House screen superstructure can be seen left of center in this c. 1908 photograph. In the foreground are two residential structures, a frame building on the right and a brick building on the left. The structures were razed around 1910. At the southeast corner of Center and Third Streets, a single-story, wood frame structure where the Newman building now stands is also visible. In 1911, it was reported that Paul Newman began relocating his hardware store and repair shop to this corner, years before constructing the current two-story, brick building at this site.

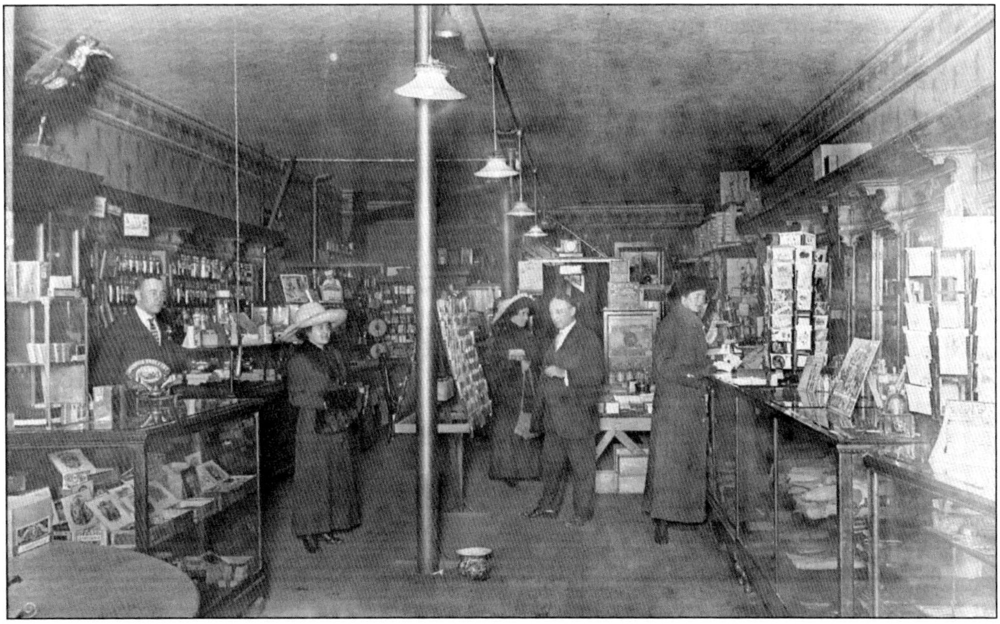

Scheddell & Reissig Drugstore. The popular drugstore was located on the south side of the 600 block of Third Street, at 607 Third Street. The heavy coats that each of the three women are wearing indicate the time of year at which this photograph may have been taken. On the right are 5¢ birthday cards, and a cigar case is visible on the lower left. An apothecary jar rack is along the back wall at left.

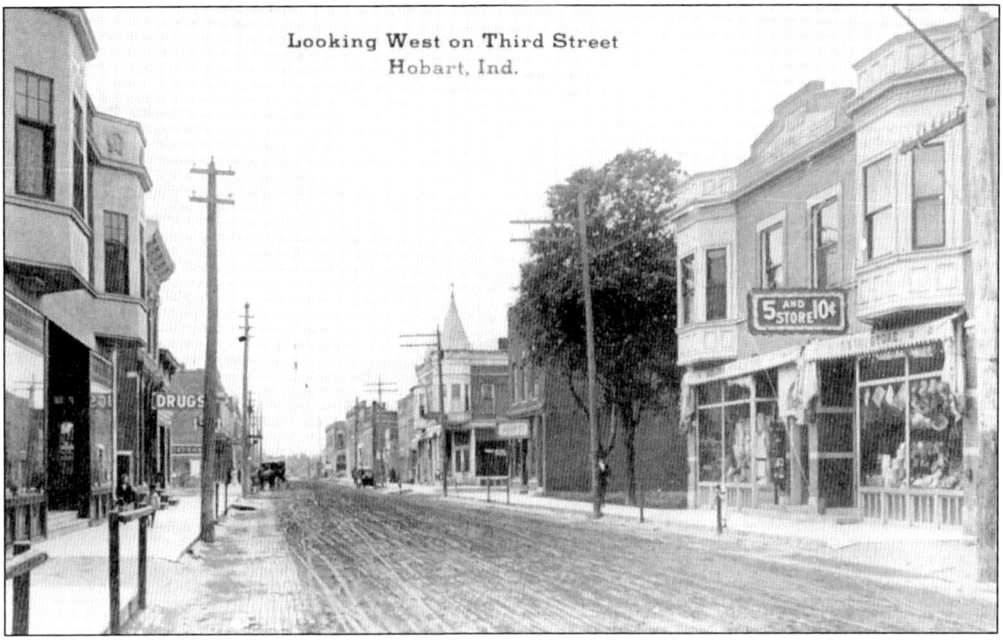

600 BLOCK OF THIRD STREET. These two west-facing photographs, taken at the same location, depict the 1910 structures of the Wild building (left) and the Friedrich building (right). The above photograph, taken around 1911, shows a gravel road and hitching posts. Missing are the 1912 streetlights and the streetcar tracks. The below photograph was most likely taken a few years later, sometime between 1914 and 1916. The hitching posts are still visible, as is the Strattan Opera House screen superstructure, which was not removed until 1917. The Gary Hobart Eastern streetcar ran east past Main Street on Third Street to the Pennsy Depot until 1919. The streetscape below depicts an interesting transition period in the Town of Hobart, with a mixture of automobiles, horse-drawn carriages, and the streetcar.

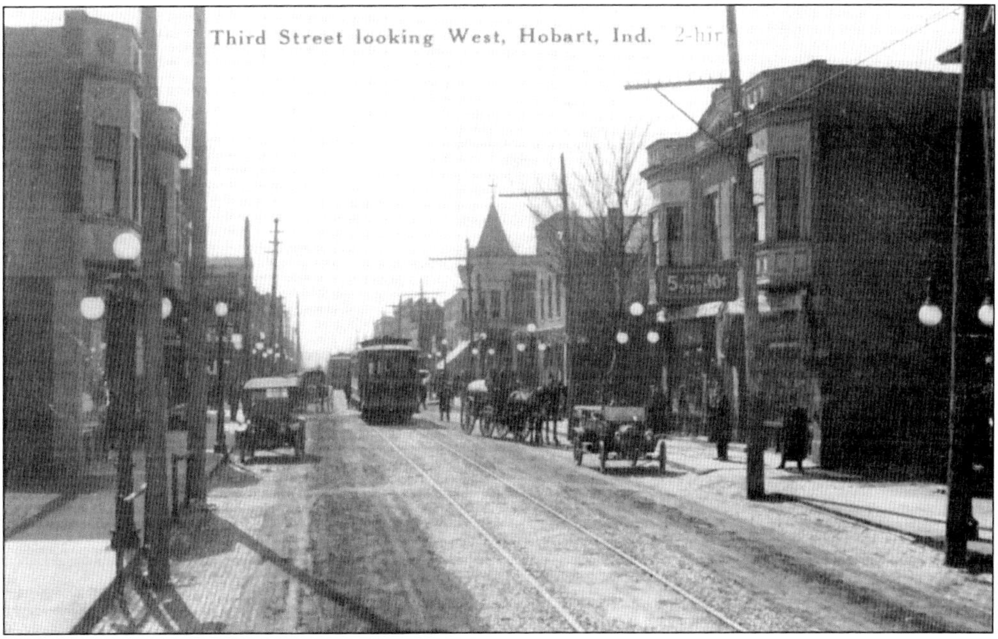

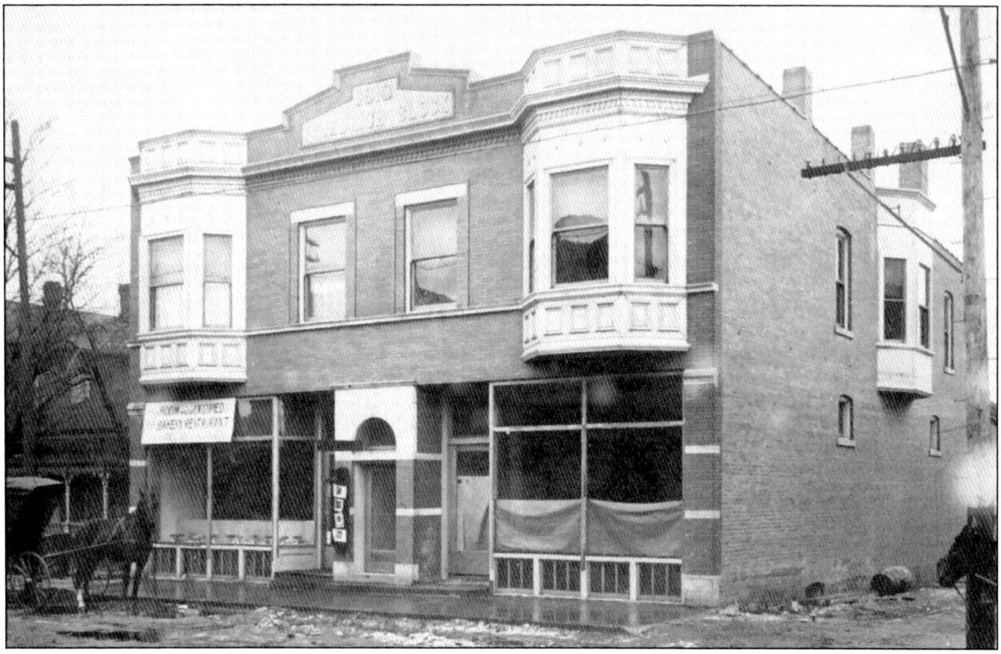

Friedrich Building. Dr. L.M. Friedrich constructed this two-story brick Italianate building in 1910. Dr. Friedrich had his residence on the second floor and his medical practice on the first floor. At one time, a photographer operated on the second floor, and over the past 100 years, there have been a variety of establishments, such as a bakery, bookstore, beauty shop, restaurant, *Hobart Gazette* offices, township trustee's offices, and the Hobart Post Office from 1923 to 1937.

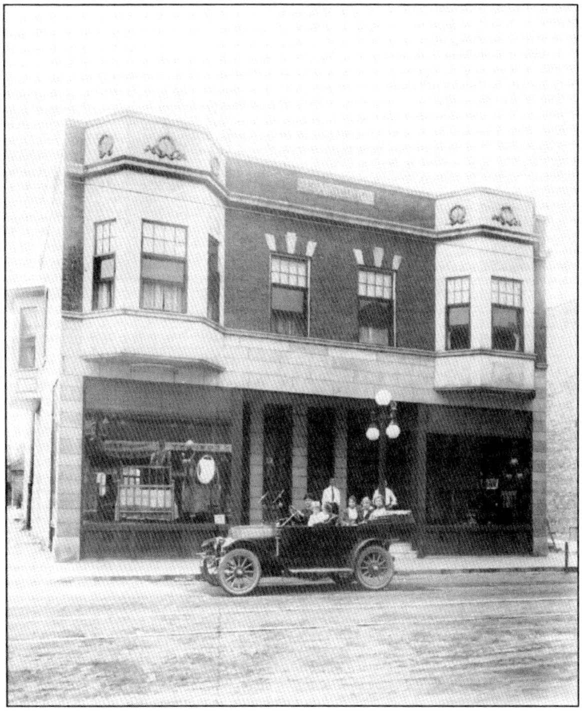

Wild Building. In 1910, Alwin Wild constructed this two-story brick Italianate building with living quarters on the second floor. The building is the current home of Like New Furniture, but Wild once operated his own furniture store from the same location. Wild, also a funeral director and embalmer, was described as a man of sterling integrity who had great foresight and excellent business ability.

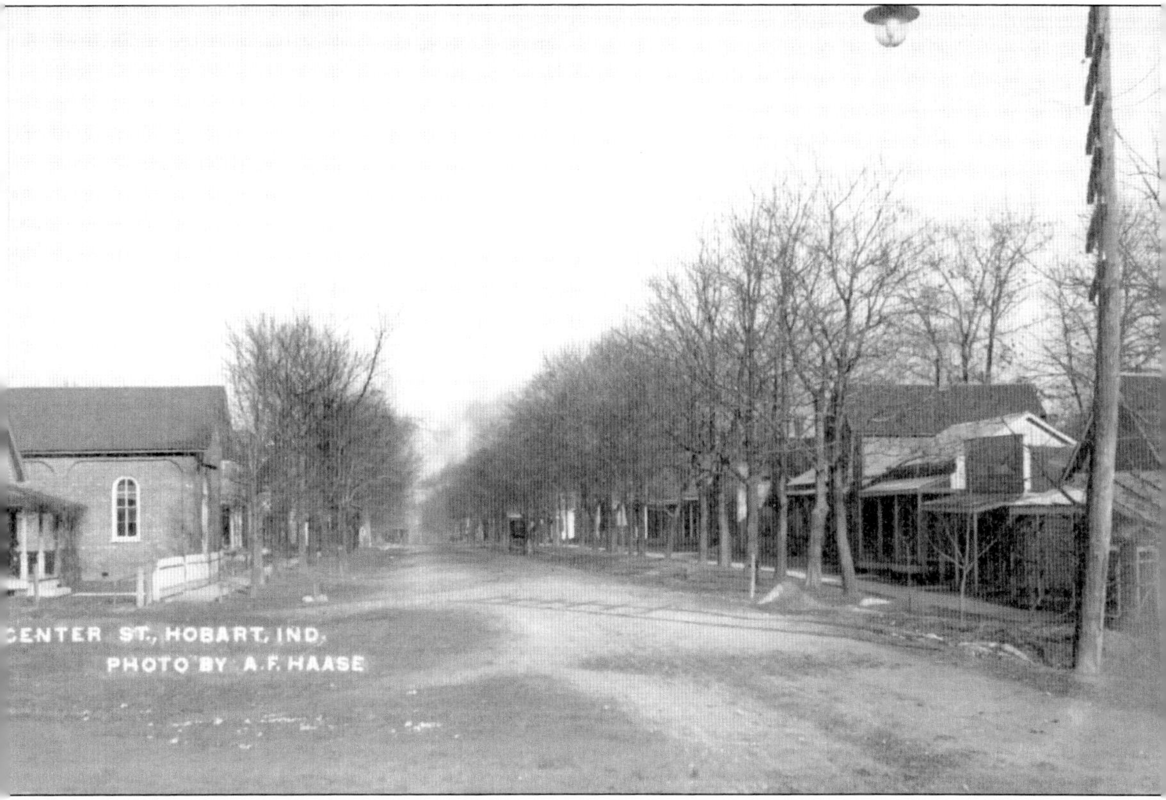

400 Block of Center Street. This north view of Center Street from the Nickel Plate Railroad shows Trinity Lutheran Church on the left. The gravel road and what appears to be a business on the right (possibly the cigar shop) date this photograph to around 1911. The Spencer family, retired circus and theater people, lived just south (right) of the cigar shop, adjacent to the Nickel Plate Railroad and across from the Nickel Plate Depot. They were said to have operated a small grocery store in Hobart. North along Center Street, lots consisted primarily of single-family homes, which still exist today along the east side of Center Street. One of the most notable is the Gordon home, at the southeast corner of Center and Second Streets. Dr. Gordon, a local physician and the county coroner from 1899 to 1909, built his Dutch Colonial Revival home with a ballroom on the third floor. The Rifenburg home, at the northeast corner of Center and Second Streets, was built by W.H. Rifenburg, who came to Hobart in 1857 and had interests in the community for over 40 years. He was elected to the Indiana state legislature in 1896.

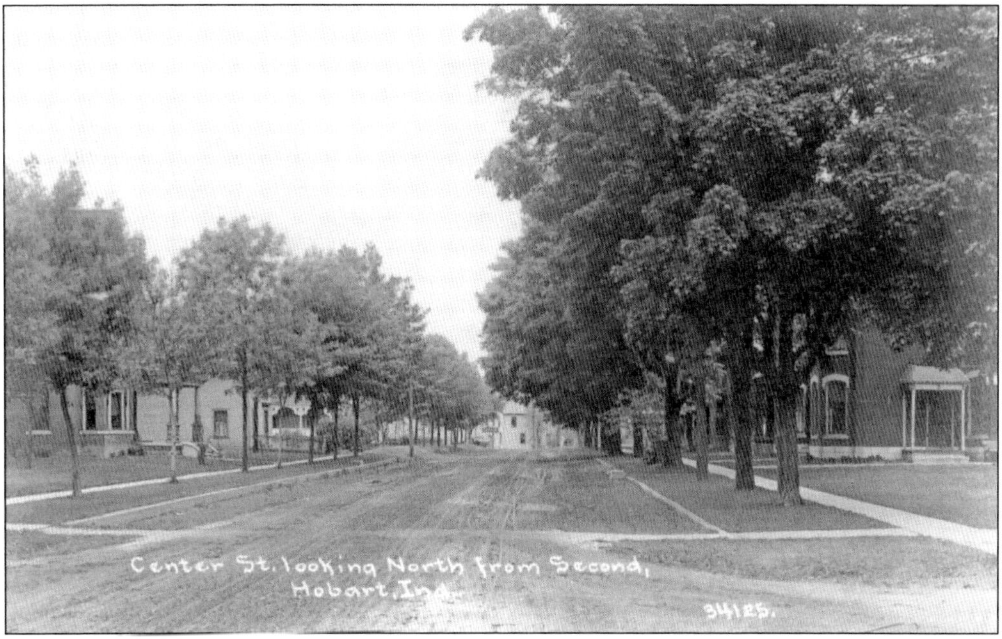

100 Block of Center Street. This north-facing photograph reveals a glimpse of the Rifenburg home, an Italianate Revival structure built in 1869 on the east side of the street. The home was the first in town to have central heating and full bathrooms. It was said that W.H. Reifenburg had a magnificent collection of books in his private library. The Reifenburg home was once featured in the *Chicago Tribune* as one of the Historic Homes of the Midwest. At the end of the street, a home can be seen with a sign reading "Garage." Eventually, that site became the Isakson garage.

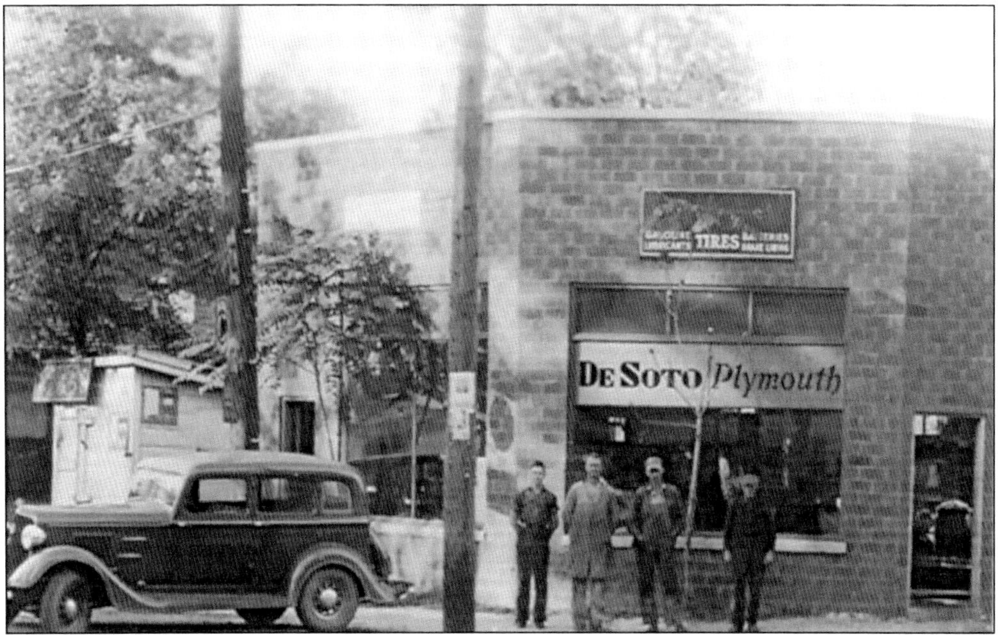

Isakson Garage. The Isakson brothers, Clarence and Walter, opened a Desoto-Plymouth dealership in 1928. They later converted the business to a Chrysler dealership in the 1960s. (Courtesy of Oyjdal Marvel Isakson.)

Five

Town of the Century

The nation's Progressive Era (1890–1920) was a period of social activism and political reform, and Hobart followed that trend. The village entered the era as a town, incorporated in 1889, and exited the era as a city, in 1921. A year before, Congress passed the 19th Amendment, establishing women's right to vote. The entire town voted on whether to become a city or remain a town. In October 1921, the votes were cast, and the decision to become a city passed by 219 votes. Candidates quickly began campaigning to become the city's first mayor, clerk, treasurer, and aldermen (council representatives).

Between 1900 and 1930, the Midwest was the most populous region in the country. The population trend was also reflected in Hobart. The 1920 census recognized a 95 percent population increase, the largest increase in Hobart's history. Before the end of the 19th century, in 1882, Hobart had taken the progressive step to grant the American Telephone Company the right to operate in town, and in 1898, the Water Works & Electric Light Plant began to provide service to Hobart's residents. Also during the Progressive Era the Hobart Women's Reading Club, with grant aid from Andrew Carnegie, helped to build a new town library. Carnegie was a Scottish American, self-made steel tycoon and national philanthropist who believed in the advancement and diffusion of knowledge and understanding.

Hobart also benefited from the nation's technological advancements in the early 20th century. In 1902, a local resident purchased the town's first automobile, a one-cylinder Oldsmobile. In 1900, a local man began to build a car, completing it in 1902. This car, also with one cylinder, was capable of speeds up to 30 miles per hour. This prompted the town, in 1904, to pass an ordinance limiting the speed of an automobile to no more than six miles per hour. Hobart shared in a global challenge when the United States entered World War I in 1917. The town had 231 men and 1 woman in military service. The city's health commissioner reported 600 cases of the influenza epidemic (Spanish Flu) in 1918, which resulted in 52 deaths, compared to the previous year's 40 cases and 9 deaths.

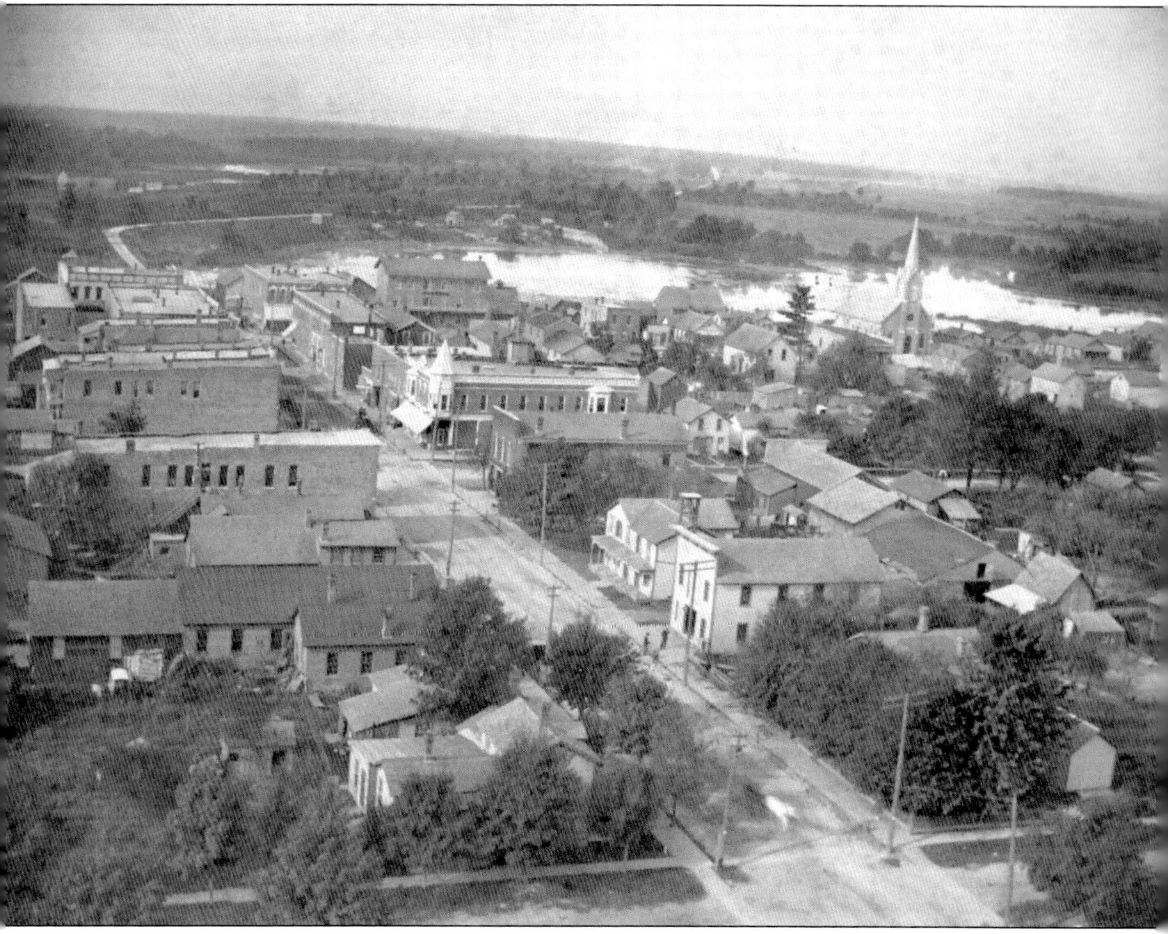

Aerial View, c. 1901. George Earle's Art Gallery, the white structure at far right, was later converted to St. Bridget's first Catholic church. Hobart House and the recently constructed Trinity Lutheran Church are seen near center right, with the church steeple soaring over Lake George, which serves as a backdrop in this early 20th century aerial photograph of the town. On the right, George Stocker's buildings are visible, excluding the two-story brick building at 315 Main Street, built the year after this photograph was taken. The building would hold the town offices. Left of center, the Guyer Building turret is visible, with the Amazon Restaurant building at center. The 1907 screen superstructure has yet to be added to the top of the Strattan Building. The wood frame, flat-front white building at lower center had a 525-pound fire bell hanging in the corner of the parapet. It was placed there in the mid-1890s and was used to alert the volunteer firefighters. It served as the town's fire alarm until 1910, when the first steam siren was installed at the light and water plant.

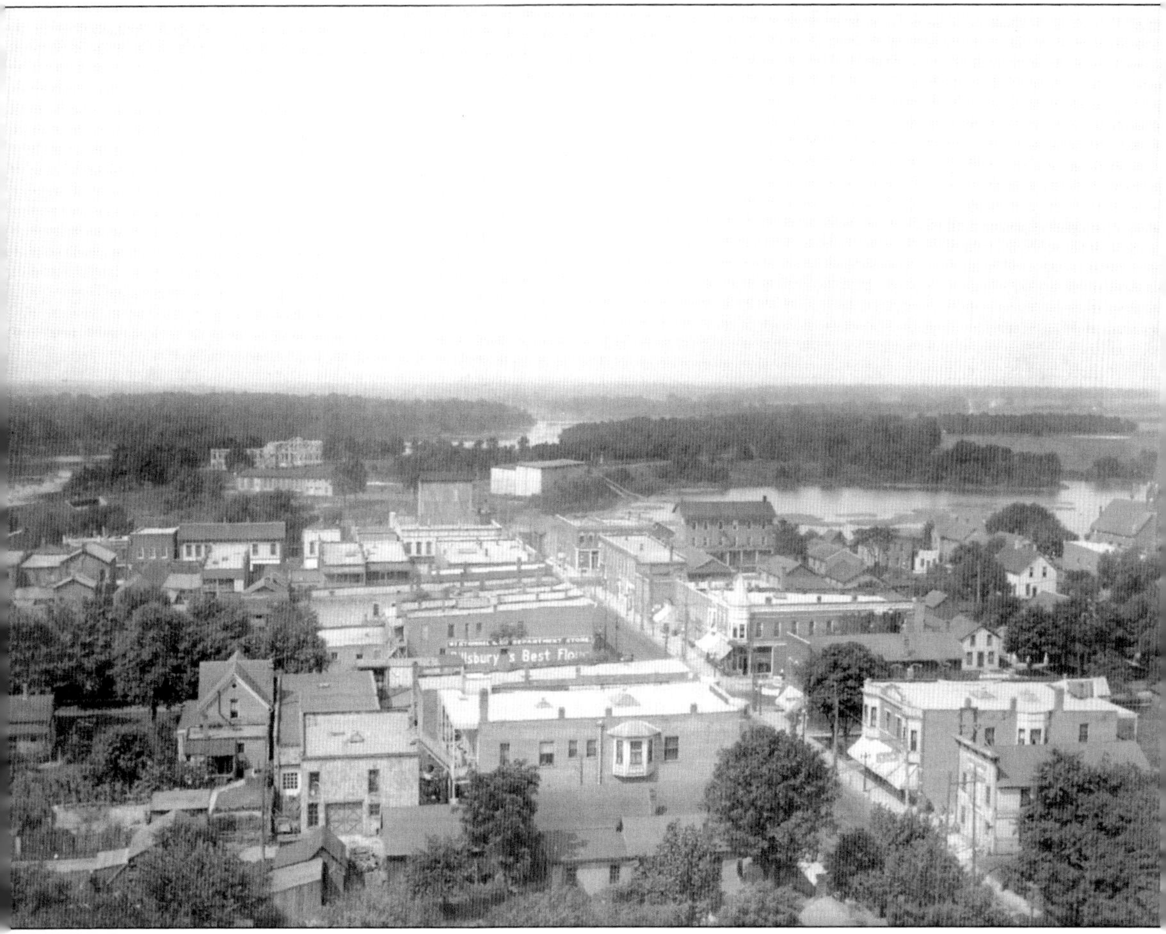

Aerial View, c. 1916. The light-colored structure in the center of this photograph is a large ice house that pulled up to two feet of cut ice from Lake George. The icehouse structure burned down in the 1920s. Across from the icehouse to the left are the streetcar barns. Left of center in the distance is the structure of a roller coaster called the Figure Eight. The coaster was part of the 1912 Hobart Amusement Company, which was contracted to develop five acres south of the Nickel Plate Railroad into the Lake George Amusement Park. Funding for the park project was secured from stock sales. Additional attractions included a merry-go-round, dance pavilion, and concessions. The plan was to coordinate the operation of an amusement park with a streetcar system. Ultimately, the Lake George amusement park project failed due to disputes in electrical rights and a delay in the development of a streetcar system, which did not become fully operational until 1914. By 1917, the park sold all of its real property to settle county tax debts. The land was acquired by the city's park system in the early 1930s.

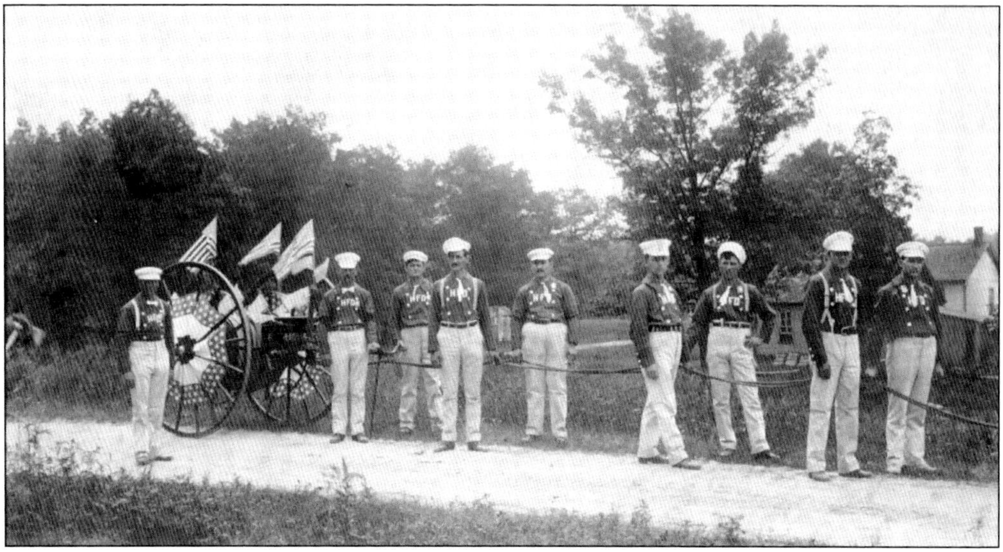

Water Bucket Brigade. At the turn of the 20th century, Hobart was a well-established and growing town. It had a bustling downtown and prosperous industry, but it lacked an organized fire department. It was said that, in the town's early days, when a fire broke out, residents would gather at the scene without much of a plan. The lack of a town fire protection plan prompted a group of prominent businessmen to meet in the summer of 1891 and discuss the creation of a volunteer fire department.

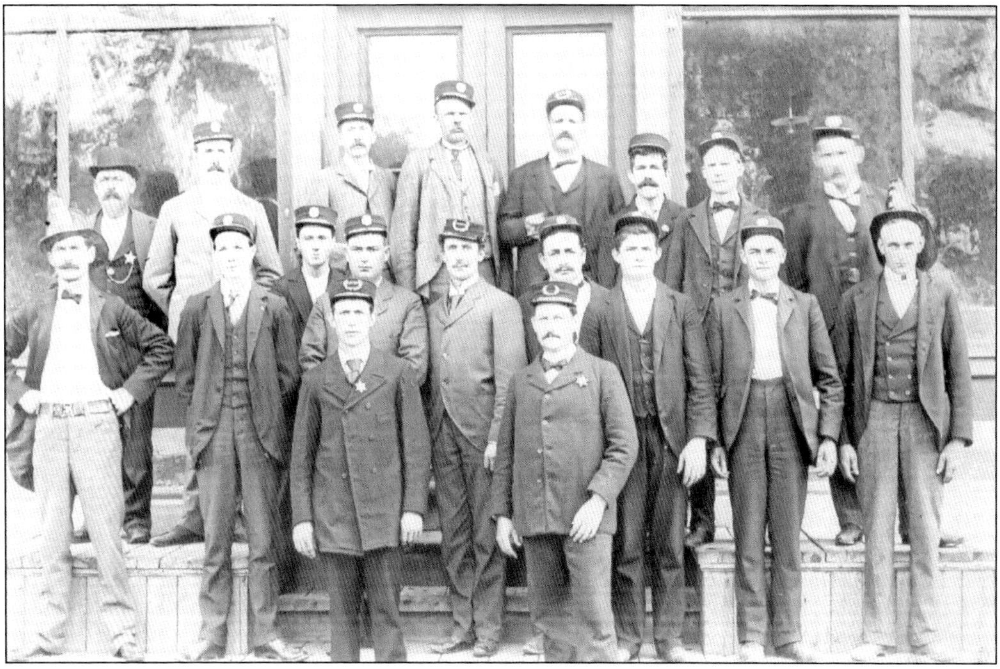

Hobart Volunteer Fire Department. On November 2, 1891, Hobart businessmen Stocker, Strattan, Owen, and Lightner organized a volunteer fire department and purchased a Howe hand pump to assist in the town's firefighting. In 1901, Hobart assigned a town fire marshal, and when the town became a city in 1921, this title was changed to that of fire chief. The Hobart Fire Department is seen here in 1895.

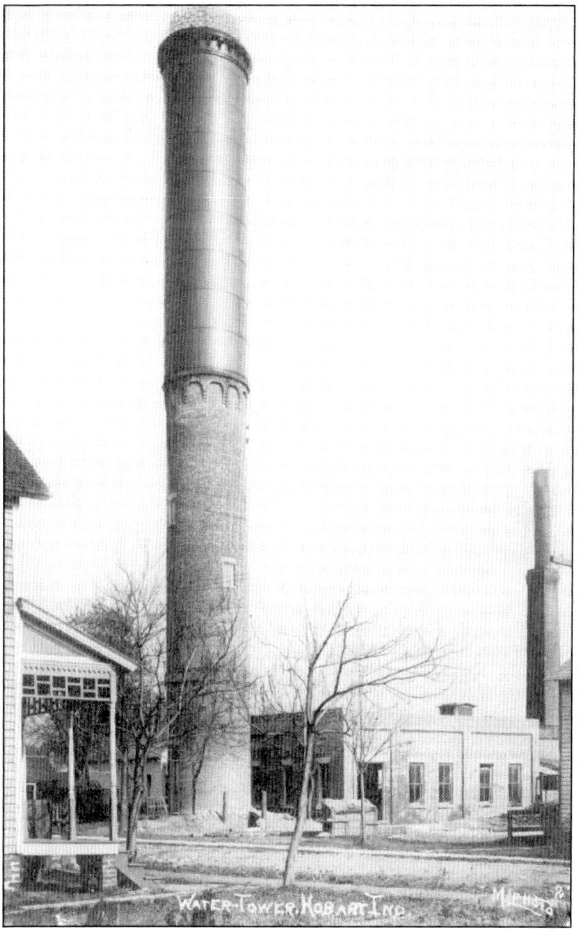

HOBART WATER WORKS & ELECTRIC LIGHT PLANT. The Hobart Water Works & Electric Light Plant was located on the east side of the 300 block of New Street. It was constructed in 1897, and in 1898, the town made two new appointments for the plant, a superintendent and a tapper. The plant's brick-and-metal standpipe (right) towered 125 feet over the town. The facility had a 60,000-gallon tank and a 75,000-gallon pump reaching four-, six-, and eight-inch water mains. The electric light plant was operated by a 100-horsepower Ball high-speed engine. The electric circuits were said to have extended to all parts of the town, furnishing street illumination and lights in nearly all private and public buildings. The Hobart Water Works & Electric Light Plant issued municipal and corporate bonds. It operated for over 32 years.

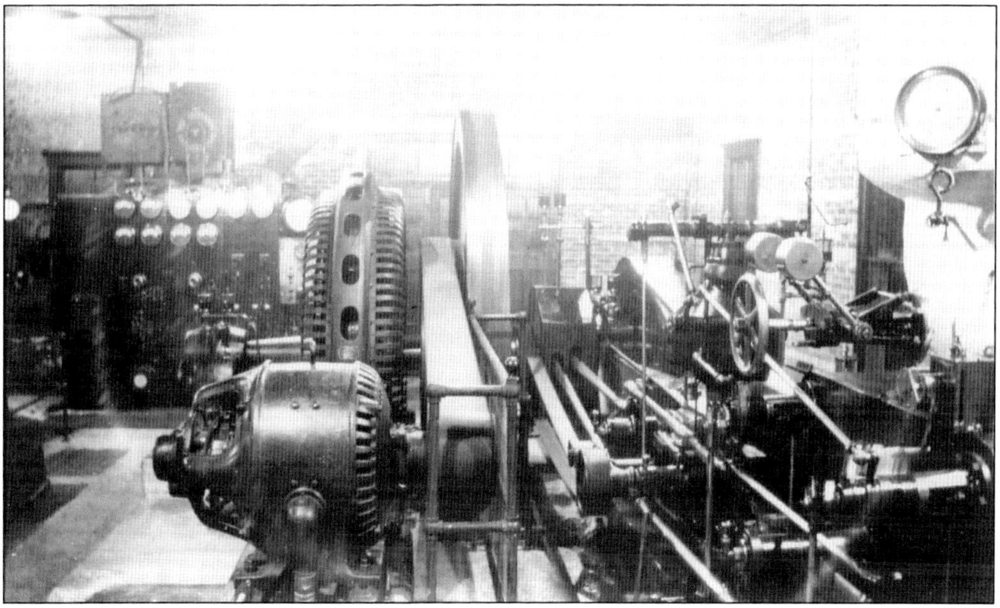

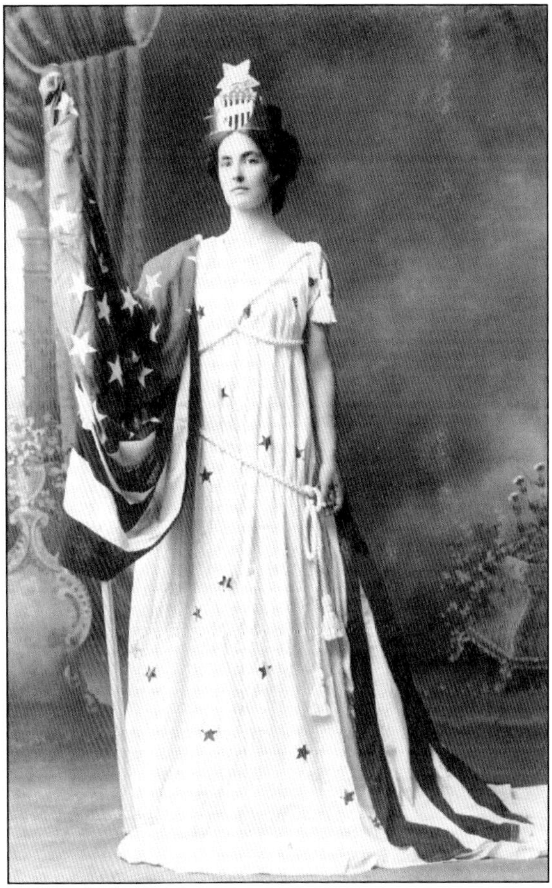

Goddess of Liberty. One of Hobart's earliest recorded Fourth of July celebrations took place in 1876, making the ongoing event at least 137 years old. Over the years, a variety of activities have been held during the Independence Day celebration, including the firing of cannons, athletic games, concerts, dances, battle reenactments, and even a public wedding ceremony in 1898. There was a time when Hobart would select a Goddess of Liberty, as seen in this c. 1910 photograph. Decades later, the celebration included the selection of a Miss Hobart.

Indian Ridge Country Club. In 1831, the future site of the golf course was a Potawatomi Village. The area had also seen numerous Sauk and Potawatomi battles. It was farmed in the early 1880s; around 1900, John Dorman, a Chicago businessman, bought the property for a summer retreat. Eventually, he designed it into a golf course. Dorman hosted a ceremony on June 18, 1931, to honor 150 Ross and Hobart Township pioneers.

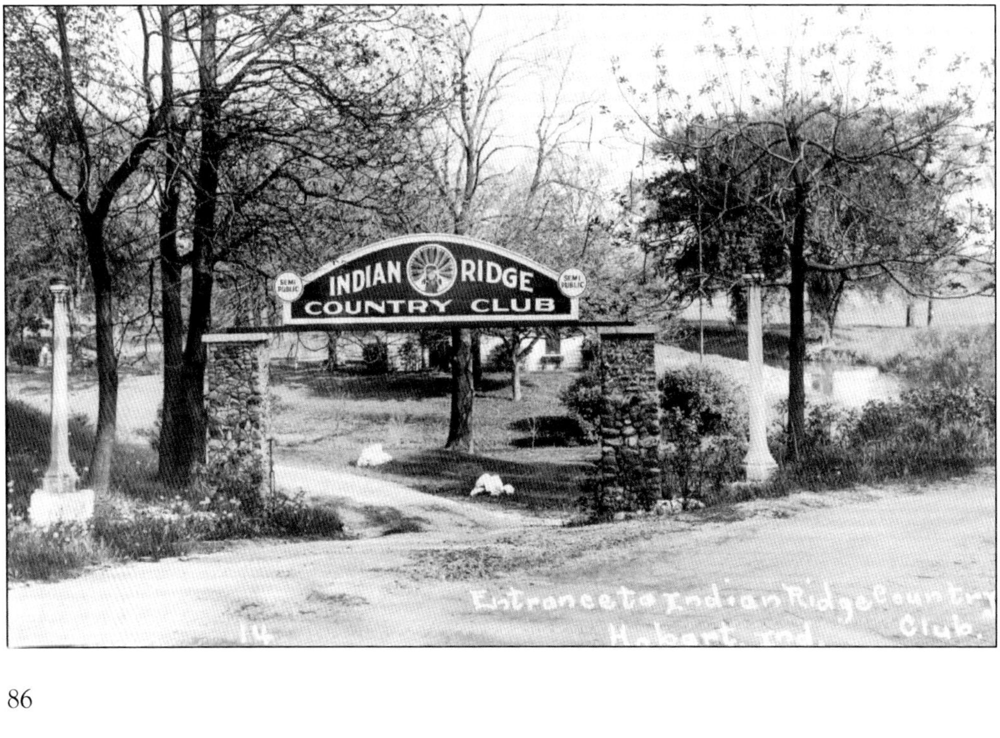

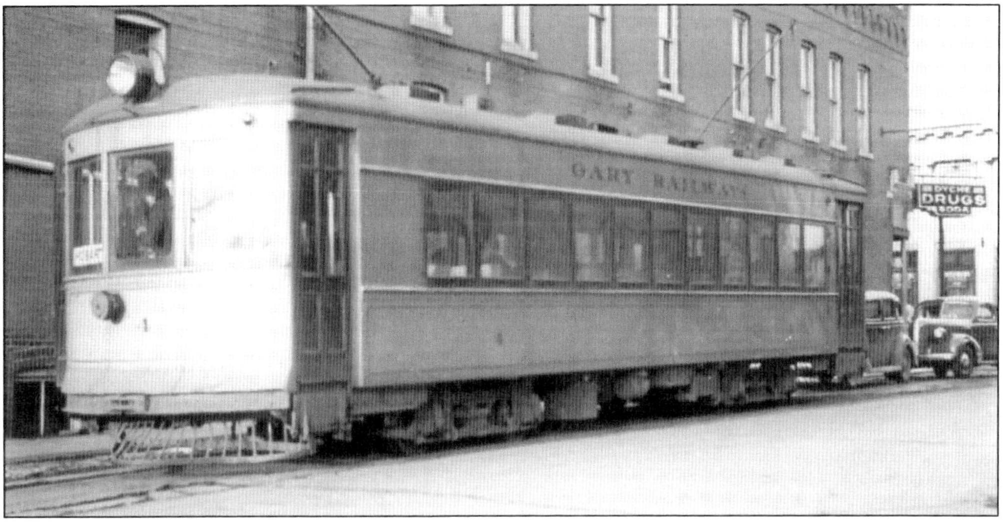

Streetcar. Around 1914, the Gary Hobart & Eastern Traction Company (GH&E) streetcar began running regular service between Hobart and Gary. The original line extended from Gary to the Pennsy Depot, but service to that stop ceased in 1919. In 1925, the GH&E merged with Gary Railways, and buses began to replace the streetcar. The streetcar rail service ended on March 18, 1939.

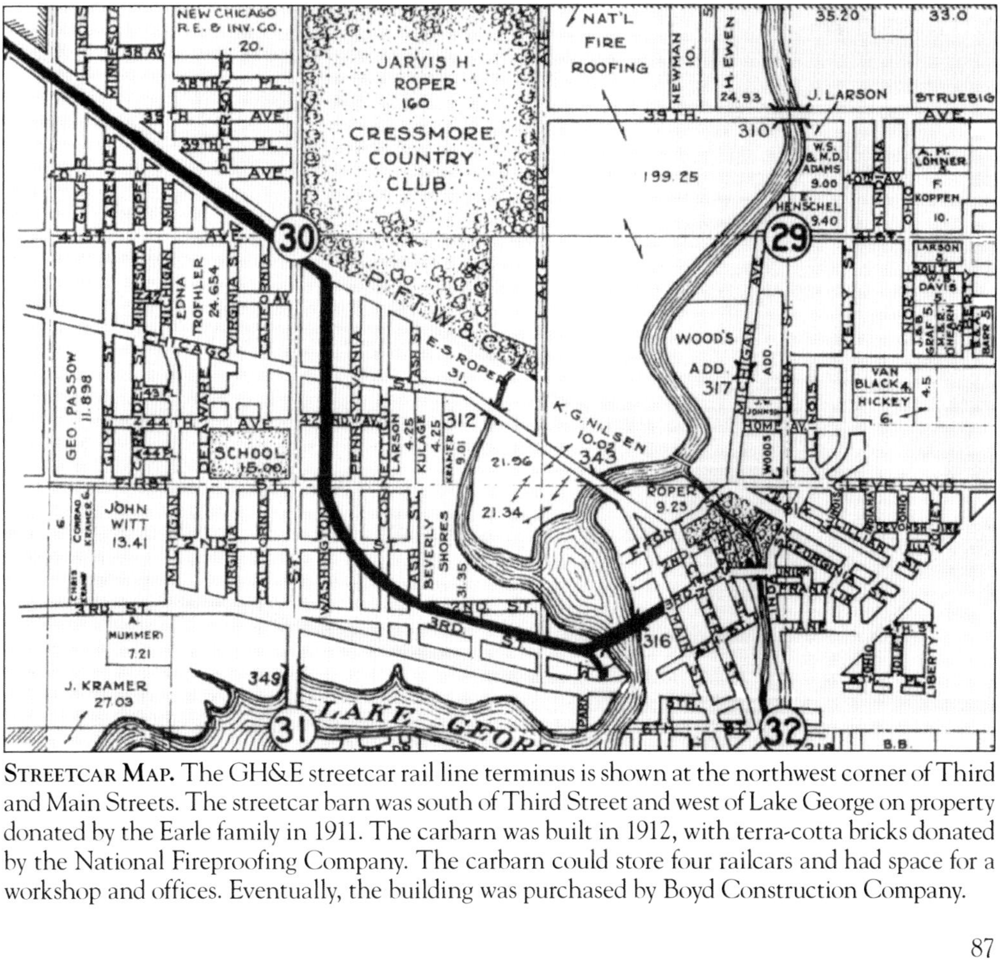

Streetcar Map. The GH&E streetcar rail line terminus is shown at the northwest corner of Third and Main Streets. The streetcar barn was south of Third Street and west of Lake George on property donated by the Earle family in 1911. The carbarn was built in 1912, with terra-cotta bricks donated by the National Fireproofing Company. The carbarn could store four railcars and had space for a workshop and offices. Eventually, the building was purchased by Boyd Construction Company.

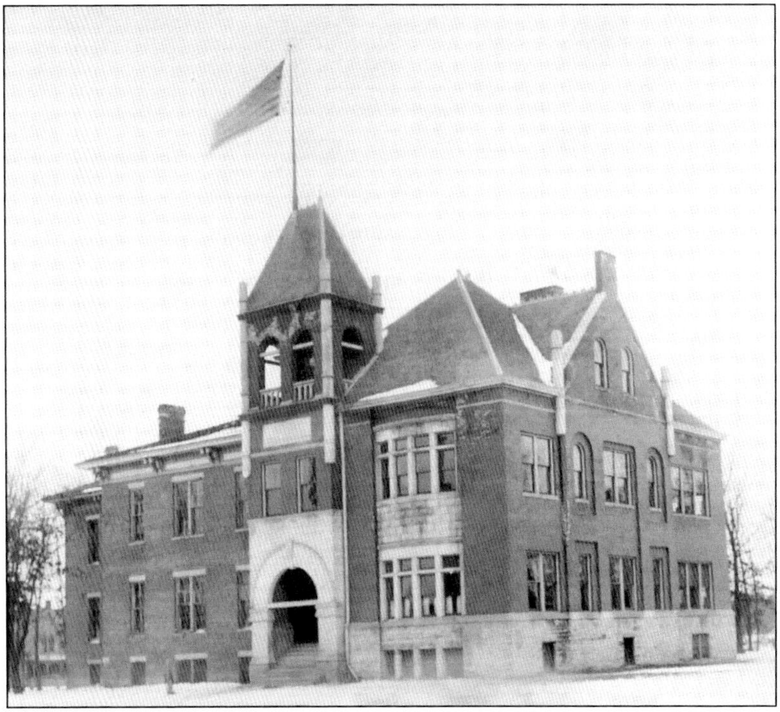

Hobart School. The original schoolhouse was constructed in 1877. The four-room building was constructed on the south side of Fourth Street between New and East Streets. As Hobart went from a village with a population of 600 in 1880 to a town in 1890 with a population of over 1,000, the school expanded in 1892 and again in 1894.

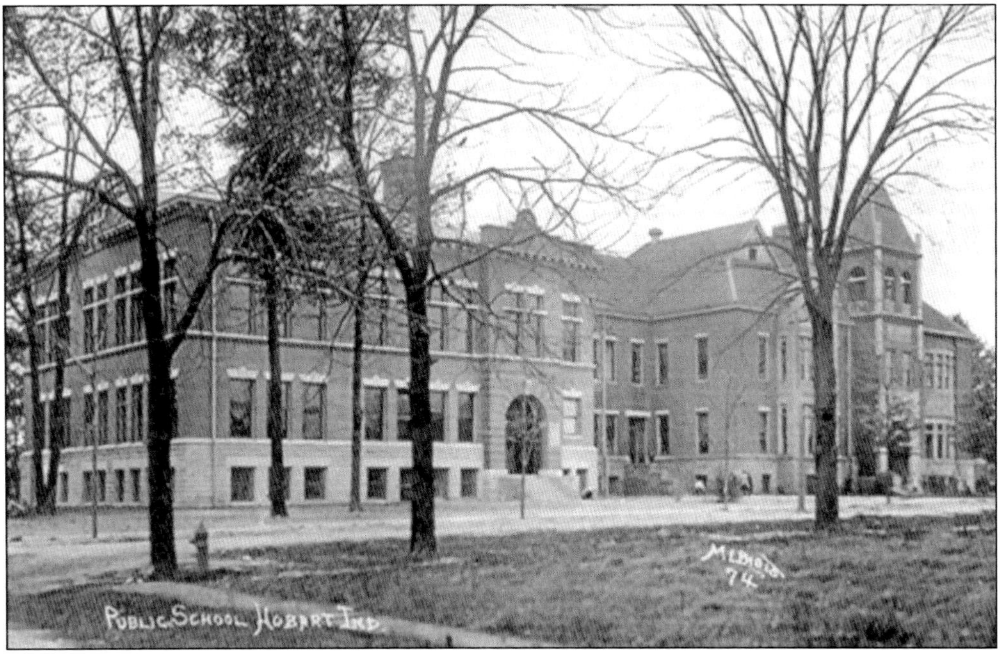

Hobart High School. The schoolhouse was divided into three educational sections: primary, grammar, and high school. Within each division, there were four grades, each consisting of one year's work. In 1898, the state Board of Education commissioned the school and recognized it as Hobart High School. The newly recognized institution, seen here around 1924, allowed its graduates to enter colleges and universities without reexamination. In 1939, the high school expanded again, as Hobart, now a city, had a population of about 7,000.

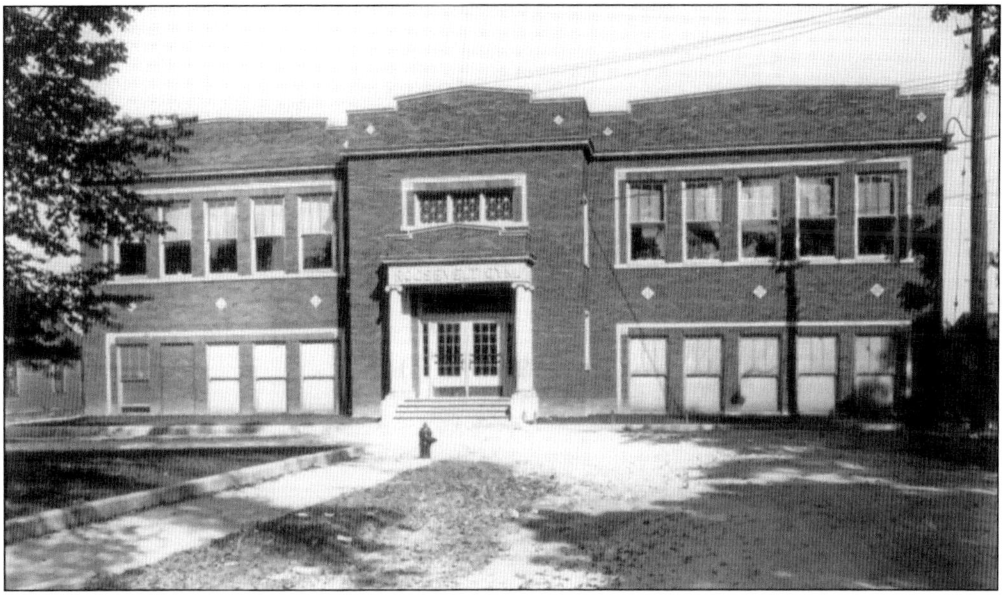

Roosevelt School. The Roosevelt School opened for the 1924–1925 school year with five classrooms on the upper level and a gymnasium on the lower level. In 1939, more classrooms were added just before the 1940 census revealed a city population increase of over 3,000 residents from when the school was built. The Roosevelt Gym/School functioned as an elementary school until the 1950s, when elementary classes were moved to the newly constructed elementary schools of Foreman (1944) and Liberty (1949).

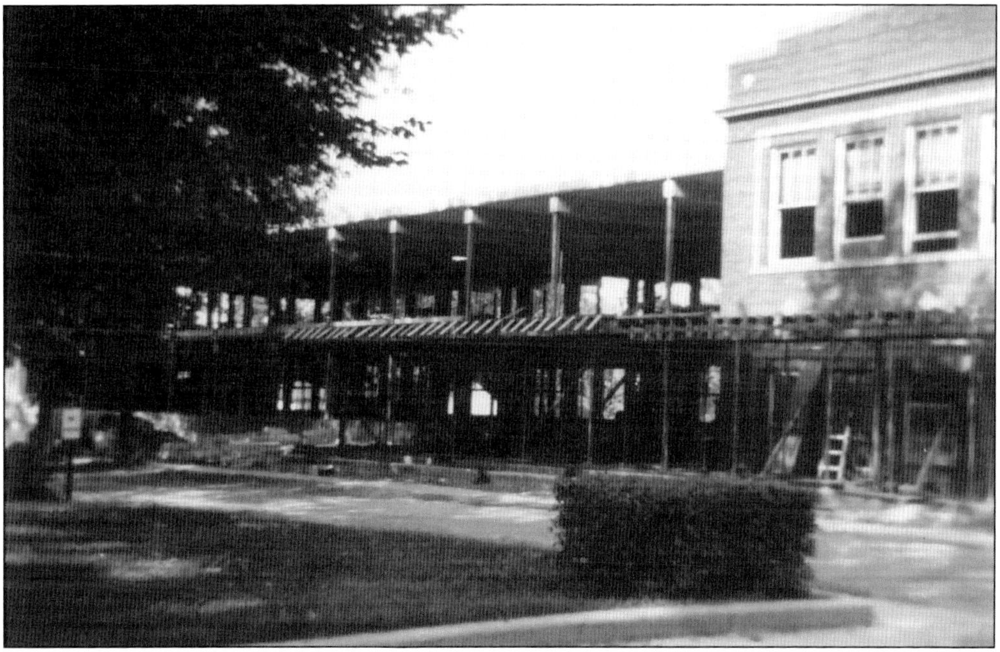

Hobart Junior High School. The elementary school was remodeled multiple times after the 1950s, with the addition of classrooms in 1954, 1961, 1967, and 1981. The building functioned as part of the Hobart Junior High School along the east side of New Street, the former site of the Hobart Water Works & Electric Power, until it was razed in 2011 to create public parking.

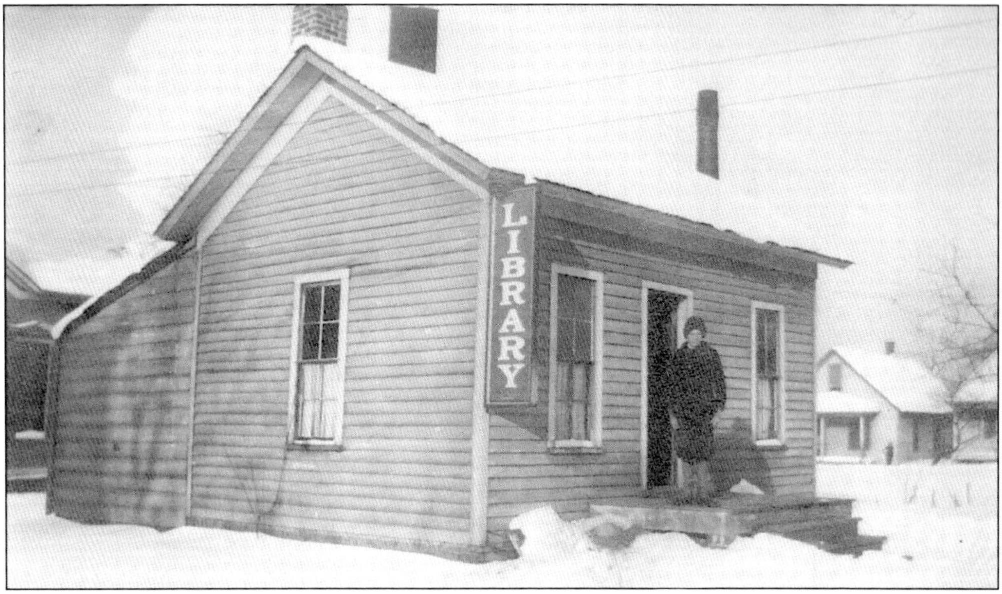

Early Library. Hobart Town Library was a hall-and-parlor home with a rear lean-to extension. The library was located on the north side of the 700 block of Fourth Street. In 1913, the Hobart Women's Reading Club helped raise money to purchase lot 73 and raze the town's early library. It was through their efforts that the Hobart Public Library was built on the site. In 1968, the Hobart Public Library was purchased by the Hobart Historical Society.

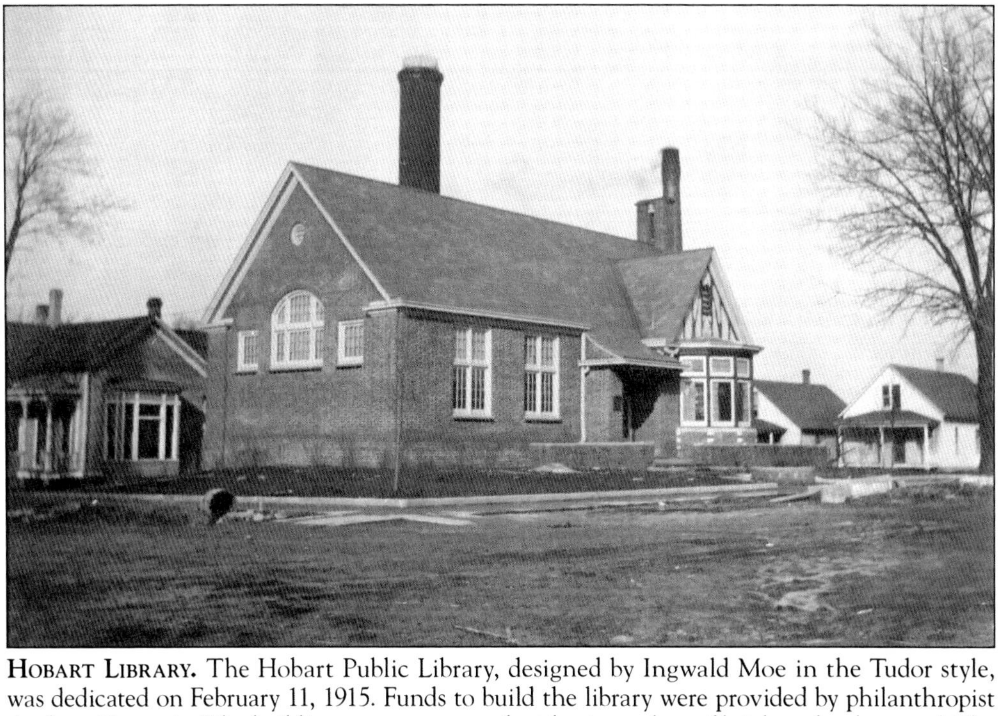

Hobart Library. The Hobart Public Library, designed by Ingwald Moe in the Tudor style, was dedicated on February 11, 1915. Funds to build the library were provided by philanthropist Andrew Carnegie. The building was constructed with nine colors of brick and a slate roof. The bay windows of leaded glass featured stained-glass medallions. On July 15, 1982, the Hobart Public Library was listed in the National Register of Historic Places.

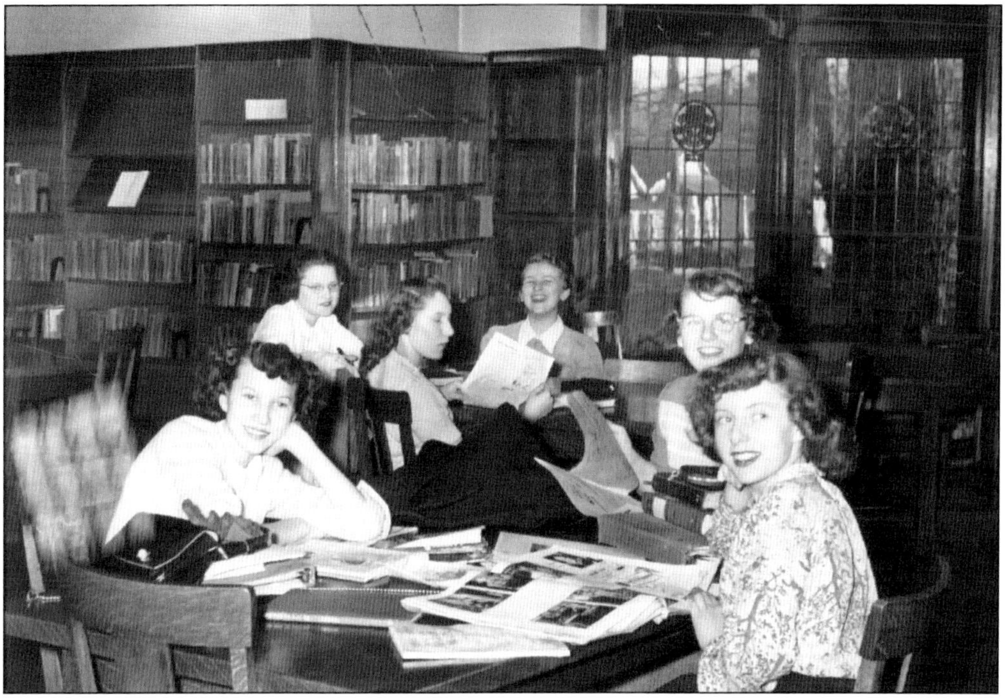

Library Patrons. The Hobart library served the public for 52 years. In 1967, the city began construction of a new public library on the southwest corner of Main and Front Streets. In 1968, the Hobart Public Library was purchased by the Hobart Historical Society, which continued the building's intended purpose of learning and research.

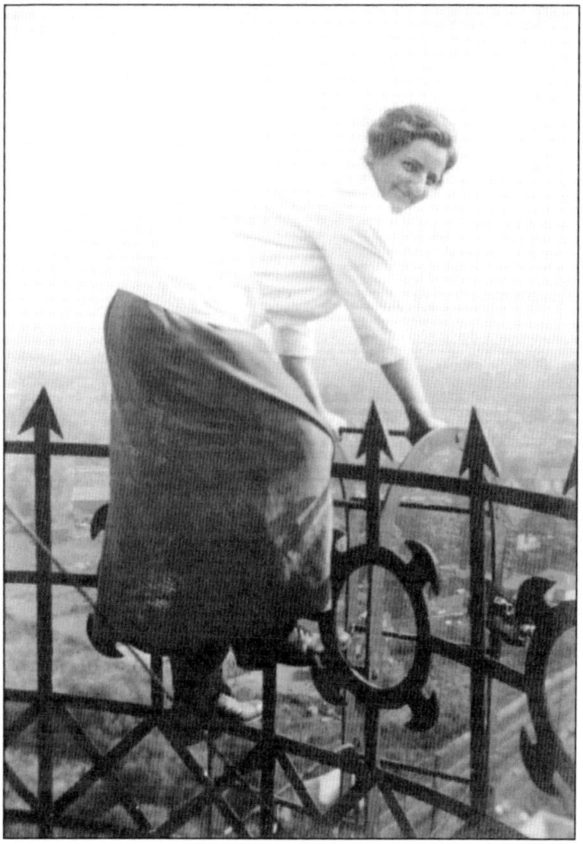

Adventurous Librarian. The librarian of the Hobart library was Dorothy Thomas. She climbed the 125-foot-high Hobart water tower one Sunday morning in August 1915. At the time, Thomas said she thought "the climb would be fun" and that she "enjoyed the view." Her photographs from the top of the water tower forever preserved spectacular views of the town for future generations.

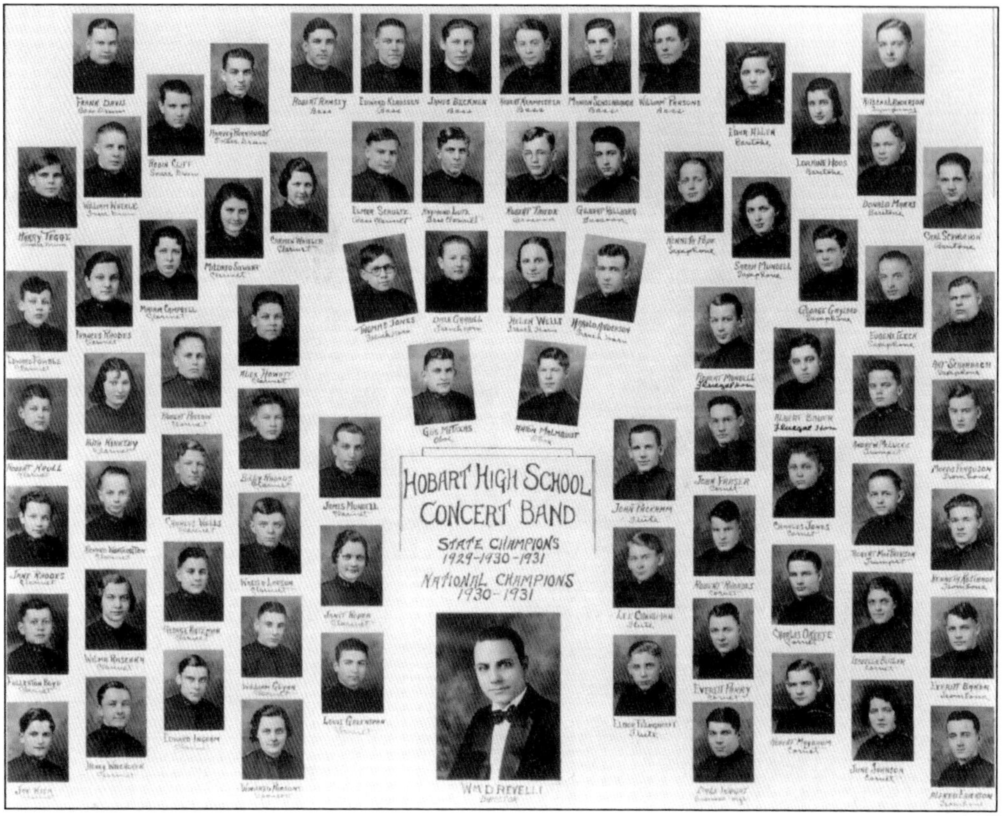

HOBART CONCERT BAND. William Revelli began his career in 1925 with a handful of Hobart students with no uniforms and borrowed instruments. Within five years, the Hobart band was famous for winning national and state contests. The band claimed state championships from 1929 to 1931 and national championships in 1930, 1931, 1933, and 1934.

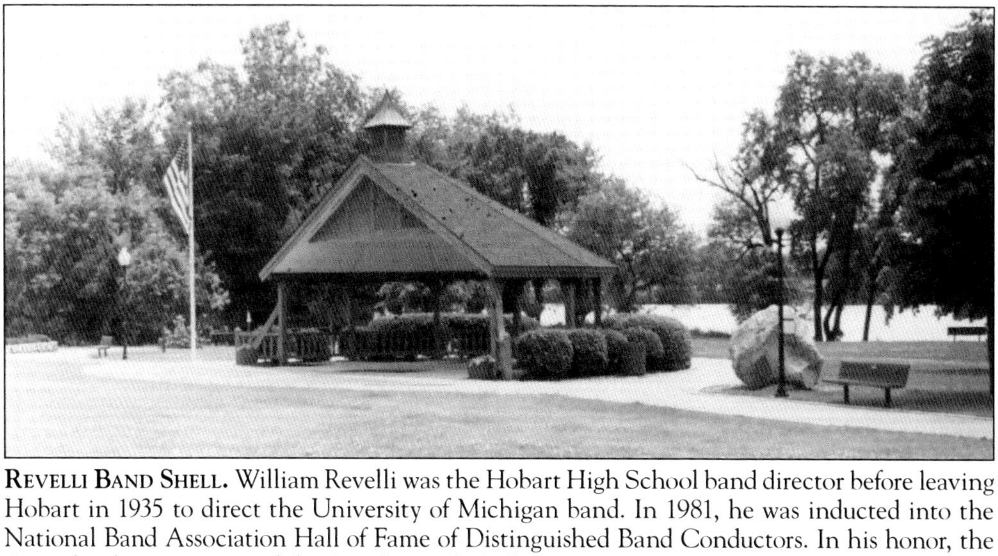

REVELLI BAND SHELL. William Revelli was the Hobart High School band director before leaving Hobart in 1935 to direct the University of Michigan band. In 1981, he was inducted into the National Band Association Hall of Fame of Distinguished Band Conductors. In his honor, the City of Hobart constructed the Revelli Band Shell in 1987 at Festival Park. In the 1920s, Festival Park was the former site of Kullage Brickworks.

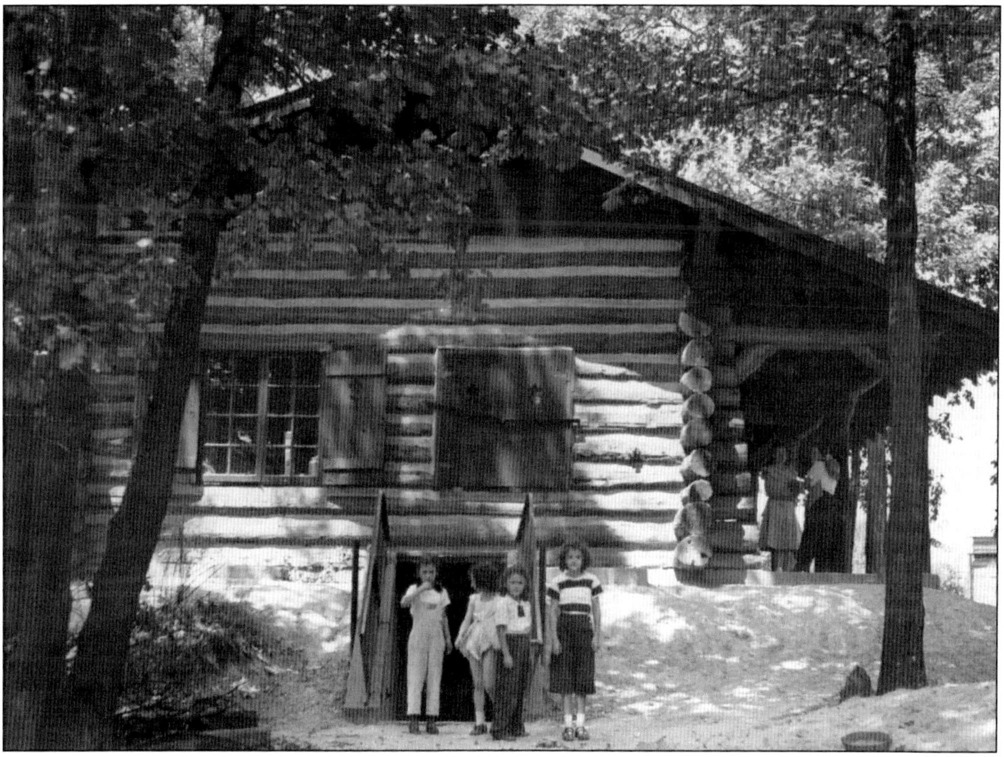

HOBART SCOUT CABIN. The Boy Scouts of America was founded in 1910, and the Girls Scouts of the United States of America was established two years later. Early records show that two Boy Scout troops formed in the Calumet area in 1921. The scoutmaster of Troop 2 was listed as Elmer Ballantyne (the little boy on this book's cover). In 1933, a scout cabin was built; it was dedicated on February 10, 1934. The land, now Pavese Park, was donated by the Barnes family for the use of Scout activities. The original cabin was destroyed by fire in 1979 and rebuilt by community volunteers for scouting use in 1985. The above photograph shows a girls' scouting event at the original cabin around 1945. Below, the new Scout cabin is seen around 1986.

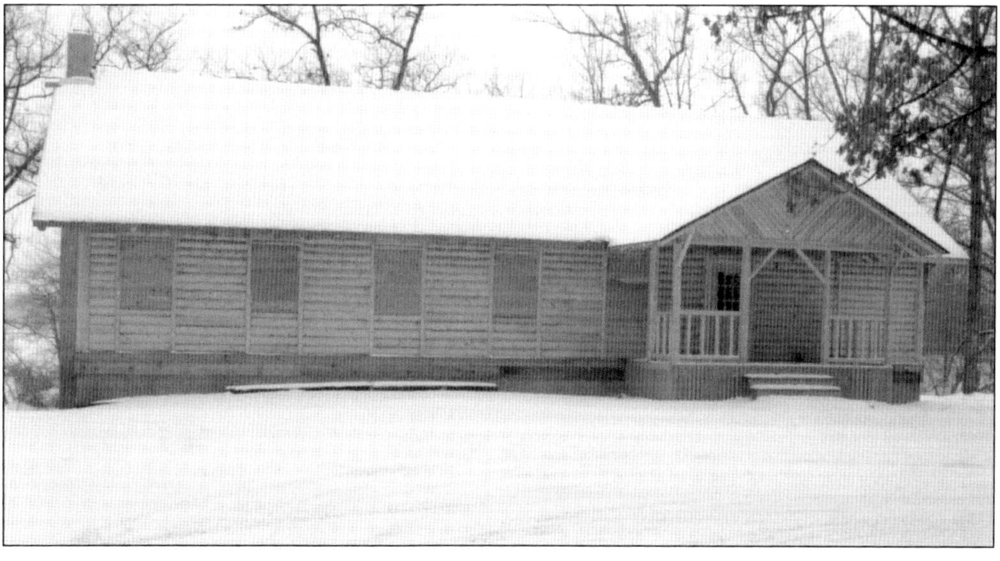

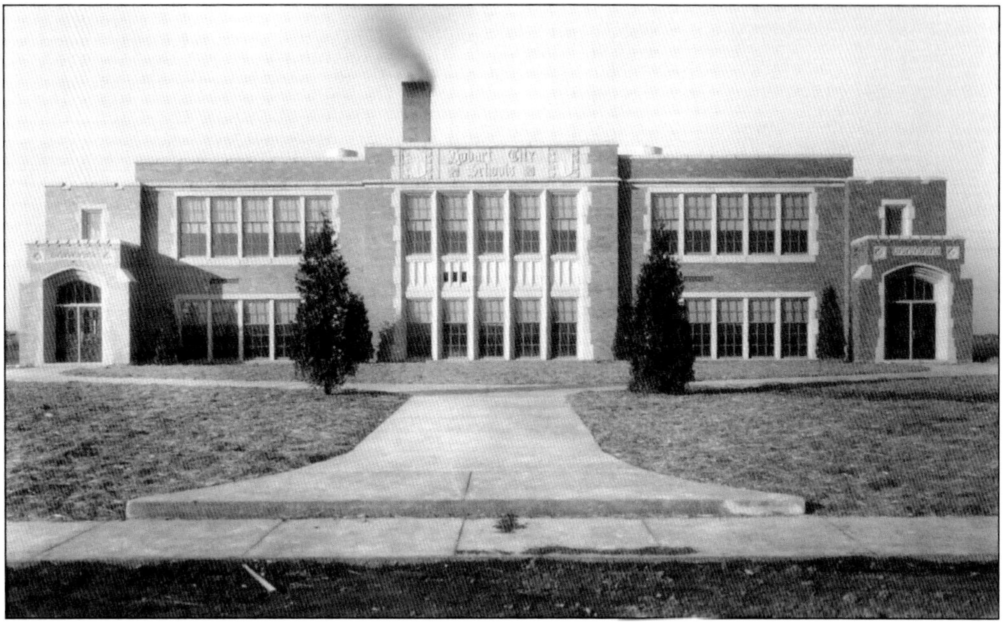

MUNDELL SCHOOL. A Gothic Revival school building was constructed on what was then the west side of the city. The Mundell Elementary School opened in 1930. It was named after the first family to settle in that area, whose descendants donated 15 acres of land at $1 an acre. In 1941, 1952, and 1956, the school was expanded. It was demolished in 1994, and the students were transferred to Joan Martin.

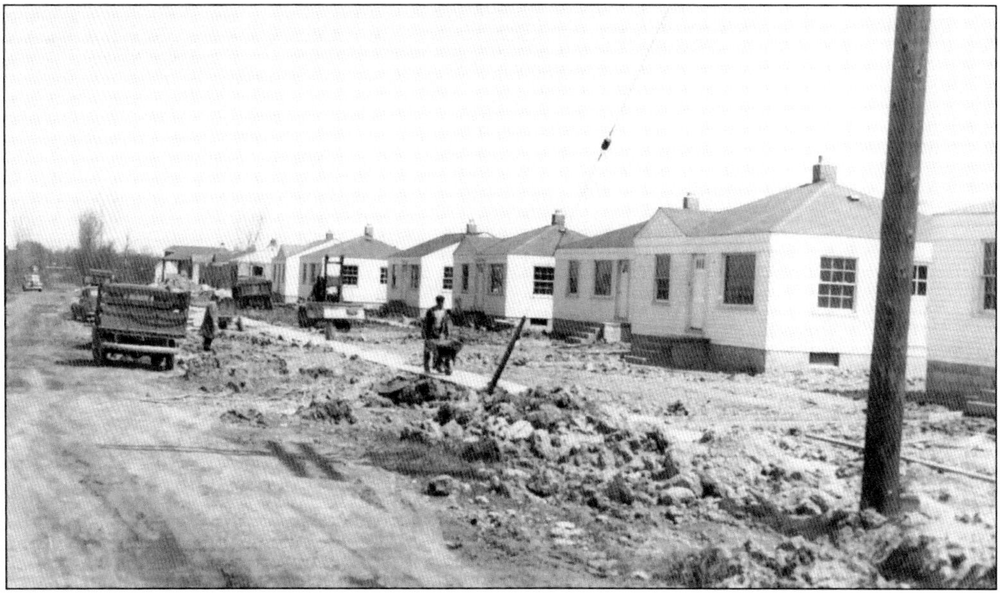

MUNDELL NEIGHBORHOOD. When Mundell School was constructed in 1931, it was in an area of undeveloped land. By 1939, it was surrounded by streets with vacant lots. Demand for the wood frame homes boomed in the late 1940s and early 1950s. The homes ranged anywhere from 800 to 1,200 square feet and were part of the response to the high demand for housing after World War II. From the construction of Mundell School to the 1950 census, the city population nearly doubled to over 10,000 people. Hobart was elevated to a fourth-class city.

Six

Yesteryears

From the mid-1930s to the 1950s, the City of Hobart operated as a fifth-class city under Indiana state law. During the Depression, Hobart relied on Lake George for entertainment and on New Deal programs to help overcome the era's economic woes. One of the New Deal agencies was the Works Progress Administration (WPA), which was funded by Congress through the Emergency Relief Appropriation Act of 1935. The WPA was charged with construction of public buildings, roads, and sidewalks, and the employment of a variety of arts-related professionals. It was the largest and most ambitious federal program, and it aided Hobart in constructing the bathhouse, post office mural, and the Brickie Bowl.

In 1938, President Roosevelt signed the Fair Labor Standards Act, which restructured the American working process and banned child labor. This act, along with the nation's high unemployment rate, changed the way schools operated. In Hobart, the existing school buildings were expanding to meet the increasing enrollment of the decade, while new schools were built in the following years to accommodate increasing populations at the end of the Great Depression. The United States entered World War II in 1941, and more than 700 Hobart residents served; 42 gave their lives. After the war, a national housing boom ensued. It was reported in 1950 that, for the first time, more than half of all occupied housing units were owned. At this time, single-family homes were constructed around Mundell School.

A national trend in the 1940s saw high schools becoming more integrated into students' social lives. Hobart was no exception to this trend. In the summer of 1945, the Hobart Hive (Ho Hive) Youth Center opened up in a home that was once near the southwest corner of Main and Fourth Streets. The Ho Hive was a popular hangout for Hobart Junior and Senior High School students. Some of the most popular programs included dancing and listening to records. In 1945, the City of Hobart installed members of the city's first planning board. The planning board commissioned the Purdue Calumet Development Foundation to do a comprehensive study on the city and create a master plan, which was approved in 1959.

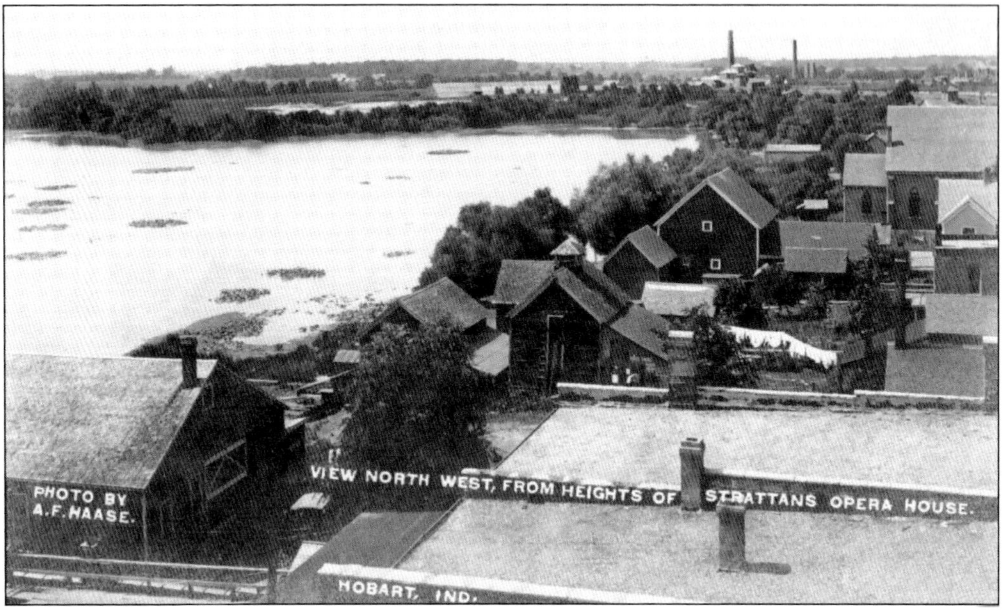

LAKE GEORGE SHORELINE. This is a north view along Lake George's shoreline, behind the 200 block of Main Street, sometime between 1902 and 1909. The shoreline was primarily for private riparian use. Some of the structures identified in the Sanborn maps along Lake George include a livery, shed, icehouse, and wagon house. In the distance at center is Otto Kulage's clay shed, and in the upper right are the brick and terra-cotta manufacturing companies.

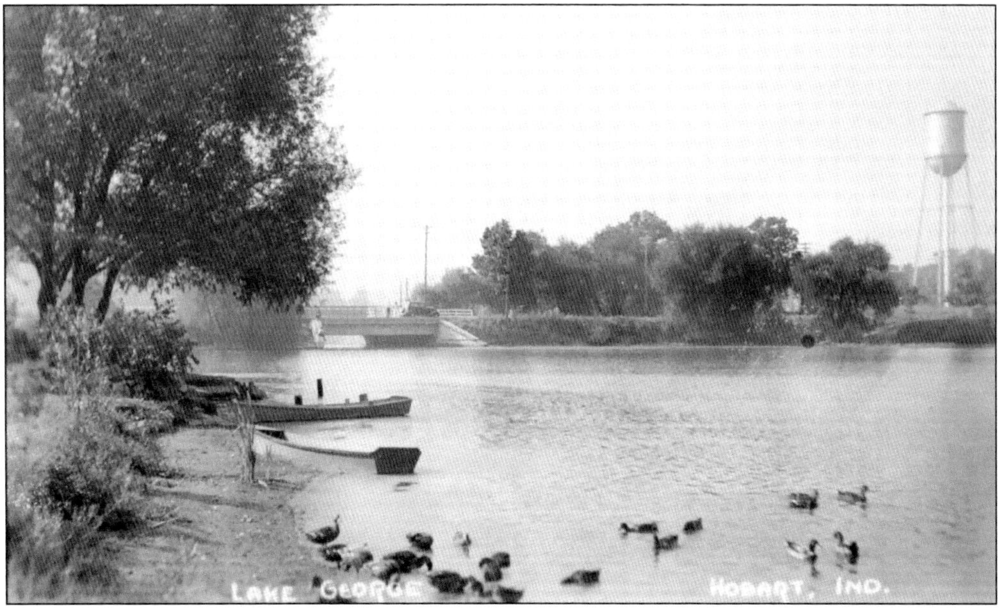

LAKEFRONT, 300 BLOCK OF MAIN STREET. A 1940s southern view along Lake George and its privately owned shoreline shows what appears to be a Desoto car parked on the Third Street Bridge. The car may have come from the Isakson Desoto Plymouth dealership on the northeast corner of Center and Front Streets. At right is the city's former water tower, which stood 150 feet tall and held 150,000 gallons of water. In 2001, the Indiana American water tower was constructed further inland on Fourteenth Street.

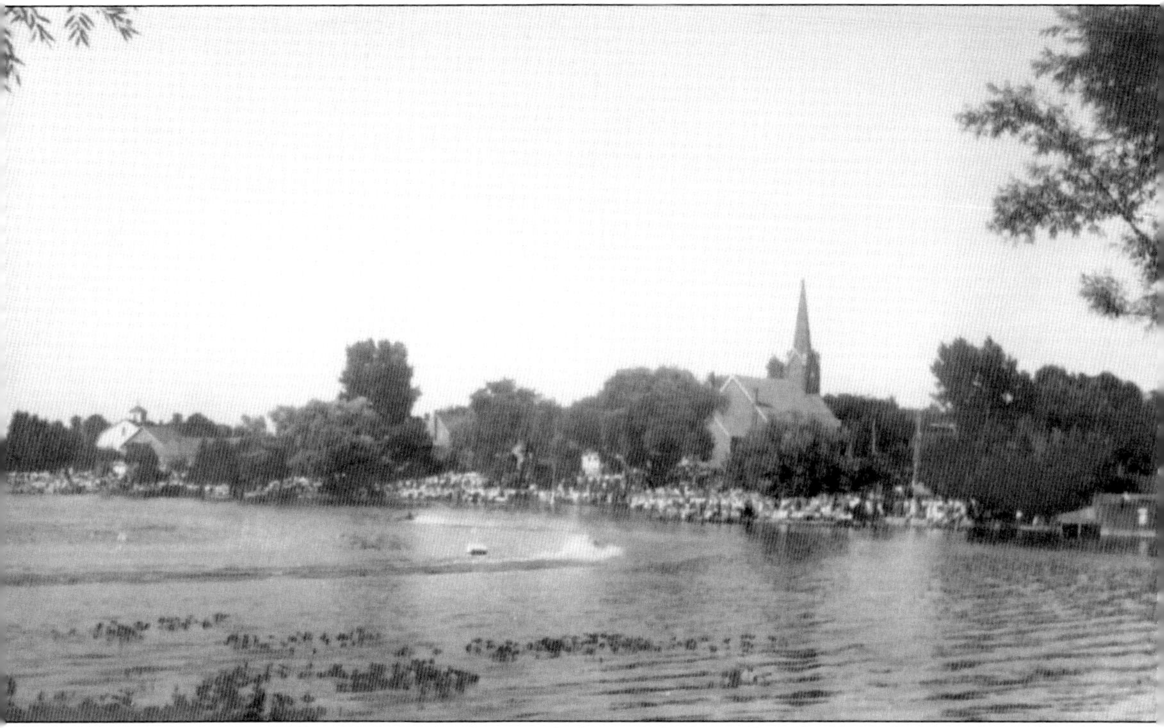

Lake George Boat Races, c. 1931. This north-facing photograph of Lake George was taken from the Third Street Bridge. Trinity Lutheran Church is on the right, and the Old Mill is on the left. At this time, the speedboats were full-sized and operated by people onboard. Today, the boat races on Lake George involve model boats that are remotely controlled from the lakefront promenade. The model boats reach speeds in excess of 90 miles per hour and are powered either by nitro methane, gasoline, or electric motors. The Clock Tower Boat Races is a three-day event, with festivities starting on a Friday. Every year, this event attracts approximately 3,000 spectators and around 60 competitors from all over the country and the world. People come to see and compete in nearly 200 different model boat races. The winner of the Hobart Clock Tower Boat Races receives the Hobart Clock Tower trophy, but everyone enjoys the venue, food, and recently incorporated model airplane show.

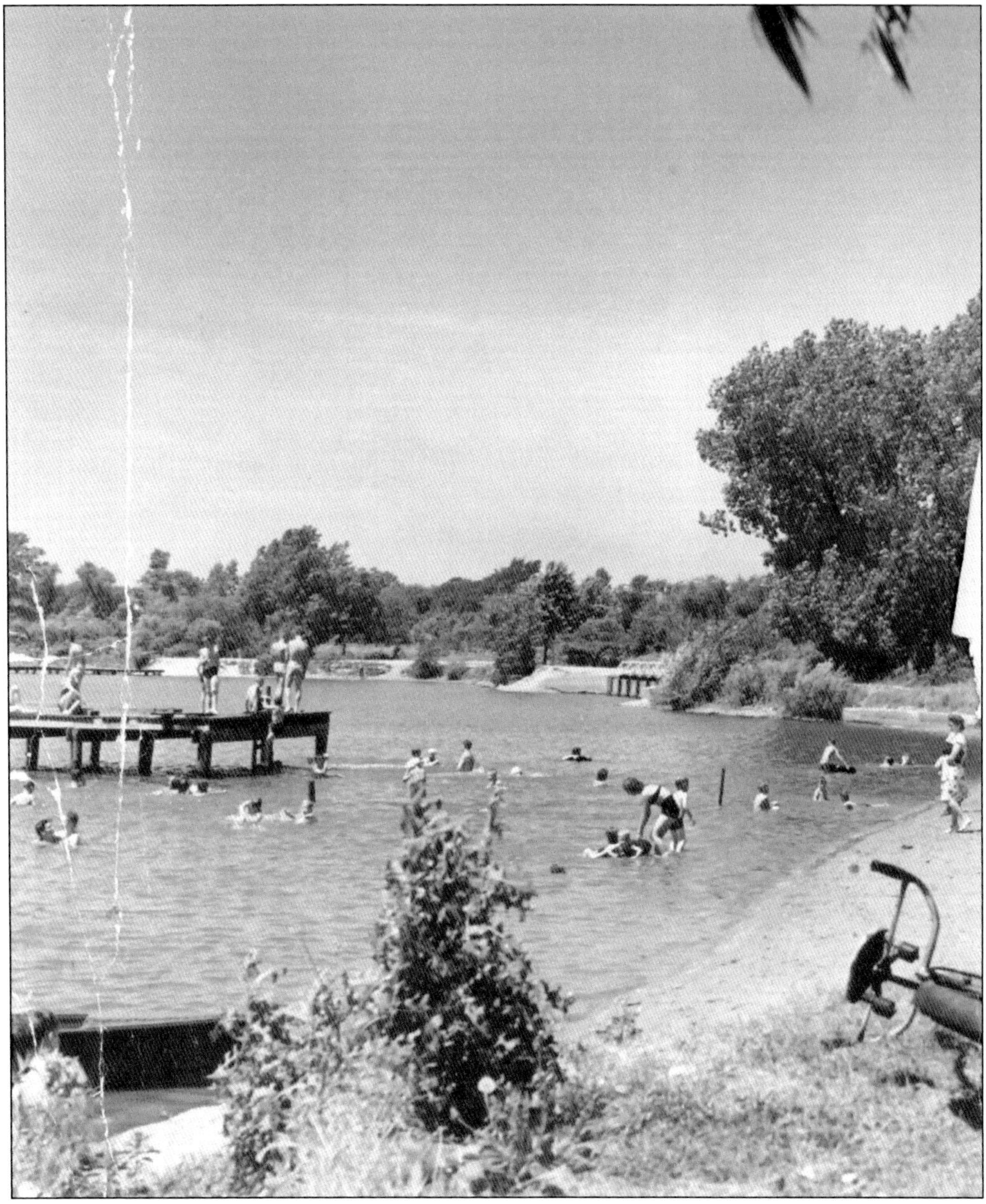

Lake George Beach Fun. In the late 1920s, Hobart residents would ice-skate on Lake George. Since 1930, Hobart officials began to purchase and acquire wooded area around the lake for park and recreation purposes. Among the facilities that were created are tennis courts, playground equipment, picnic facilities, and the Boy Scout cabin site. In the late 1930s, the city brought in sand and constructed a beach and bathhouse at the end of Front Street west of Main Street. The beach offered a sunbathing and jumping platform located about where the current fishing gazebo now stands. The fun lasted for about 20 years, until a bipartisan committee was formed in the 1950s to study a lake cleanup and lakefront beautification plan. The idea was put to a referendum, and the residents voted against it. However, interest in recreational opportunities continued on Lake George, and in July 1962, the lake was used for a three-day state water ski championship competition hosted by the Hobart Boat and Ski Club.

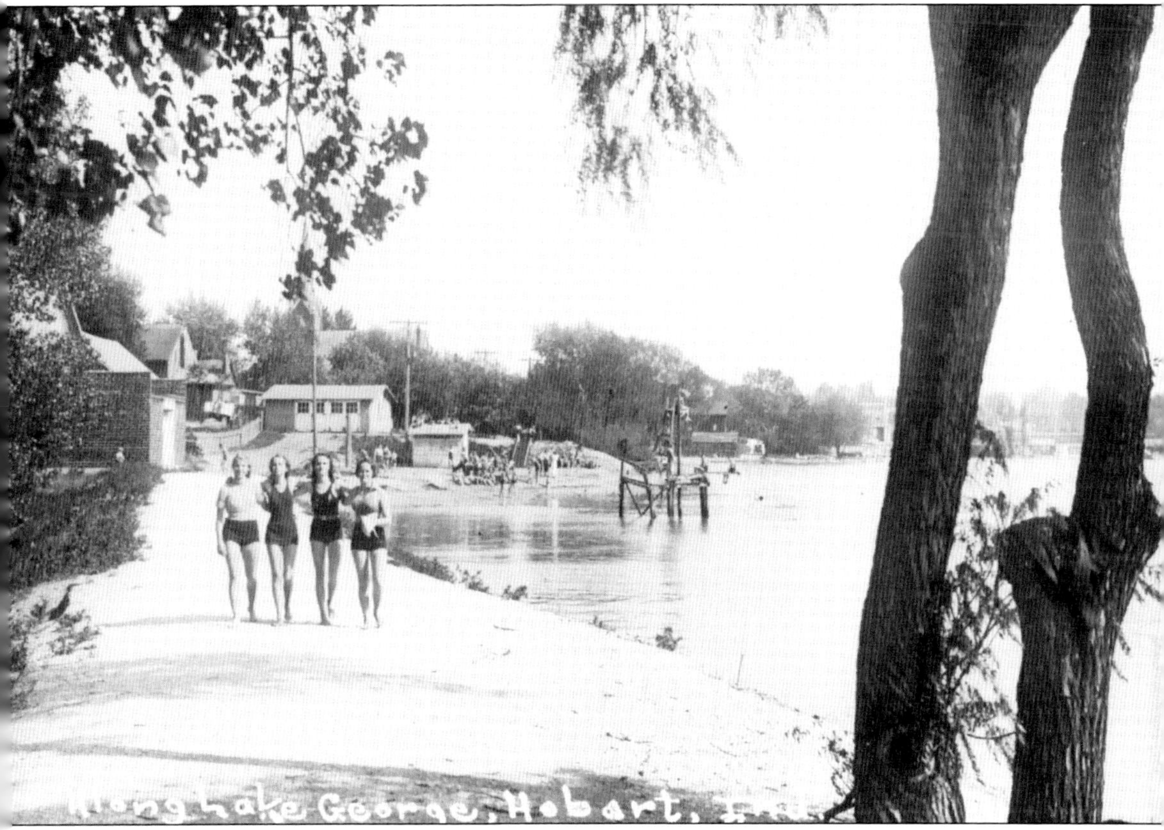

Beach Walk. This south-facing photograph of Lake George, taken around 1933, shows the sunbathing and jumping platform in the background. The four sun-seeking ladies are walking along an earthen dam towards an open pedestrian bridge, now a covered bridge, and the Izaak Walton fish hatchery, now Festival Park. The Lake George Dam and pedestrian bridge were engineered by Krull & Son and constructed by Boyd Construction. The Boyd firm was founded in 1911 by Vincent R. "Doc" Boyd Sr. at a time when horses were used instead of heavy equipment. Among Boyd Construction's most notable Hobart projects are the Hobart Water Works & Electric Plant Building, the Third Street Bridge over Lake George (1916), and the Lake George Dam (1928). Krull & Son was founded in 1914 by William Krull after he purchased Walter Black's engineering company and served as the city's engineer. Many of the city's plat records were created by Krull & Sons. Today, Krull Survey Inc. is a fourth-generation-owned company led by William Krull's grandson and two great-grandchildren. Both the Krull and Boyd businesses continue to serve the City of Hobart and surrounding municipalities.

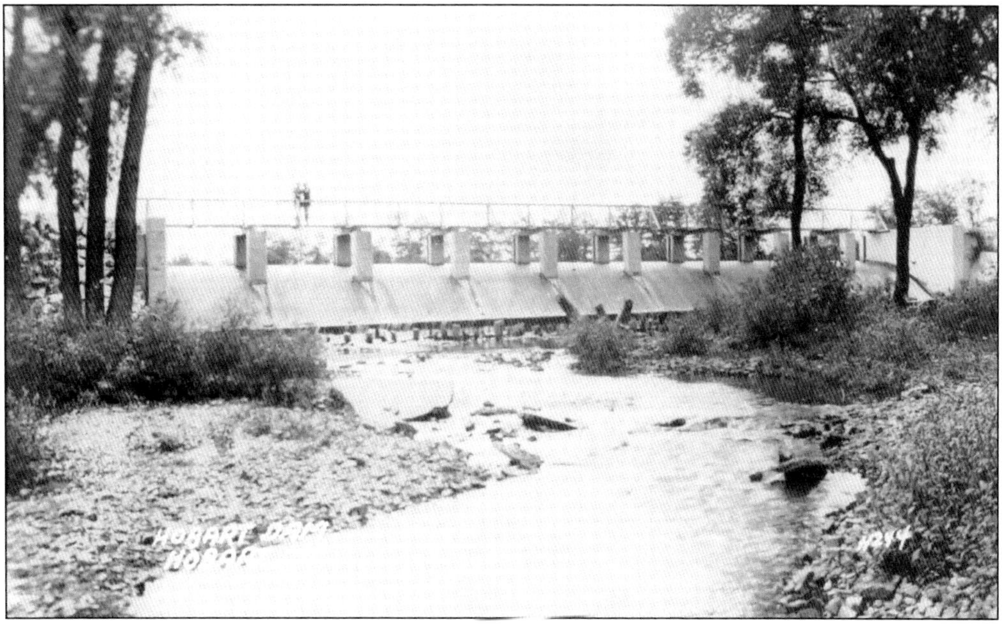

Dam Bridge. George Earle's original tumble dam was reconstructed in 1928 by Boyd Construction. It is seen here around 1929. The upgrades to the dam ultimately connected two future parks, Lakefront Park and Festival Park. Prior to the creation of these parks, the shoreline was owned by individual property owners. The new dam connected commerce and entertainment in Hobart. In 1988, the dam was once again upgraded to a more attractive covered pedestrian bridge.

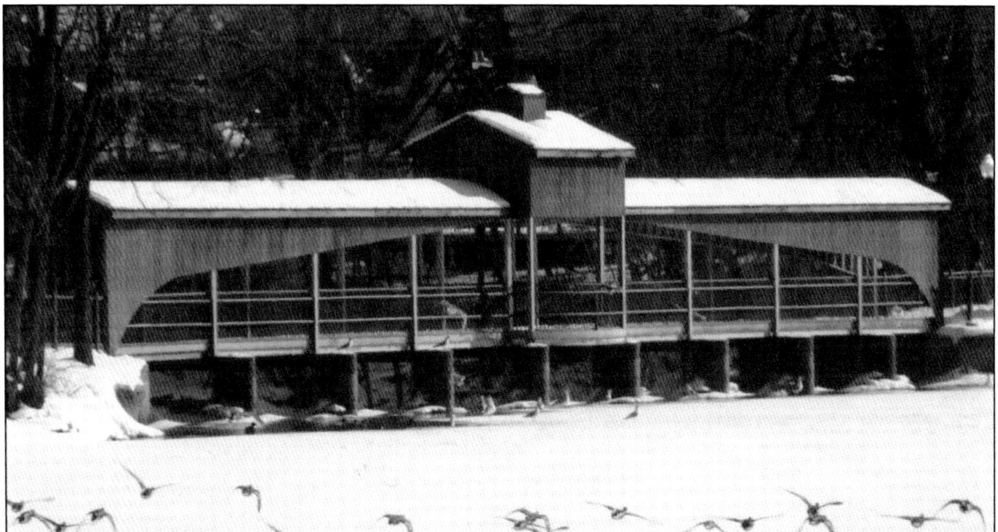

Covered Bridge. In 1988, the six-foot-wide Kuchta Covered Bridge was constructed over the 144-foot Lake George Dam. This bridge connected recreational opportunities at the community center in Festival Park to downtown. The covered bridge was constructed by volunteers from donated funds and material. At the center of the bridge, which was designed by an architecture professor, is a two-tier roofline of the bridge steeple. Its design mirrors the top of the Old Mill.

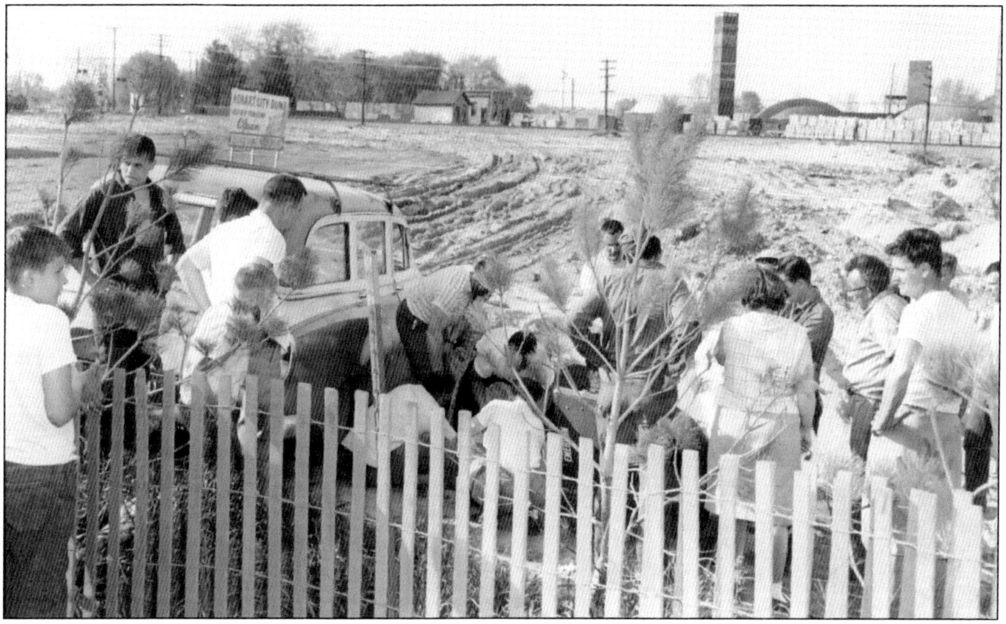

CITY LANDFILL. After the brick and terra-cotta companies closed operations in Hobart, they left several open clay pits around the community. One pit, a 14-acre site north of Old Ridge Road and south of the Pittsburgh, Fort Wayne & Chicago Railway, between Lake Park Avenue and Deep River, became a landfill site. After this pit was filled and covered, it became Riverfront Park, also known as the rugby field. The landfill is seen here in the 1950s.

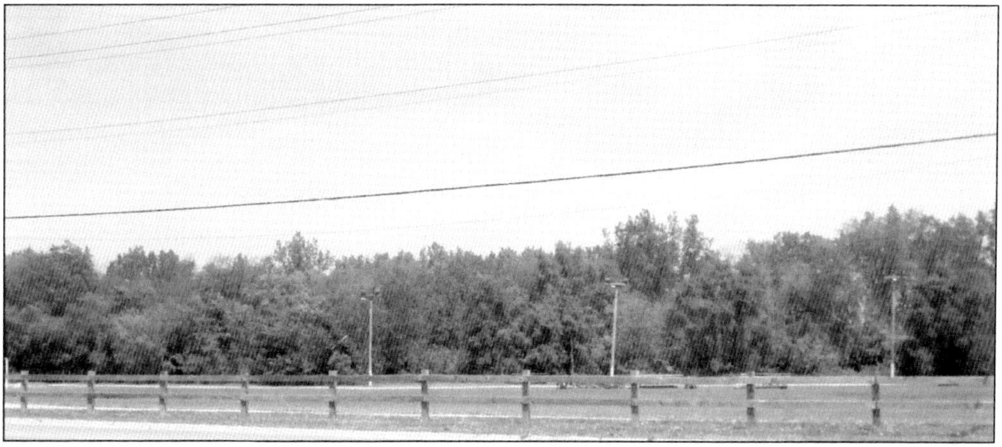

RIVERFRONT PARK, C. 2013. Riverfront Park is located near downtown Hobart and borders Deep River on the east. The park's open field is flanked on either side by gravel parking lots. These lots provide overflow parking and staging for events occurring across the street at Festival Park. The park has a walking/running track around the field. The space is used primarily by the Northwest Indiana Exiles men's rugby club. (Courtesy of Sergio Mendoza.)

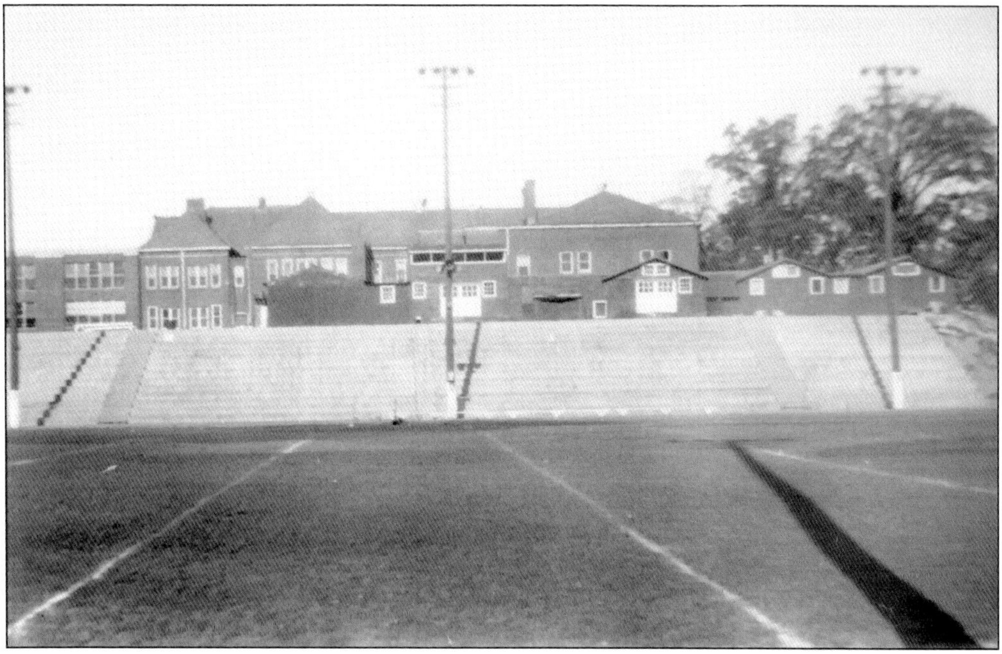

Brickie Bowl. Work on the Brickie Bowl began in 1936 through the WPA. A succession of trucks carried fill to create the field area. Between 1938 and 1939, the concrete bleachers were constructed by students as part of a high school class.

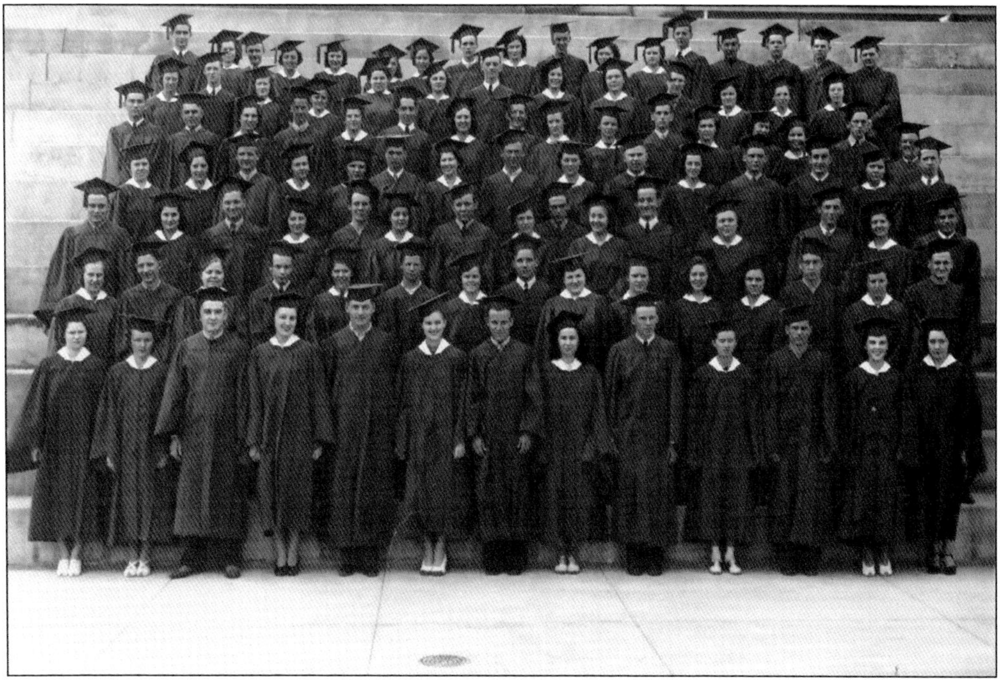

1940 Graduating Class. The Hobart High School Brickie Bowl was dedicated in May 1940. Shown here is the 1940 graduating class of Madge (Dockter) Smith. The class is posing in front of the newly completed concrete bleachers. (Courtesy of Richard Smith.)

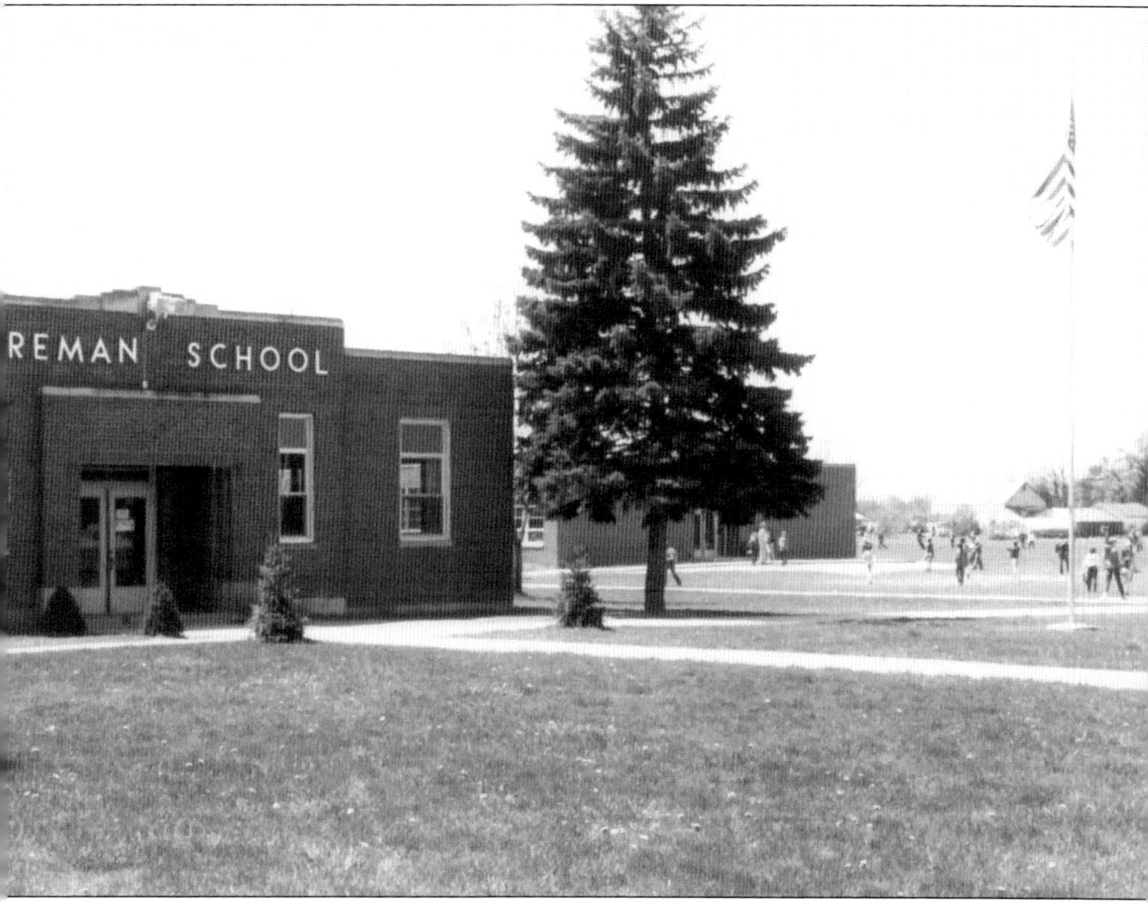

FOREMAN SCHOOL. The Foreman School, which sat on the current Joan Martin School site, was constructed in 1944 with seven rooms. The school was named after "Uncle Billy" Foreman, who served as a school janitor from 1906 to 1939. The building was razed in 1994. Liberty School was constructed in 1949, Ridgeview was built in 1955, and George Earle School opened in 1962. The newest elementary school, Joan Martin, was built in 1994 and replaced the Mundell and Foreman Schools. In 2009, Hobart opened its new high school, and the former high school, built in 1967, was renovated for use as a middle school. The original Hobart High School site on Fourth Street is now the home of the Hobart Police Department, Hobart City Court, and the Maria Reiner Senior Center. Maria Reiner was a German immigrant who married and settled in Hobart and lived a modest life. The Reiners never had children, and Maria—preceded in death by her husband—left all her possessions to the senior citizens of Hobart, resulting in an endowment for a social environment that provides onsite activities.

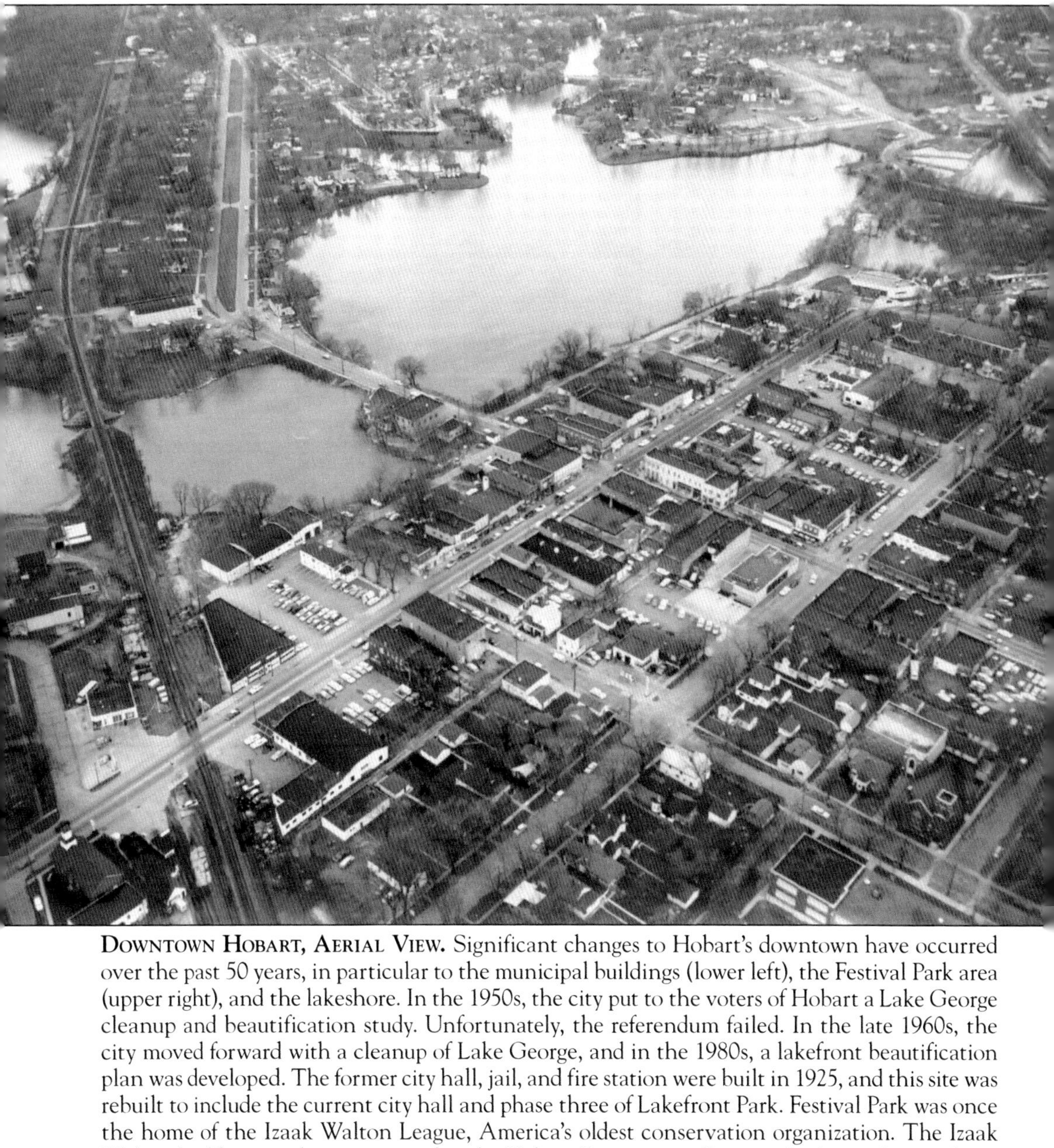

Downtown Hobart, Aerial View. Significant changes to Hobart's downtown have occurred over the past 50 years, in particular to the municipal buildings (lower left), the Festival Park area (upper right), and the lakeshore. In the 1950s, the city put to the voters of Hobart a Lake George cleanup and beautification study. Unfortunately, the referendum failed. In the late 1960s, the city moved forward with a cleanup of Lake George, and in the 1980s, a lakefront beautification plan was developed. The former city hall, jail, and fire station were built in 1925, and this site was rebuilt to include the current city hall and phase three of Lakefront Park. Festival Park was once the home of the Izaak Walton League, America's oldest conservation organization. The Izaak Walton building was later converted to the Hobart Community Center, which was damaged in a 2008 flood. It was rebuilt in 2011 with a 150-person-capacity conference/banquet room. Festival Park was the site of a former clay pit, which was used as a fish hatchery by the Izaak Walton League. In 1976, the fish hatchery was filled in with dredge material to create Festival Park. This aerial photograph was taken around 1961.

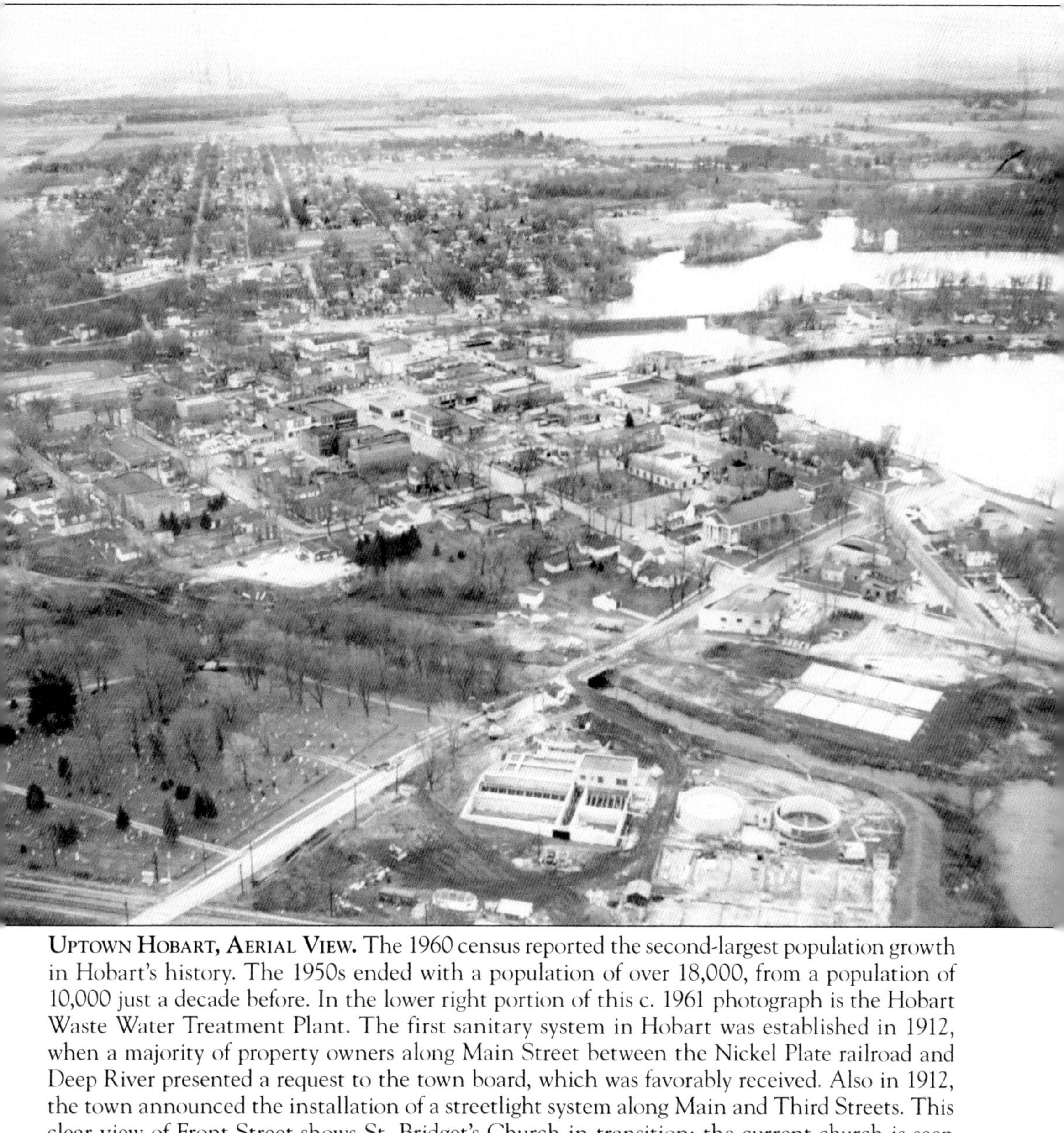

UPTOWN HOBART, AERIAL VIEW. The 1960 census reported the second-largest population growth in Hobart's history. The 1950s ended with a population of over 18,000, from a population of 10,000 just a decade before. In the lower right portion of this c. 1961 photograph is the Hobart Waste Water Treatment Plant. The first sanitary system in Hobart was established in 1912, when a majority of property owners along Main Street between the Nickel Plate railroad and Deep River presented a request to the town board, which was favorably received. Also in 1912, the town announced the installation of a streetlight system along Main and Third Streets. This clear view of Front Street shows St. Bridget's Church in transition; the current church is seen on Center Street, and the previous church faces Main Street. Across from St. Bridget's Church, on the west side of Main Street, is Trinity Lutheran Church. Also visible is the former Hobart Beach Bathhouse, operating as the Hobart Chamber of Commerce office. At lower left is the Hobart Cemetery and the abandoned Elgin, Joliet & Eastern railroad spur crossing Third Street to Front Street.

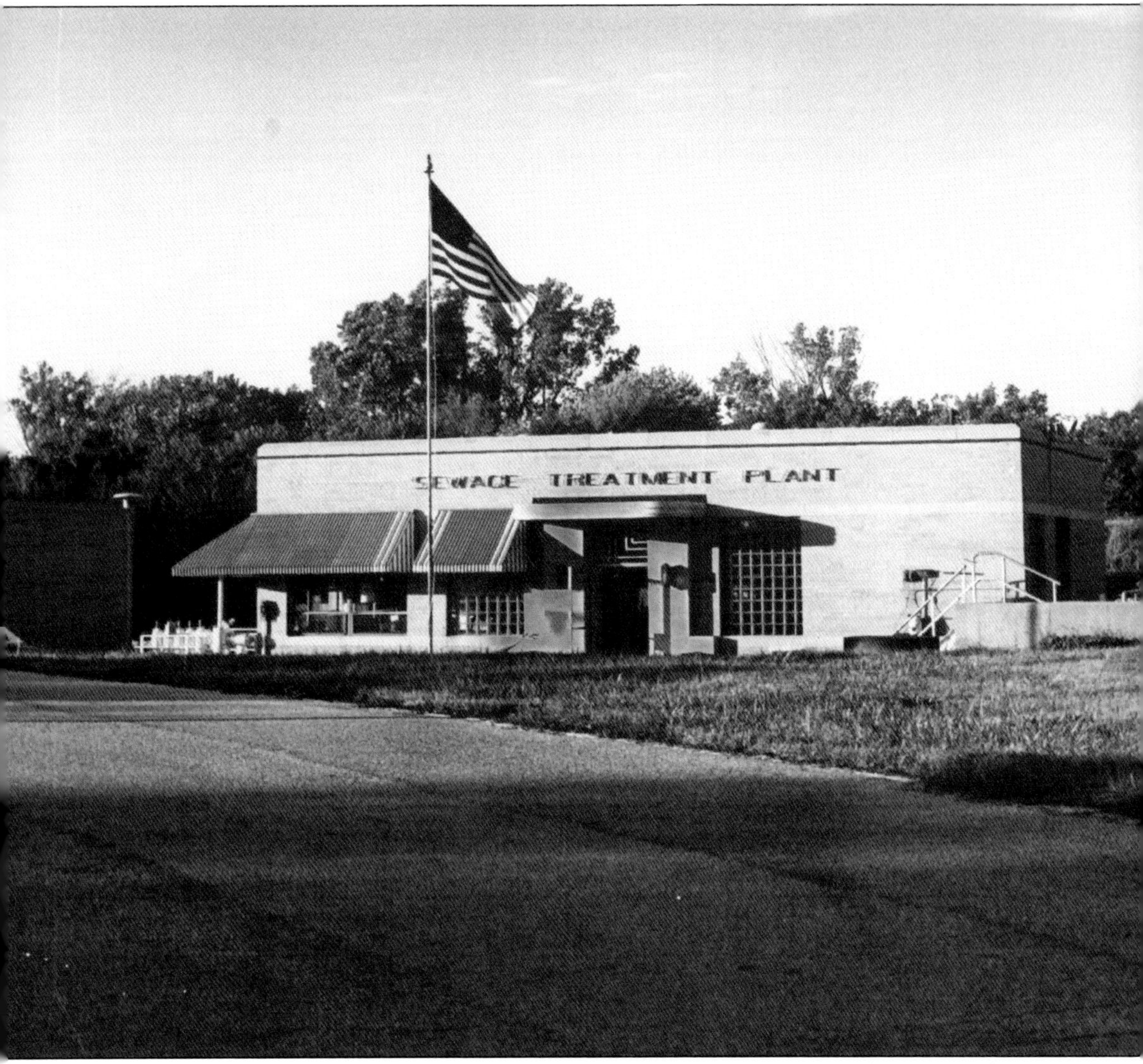

Sewer Treatment Plant. In 1949, the city began to prepare a site along the north side of Front Street, just south of the PFW&C railroad, for a sewage disposal treatment plant. Construction began in 1952, and in October 1953, the plant was in operation. In 1974, the Indiana Department of Environmental Management ordered a shutdown of Hobart's sewer plant, citing capacity concerns. The wastewater treatment plant closed in 1988, and Hobart's sewer system was connected to the City of Gary sanitary system. The 1974 state-imposed sewer moratorium on Hobart stunted community growth opportunities, skewed population cohorts, and created a tax-assessment imbalance. In the 1980s, for the first and only time in Hobart's history, the city experienced a population decline. In an effort to regain control of the community's services and growth opportunities, Hobart proposed the construction of a new sewer treatment plant, which would result in increased capacity and improved water quality discharge into the Lake Michigan tributary. The proposed plant also aimed to eliminate untreated sewage discharge caused by Gary's combined sewer system. The Hobart permit to construct a new wastewater plant was approved in 2004, but the City of Gary expressed concern and filed for administrative review. A recent legal decision went in Hobart's favor, but the lengthy review process has increased construction costs. Hobart is now required to reassess the construction of a new wastewater treatment plant.

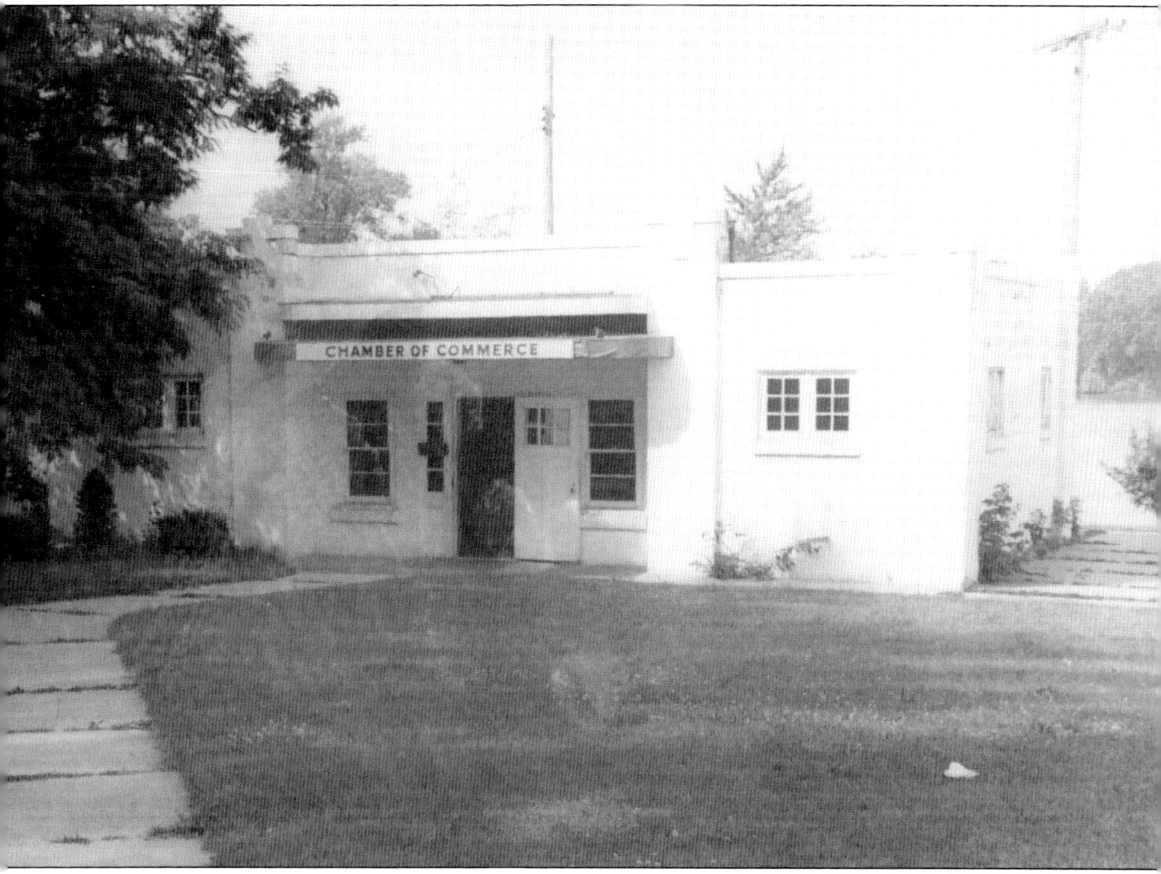

HOBART BATHHOUSE. The Art Deco Hobart bathhouse, built by the WPA, provided facilities for bathers at the Hobart Beach. After the beach was closed, the facility served as Lake Shore School. In 1955, it was acquired by the Hobart Chamber of Commerce for its offices. Shown here in 1967, the building stood on the southwest corner of Front and Main Streets. It was demolished the following year to make way for the Hobart Public Library. Hobart's business leaders have always been essential to the community's growth. Early on, there was Earl's Mills and Black's trading post. The formation of the Commercial Club in 1890 led a premature charge for the town to become a city. In 1901, the Hobart Commercial Association was formed, and in 1912, the Hobart Improvement and Commercial Club organized and urged the town to regulate water levels in Lake George. In 1933, the Hobart Retailers Association met at city hall to formulate plans for a better Hobart. A year after the city's 1947 centennial celebration, the Hobart Business Association was formed. It eventually became the Hobart Chamber of Commerce. The chamber and its many subcommittees continue to vie for a better community where Hobart businesses can thrive.

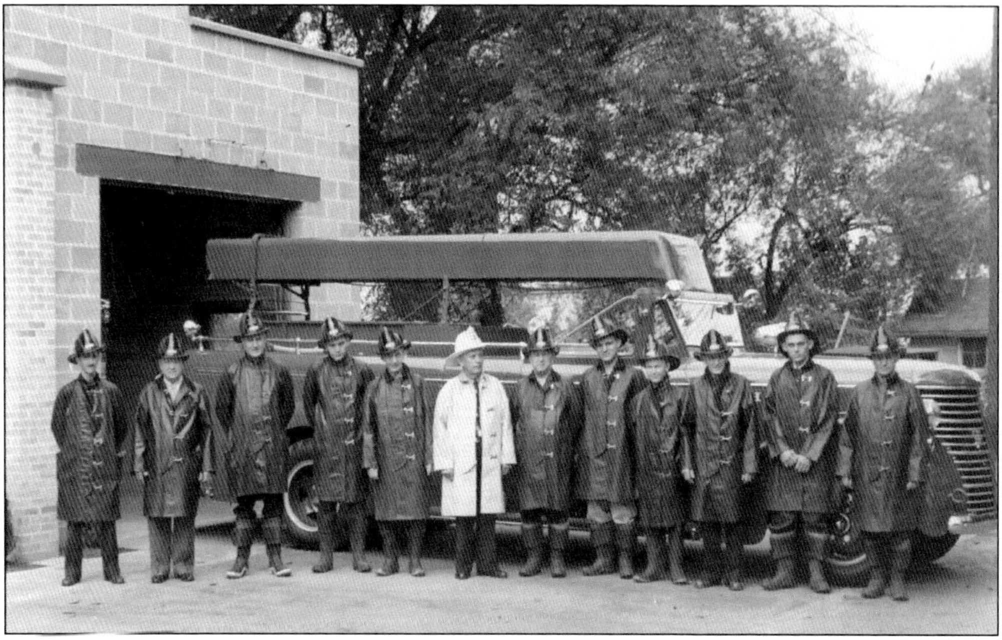

FIRE DEPARTMENT. Some of these men from the Hobart Fire Department would have been on the department when the Hobart House was declared a firetrap and condemned in 1939. At the time, this station, at the end of Fourth Street and east of Lake George, was the only one in town. It shared space with the police department in a single-story brick building. This photograph was taken around 1941.

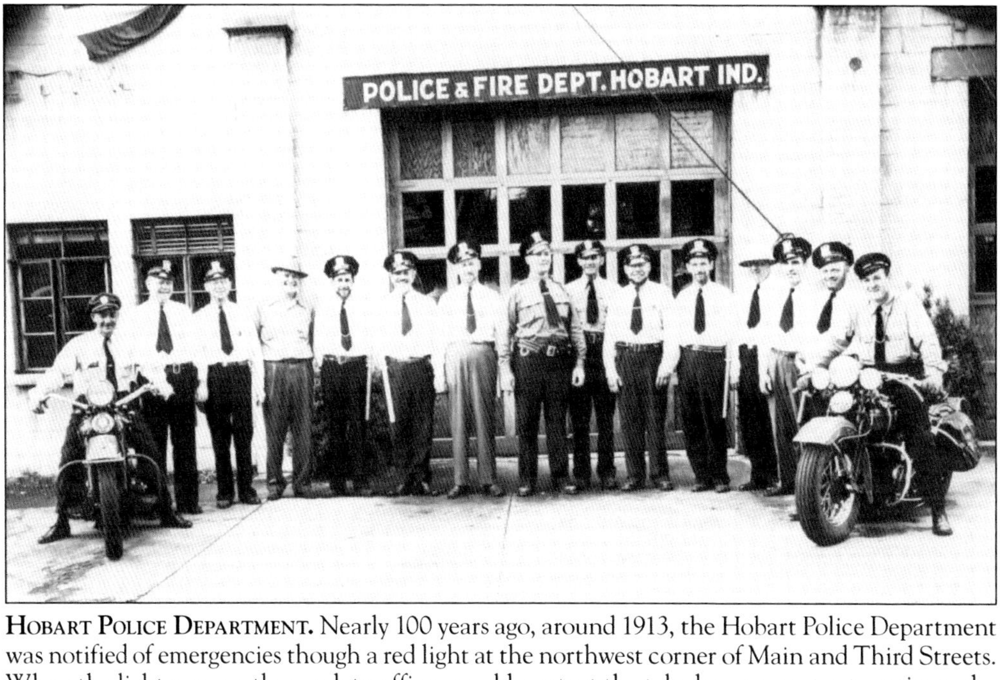

HOBART POLICE DEPARTMENT. Nearly 100 years ago, around 1913, the Hobart Police Department was notified of emergencies though a red light at the northwest corner of Main and Third Streets. When the light was on, the on-duty officer would contact the telephone operator to activate the emergency notice. Today, a 100-foot-tall communication tower aids the police department with transmitting emergency alerts. The police department is seen here around 1945.

Seven

Double Down Days

In the mid-1950s, the nation moved forward with the 1956 Highway Act, with the goal of connecting state capitals to major cities. This national effort presented opportunities in Hobart when Interstate 65 was constructed in 1968. The highway went from Gary to Indianapolis along the west side of Hobart. The 1970 census reported a 15 percent population increase. But, 10 years later, Hobart experienced its only population drop, reported in 1990. Hobart rebounded with tax incentives, and in 2010, the census revealed a population increase of over 7,000 people. Despite the minor population drop in the 1970s, Hobart continued to move forward with the construction of new postmodern public buildings and a modern medical facility expansion. In the early 1990s, the city made the decision to physically double in size and become home to a 1974 interior shopping mall and a mid-1800s commercial district. Also in the early 1990s, the city brought into its boundaries the historic interests of Ainsworth, the Lincoln Highway, and tales of Michael Carrozzo, mobster turned dairy farmer.

Ainsworth is an old settlement surrounded by acres of farmland located near the intersection of Indiana State Road 51 and Ainsworth Road. Access to this early settlement was reached through the east-west route of Ainsworth Road, or from State Road 51, which ran north from the Historic Lincoln Highway (Seventy-third Avenue) and ended just north of the Grand Trunk Rail Road. East of this intersection was once the 900-acre estate of Michael Carrozzo, gangster friend to notorious Al "Scarface" Capone. Carrozzo was known as the head of the street laborers' union in Chicago. Also included as part of the annexation is a portion of the historic Lincoln Highway. The highway turned 100 years old in 2013. It was the first transcontinental highway, stretching over 3,000 miles from New York to California.

Even though Hobart's boundaries reach beyond its original platting, the city has maintained its original small-town appeal. This can be attributed to the Historic Preservation Act of 1966. This act declared it the policy of the federal government to foster partnerships for the preservation of historic and cultural resources. In 2007, Hobart gave itself the opportunity to declare local historic and cultural resources through the creation of the Hobart Historic Preservation Commission. It is up for debate if Hobart has become the thriving western city George Earle envisioned nearly 170 years ago. In any case, this old settlement has positioned itself for a sustainable 21st century.

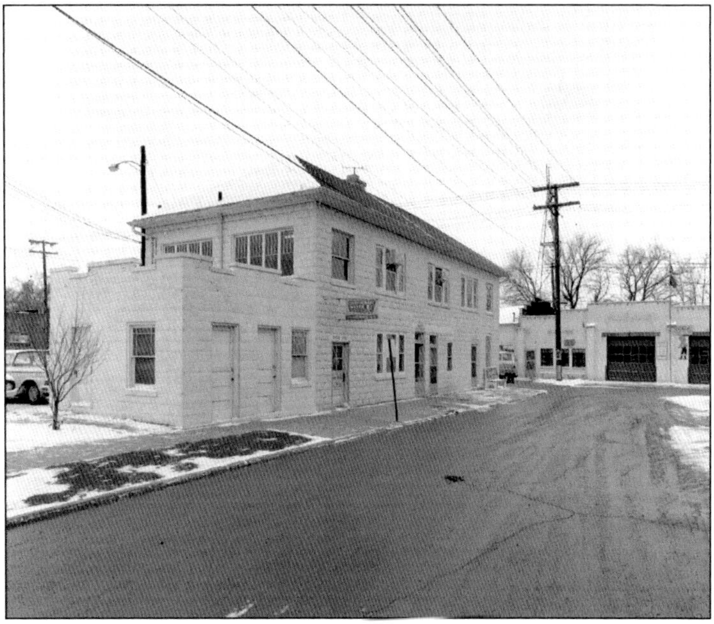

City Hall. In 1939, the city located its municipal services at the end of Fourth Street along the eastern edge of Lake George. The cluster of buildings included the street services building, city hall, and the police and fire departments. City hall, constructed from split-face brick, housed the offices of the mayor, clerk-treasurer, city engineer, license bureau, sewage works, Gary-Hobart Water Corporation, and the common council room.

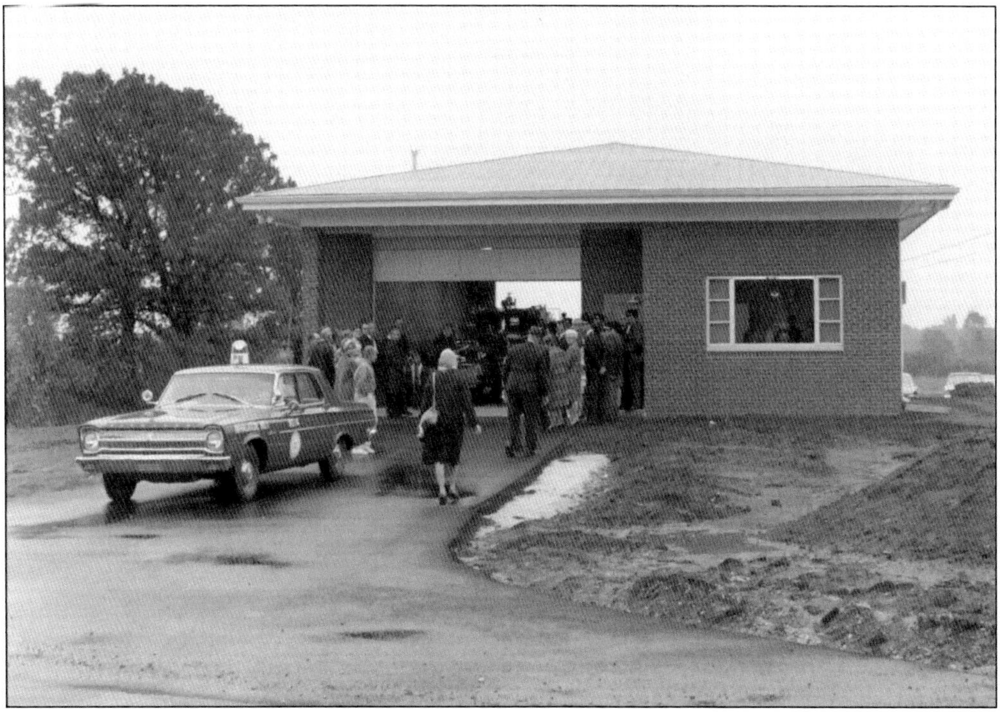

Fire Stations. In 1967, the city added a second fire station. Seen here is the open house for fire station No. 2, which was built along Old Ridge Road near Hillman Park to provide service and protection to the west side of the city. Currently, this station is going through a cost-of-services review. In 1974, a fire station was constructed along Tenth Street, west of Lincoln Street. This structure became fire station No. 1, replacing the station at the end of Fourth Street. Station No. 3, located along Ridge Road and west of State Road 51, was dedicated in 1999. A fourth fire station was dedicated in 1996 on Colorado Street as a result of the city's 1993 annexation.

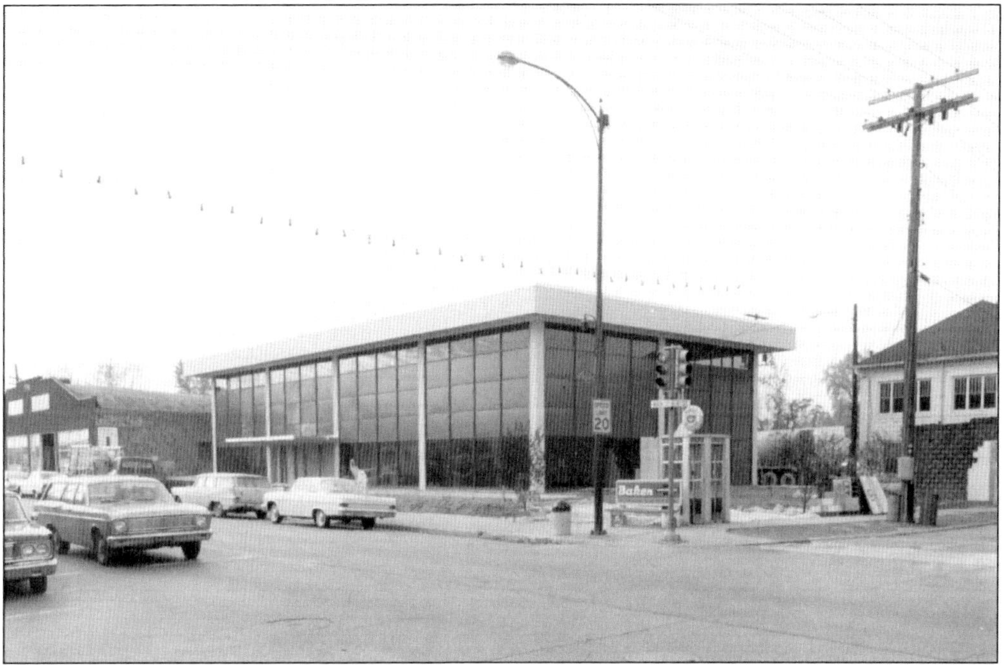

CURRENT CITY HALL. In 1967, a Postmodern-style city hall opened to the public. The police department and jail at the end of Fourth Street were located in this building until 1994, when they were relocated to the southwest corner of Second and Main Streets. In 2011, those services, along with the court system, were once again relocated to a renovated and upgraded former school site along Fourth Street.

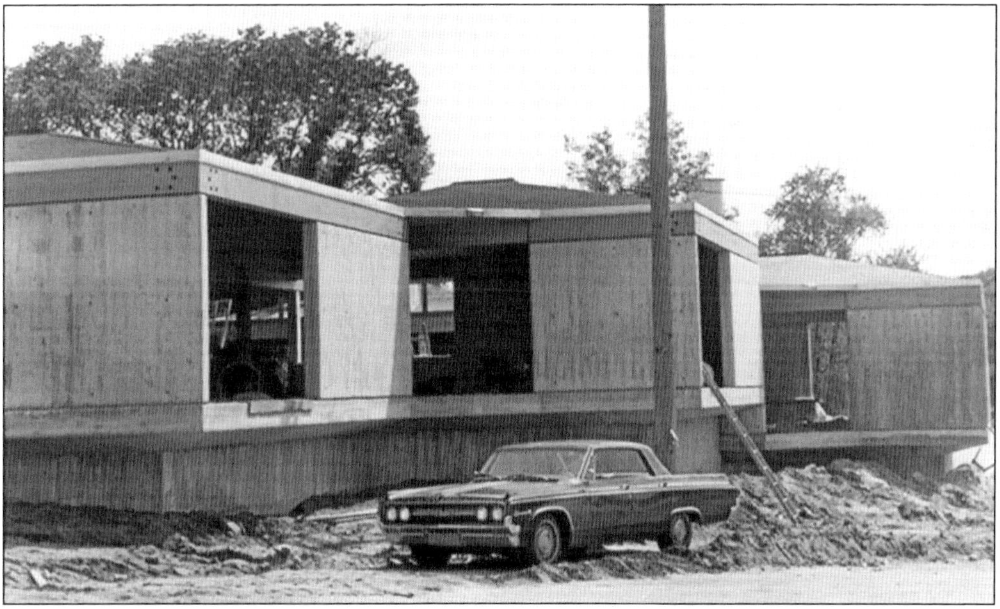

HOBART PUBIC LIBRARY. The Postmodern library building was constructed in 1968 on the former site of the Hobart Beach bathhouse. In the 1850s, this was the site of Lewis Hammond's Tavern House, a two-story wood frame coach house and tavern with a second-floor dance hall. The library is seen here under construction around 1967.

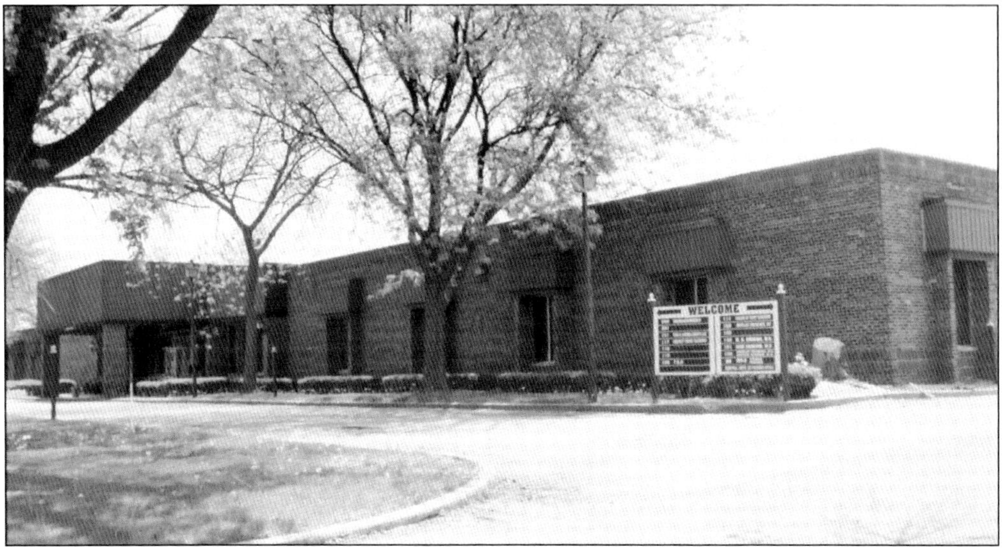

Prudential Building. In 1972, Prudential Insurance Company selected the City of Hobart as the location for its new building. Prudential constructed a modern, 30,000-square-foot building at the southwest corner of Tenth Street and Lake Park Avenue. In 1974, it built an additional 20,000 square feet. There are multiple businesses in the offices today, one of which has the distinction of being the city's only college, College of Court Reporting. (Courtesy of College of Court Reporting.)

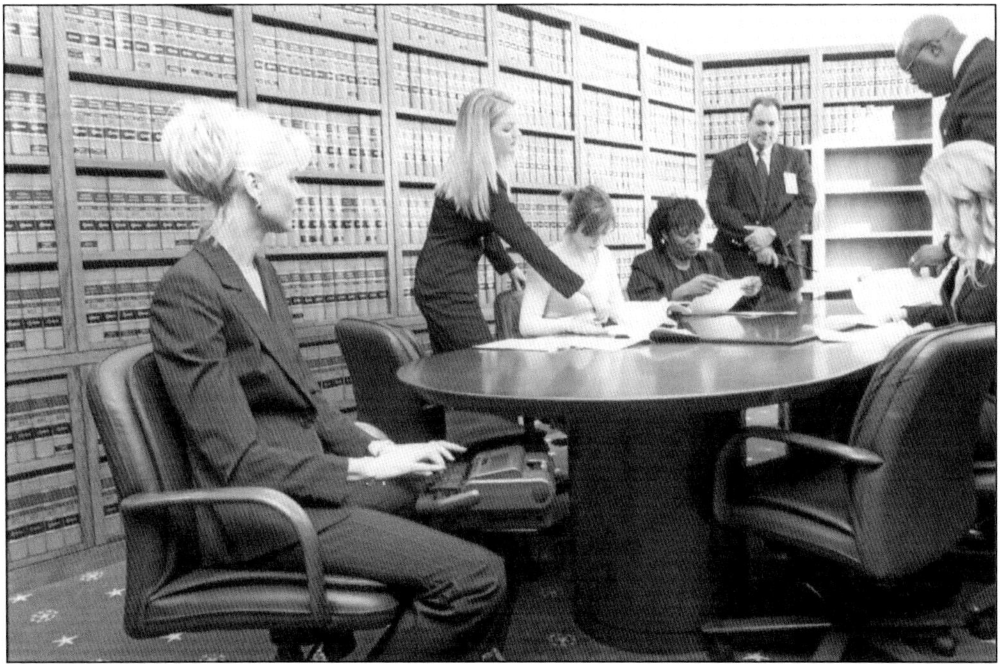

College of Court Reporting. College of Court Reporting, accredited by the Accrediting Council for Independent Colleges and Schools, began in 1984. The founder and director of education, Kay Moody, saw a need for creating leaders in the field of court reporters, stenographers, broadcast captioners, and communication access real-time translation workers. Moody started teaching courses out of her Hobart home. Now, students both local and worldwide can take courses in Hobart or online. (Courtesy of College of Court Reporting.)

YOHAN. Yohan Petrovich "came" to Hobart High School in 1942–1943. He was registered as a fictitious student in a study hall by George Zuppko. As a joke among the students, Yohan's name kept appearing during study hall roll call, and someone always responded with "Here!" Eventually, the school had a contest to name the Hobart High School mascot, and "Yohan Petrovich" was the winning selection. At that time, he was a man of brick. A 1949 Hobart High School graduate, Floyd "Duke" Swynenberg, drew the caricature that is used today. Yohan is said to always be "Here!"

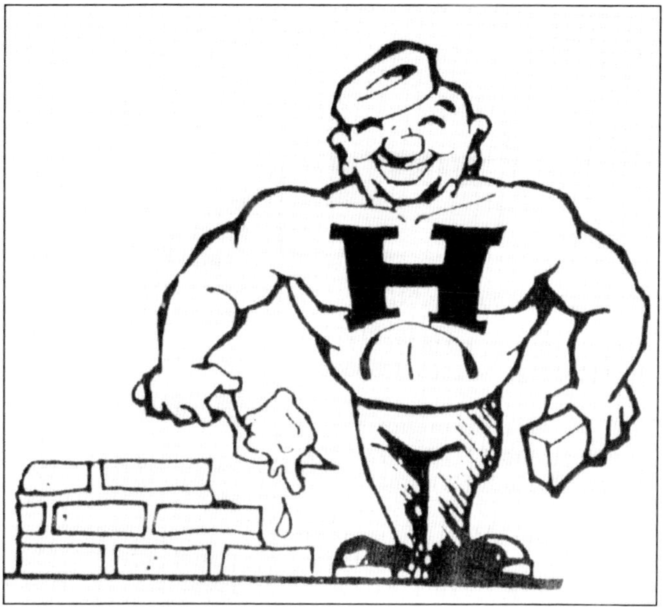

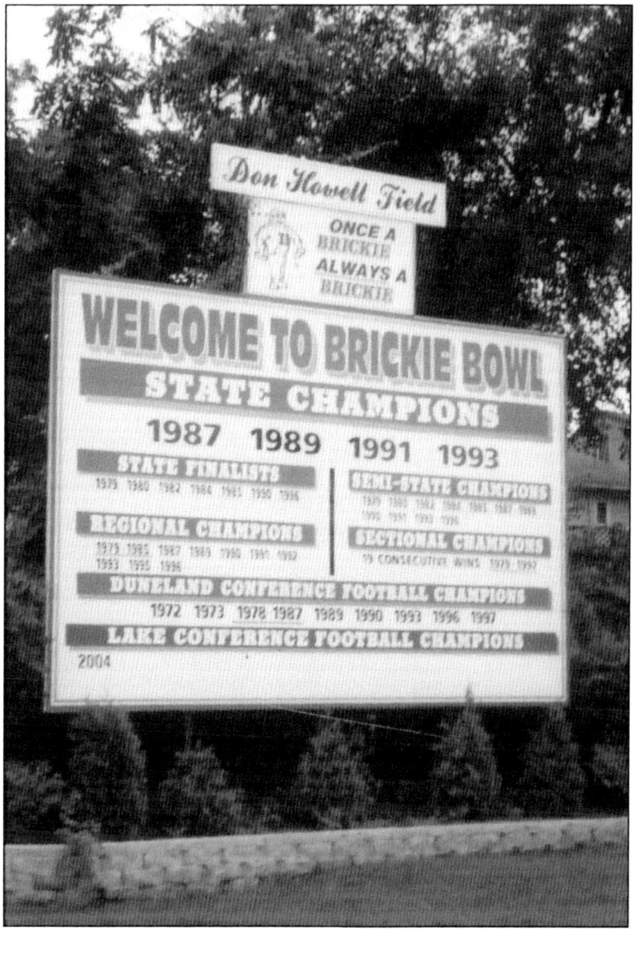

BRICKIE CHAMPIONSHIPS. Hobart High School's athletics program began in 1891, with the formation of a basketball team. A cross-country team was established in 1926, and the football team was formed in 1927. The girls' basketball team won the state championship in 1907, and the boys' cross-country squad won state championships in 1957 and 1960. The school has won football state championships in 1987, 1989, 1991, and 1993, and the gymnastics team won the 2004 state championship. (Courtesy of Steve Euvino.)

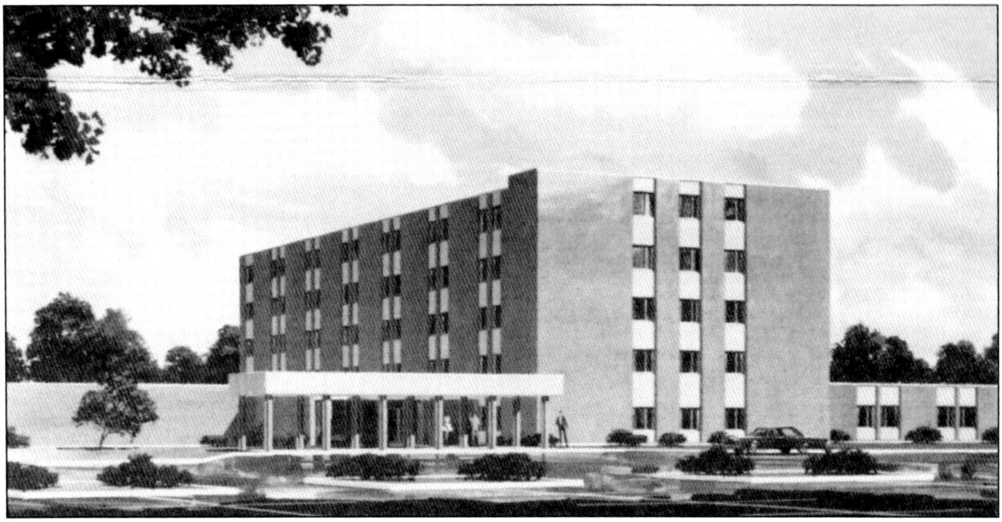

St. Mary Mercy Hospital Southeast. In 1971, a "coming soon" sign was posted on the future site of St. Mary Medical Center. On November 28 of that year, the ground-breaking ceremony was held. In May 1973, a grand-opening celebration hosted over 5,500 people, who toured the five-story, 100,000-square-foot, 159-bed general hospital. In 1974, the hospital changed its name to St. Mary Medical Center. (Courtesy of St. Mary Medical Center.)

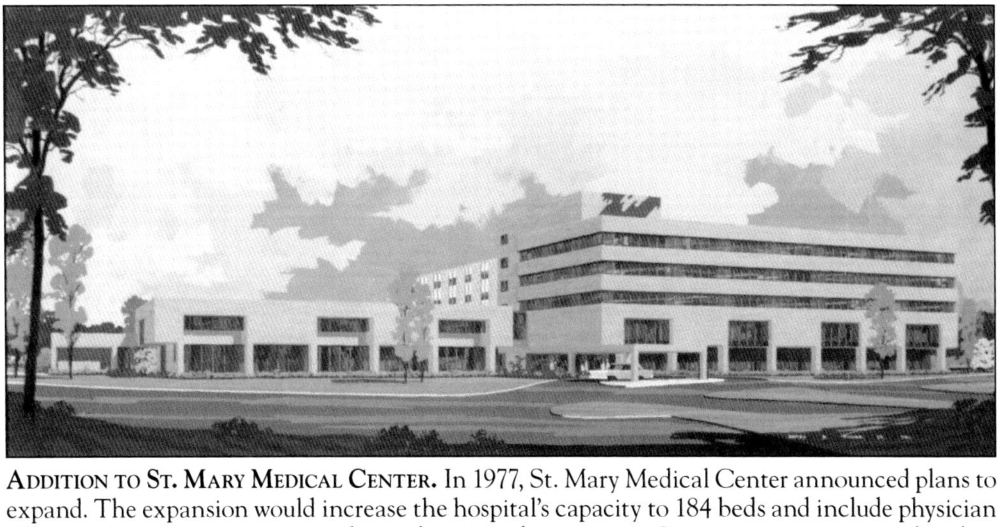

Addition to St. Mary Medical Center. In 1977, St. Mary Medical Center announced plans to expand. The expansion would increase the hospital's capacity to 184 beds and include physician offices, an emergency room, and an education department. Construction was completed in 1979. In October 2000, Hobart (population 21,000) was recognized as a "Well City" by the Wellness Council of America, the first Indiana city to be so recognized. (Courtesy of St. Mary Medical Center.)

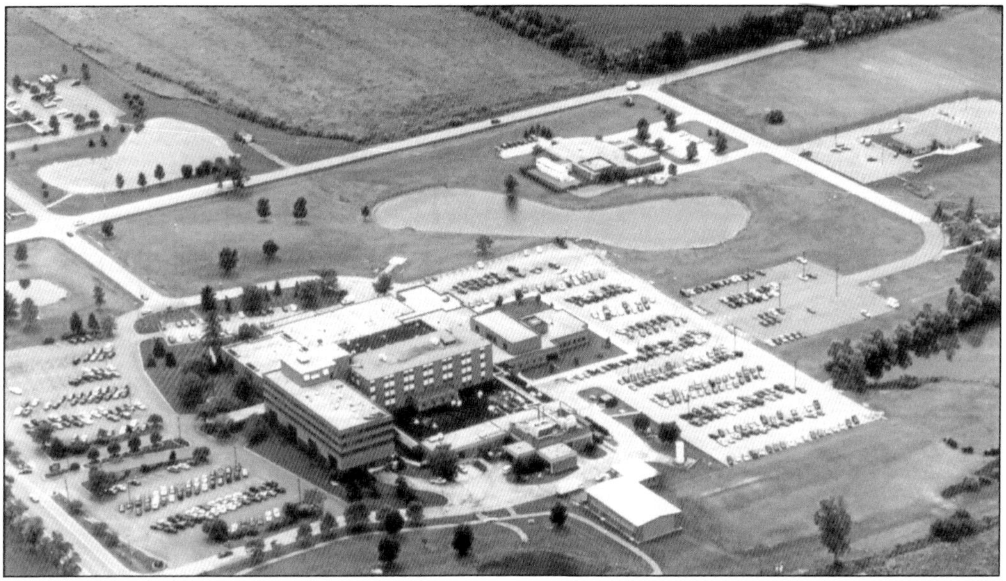

Aerial View of St. Mary Medical Center. Hobart's local hospital has roots in the Poor Handmaids of Jesus Christ, which founded St. Mary Mercy Hospital in Gary in 1913. In the 1950s, a Hobart town study revealed that a hospital would soon be needed in the community. Approximately 25 years later, St. Mary Medical Center was established. The original hospital building was erected as a tear-down, to be used for only 10 years, with long-range plans to build a new facility and expanded services. That first building still stands 40 years later, and the facility has seen many additions and expansions of services. The hospital, seen here around 1999, remains dedicated to its Roman Catholic tradition. (Courtesy of St. Mary Medical Center.)

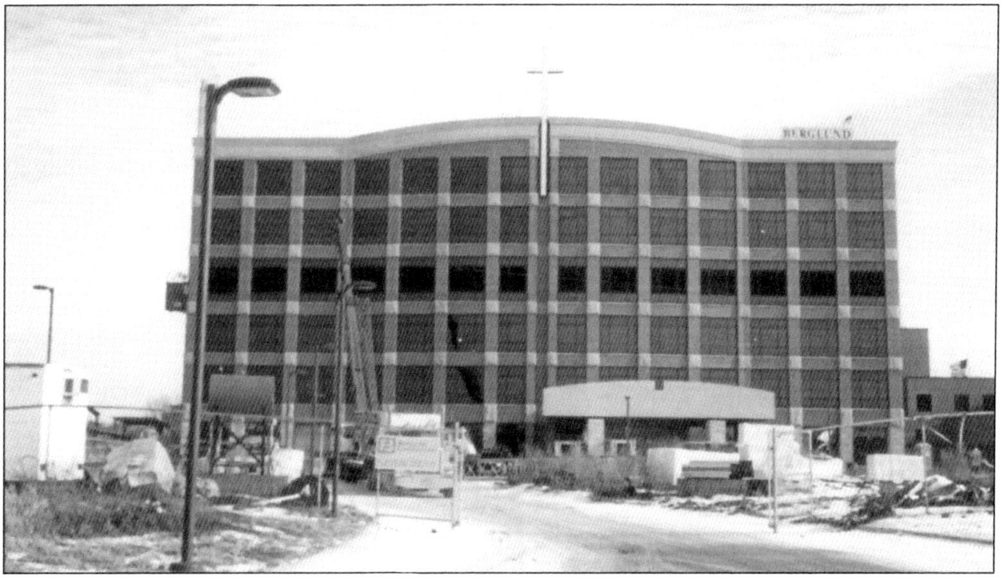

St. Mary Medical Center Patient Tower. On November 20, 2002, a ground-breaking ceremony was held for a six-story, 124,000-square-foot addition. The new patient tower with private rooms was completed in September 2004. Over the years, the hospital has continued to expand its services and facilities, including the emergency room, servicing center, and offices. The hospital has plans to add a four-story surgical/ICU pavilion. (Courtesy of St. Mary Medical Center.)

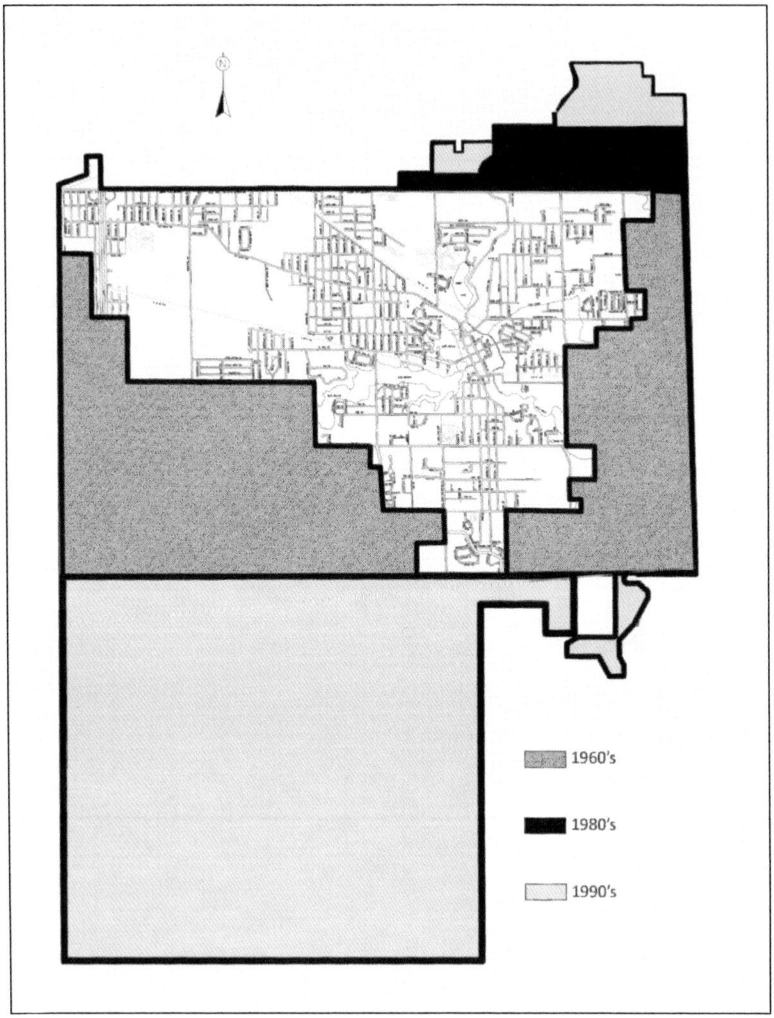

ANNEX MAP. In the 1960s, the city had grown to 15 square miles, almost doubling in size from its previous 9 square miles. In the 1990s, the city nearly doubled again, to approximately 27 square miles. The annexation of the 1990s incorporated the early settlement of Ainsworth, the Lincoln Highway, the residential borough of Green Acres, and a regional shopping mall into Hobart's municipal boundary. The Ainsworth settlement first appears on an 1882 H.C. Tunison Lake County map. Prior to that, the area was identified as Hickory Top. In 1872, Hickory Top School reported 40 students. It was located just south of the Grand Trunk Railroad and west of the current Grand Boulevard (SR 51). However, it is believed that schooling occurred in this area before the 1860s by the women of the Underwood, Lathrop, Harper, and Castle families. In 1880, the Grand Trunk bisected what is now known as Ainsworth, and by 1884, Ainsworth School was being referenced. It is believed that the Ainsworth name came from two well-respected educators in the area during the 1870s: Cephas Willard and Sara (Marrow) Ainsworth, who were married in 1869. C.W. Ainsworth (1840–1908) was said to be second to none in Northern Indiana in experience, knowledge, and general ability to discuss educational matters. He received a Yale law degree in 1868. Shortly after graduation, he served as the superintendent for the State of Indiana Industrial Schools, and assistant superintendent of the Indiana House of Refuge for Delinquent Boys. In 1875, he was listed as a co-owner of The Crown Point Register. (Courtesy of Hobart City Hall, modified by Sergio Mendoza.)

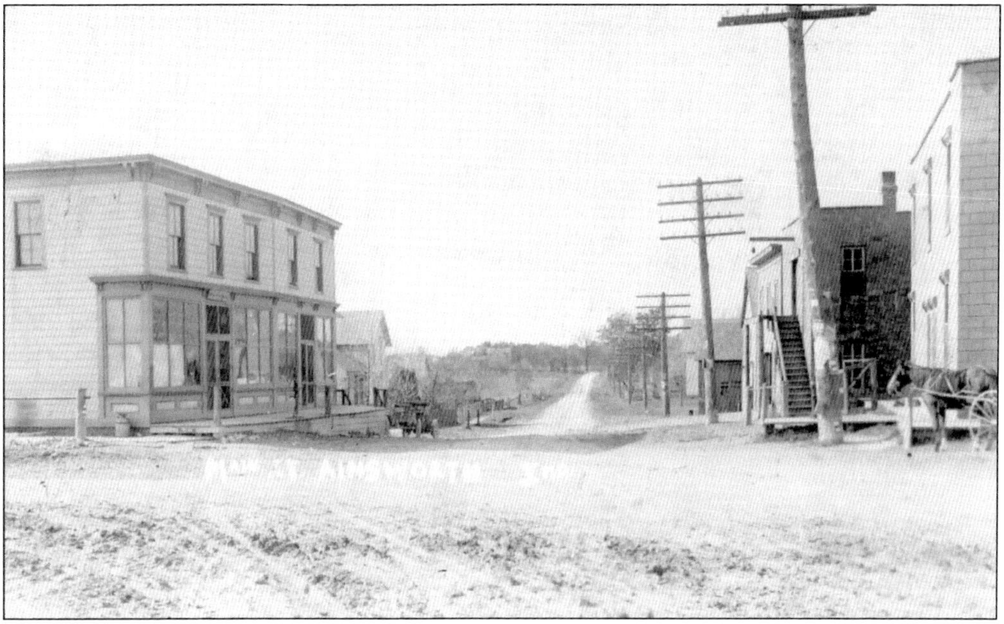

AINSWORTH ROAD. A westward view of Ainsworth road from Grand Boulevard around 1910 shows the Sauter enterprises on the right (north). On the left (south) is the Ainsworth post office and Raschka's Grocery Store. Some early homes from 1869, 1874, and 1899 are still in the area along Ainsworth Road and Grand Boulevard.

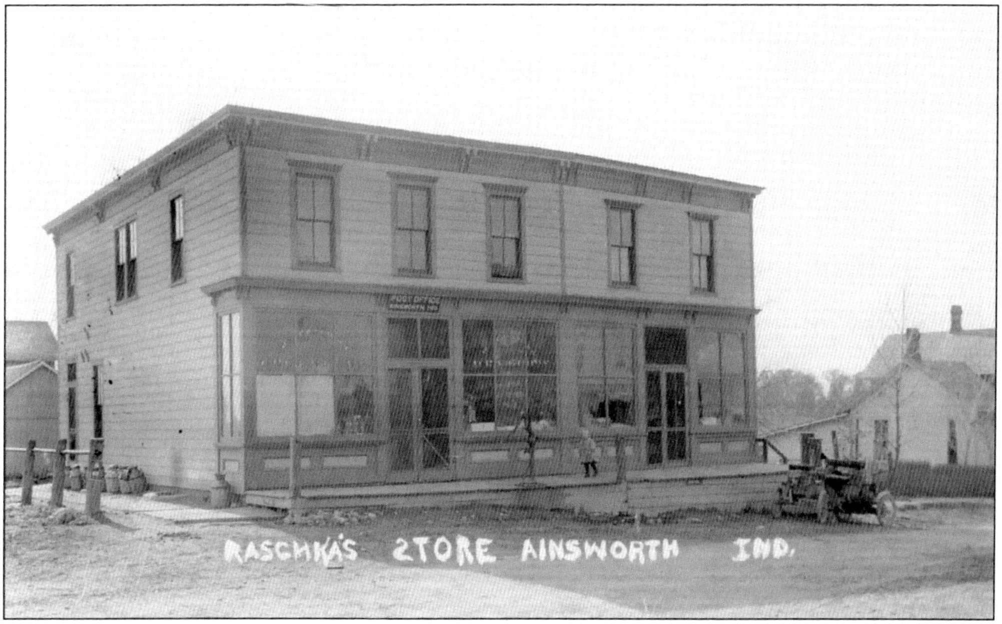

AINSWORTH POST OFFICE. At the southwest corner of Ainsworth Road and Grand Boulevard was the settlement's post office, which operated rural route delivery out of Hobart from 1882 to 1934. Henry Chester was the first postmaster. Lucy Popp was the first postmistress in the late 1920s. Popp operated the post office out of the Popp Grocery Store, formerly Raschka's Groceries. The home on the right (west) was constructed in 1869 and still stands.

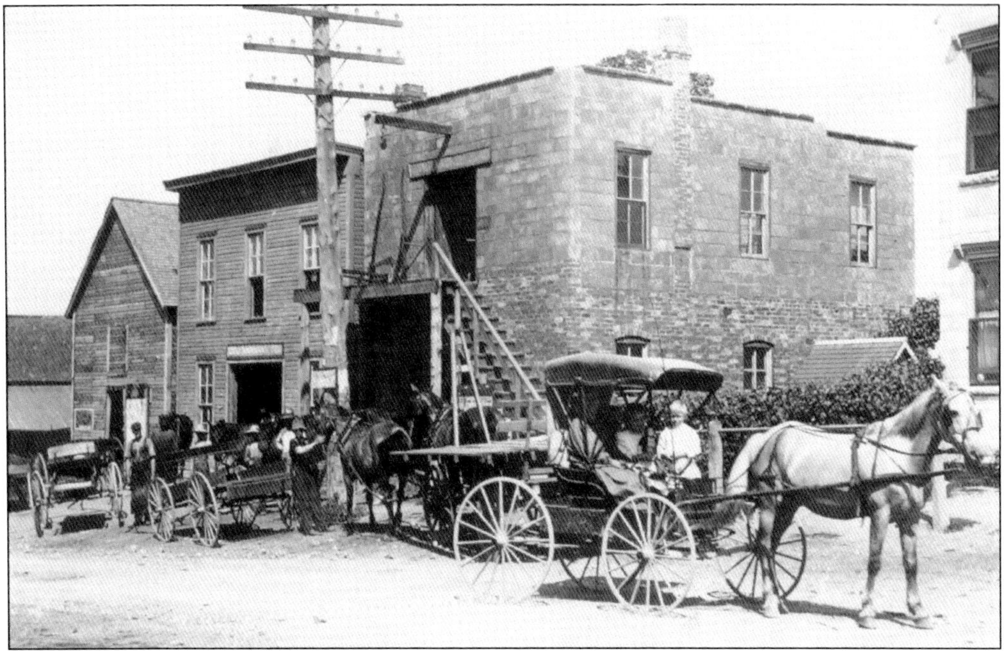

Sauter's Businesses. Edward Sauter came to Ainsworth from Hobart in the late 1890s. He constructed a two-story building at the northwest corner of Ainsworth Road and Grand Boulevard in 1899. A saloon was on the lower level of the building, and his residence was on the second floor. Behind the home and saloon, he erected a two-story brick building to operate his blacksmith shop. The second floor was said to have housed a barbershop.

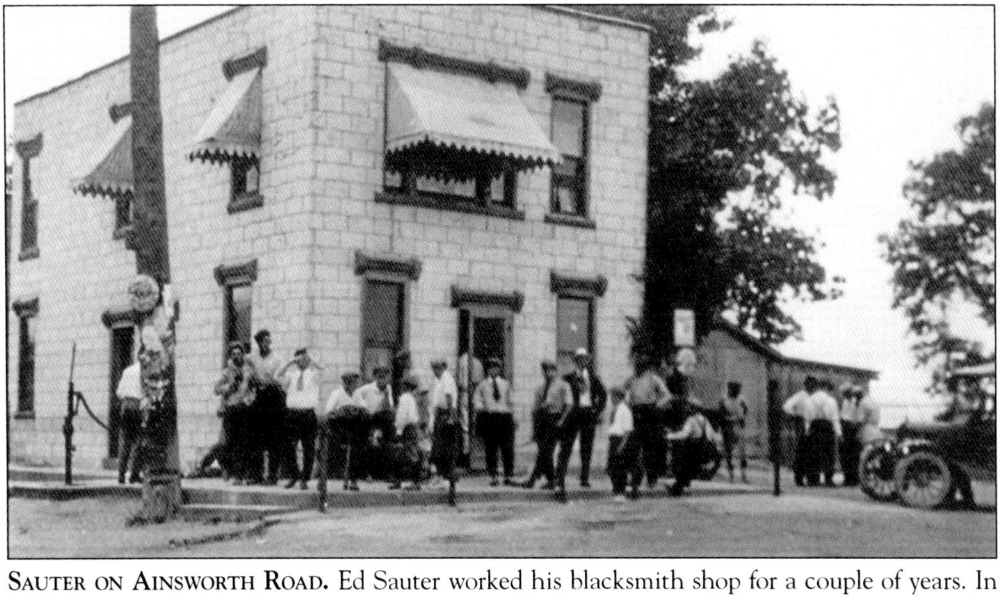

Sauter on Ainsworth Road. Ed Sauter worked his blacksmith shop for a couple of years. In 1901, he diversified his business investments and built a two-story frame structure next to the blacksmith shop. He used this building for storage and operated a popular dance hall on the second floor. In 1906, a sheriff's sale was publicized for Ed Sauter's Ainsworth investments. It appears that Sauter left the area in financial hardship and was only heard from occasionally in Hobart, where his son George Sauter operated Sauter Grocery store in the 1920s.

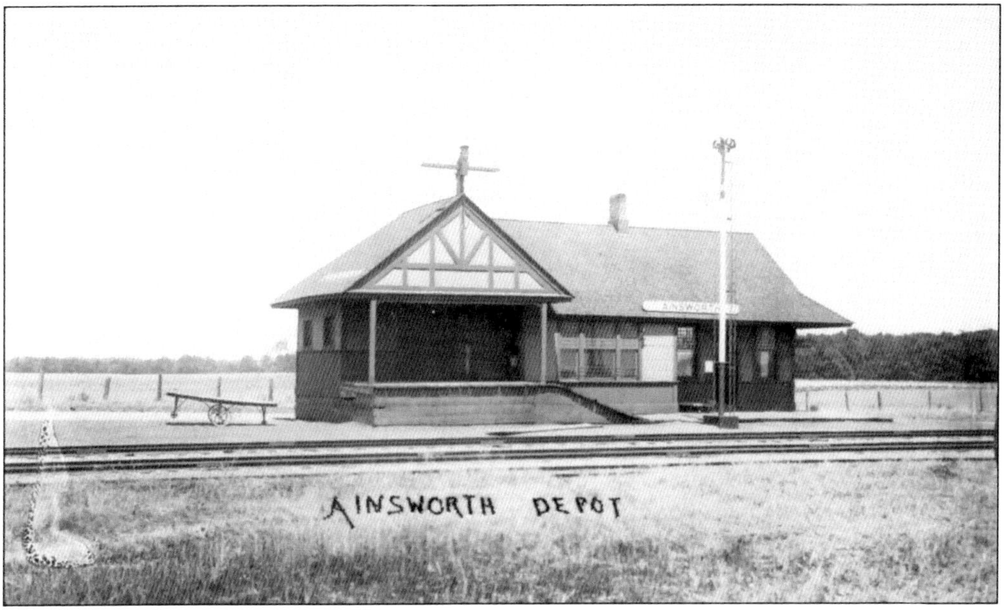

AINSWORTH DEPOT. In 1880, the Grand Trunk Railroad came through Ross Township. In 1883, it was running scheduled stops at the Ainsworth depot, which proved to be a valuable agriculture exporting location due to the surrounding farms. The Ainsworth depot is seen here around 1910. It was used for passenger transport and was particularly popular for the export of milk.

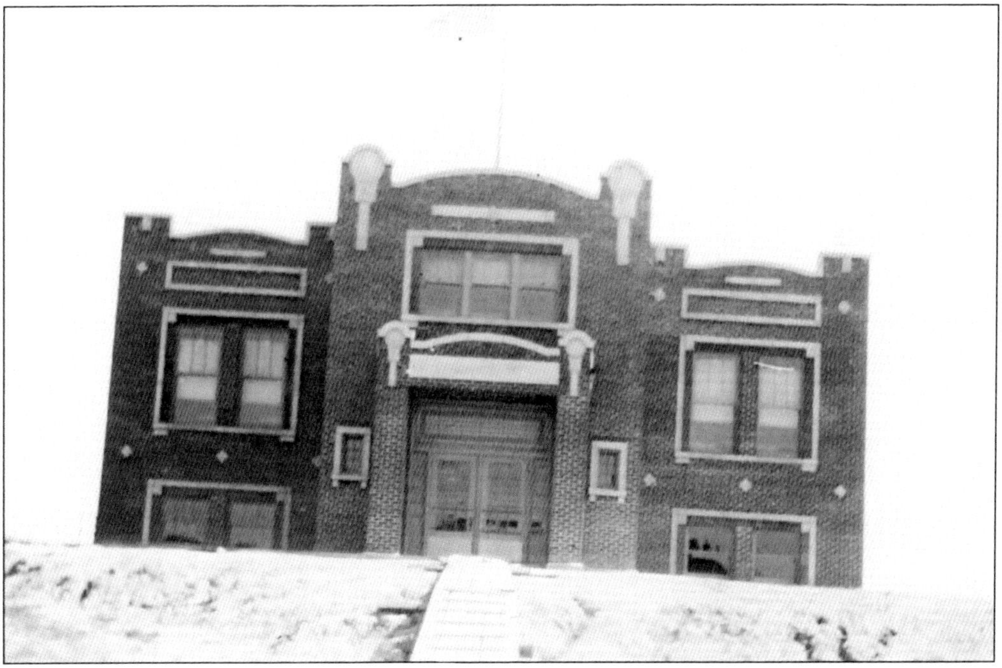

HAAN SCHOOL. The Haan School was constructed in 1915 and was originally referred to as Ainsworth School. It was later renamed after Maj. Gen. W.G. Haan. The school currently stands on the east side of Grand Boulevard, south of the former Grand Trunk Railroad. William Haan had a varied and honored military career. He was born at Crown Point in 1863 and graduated from West Point in 1889. He died in 1924 in Washington, DC.

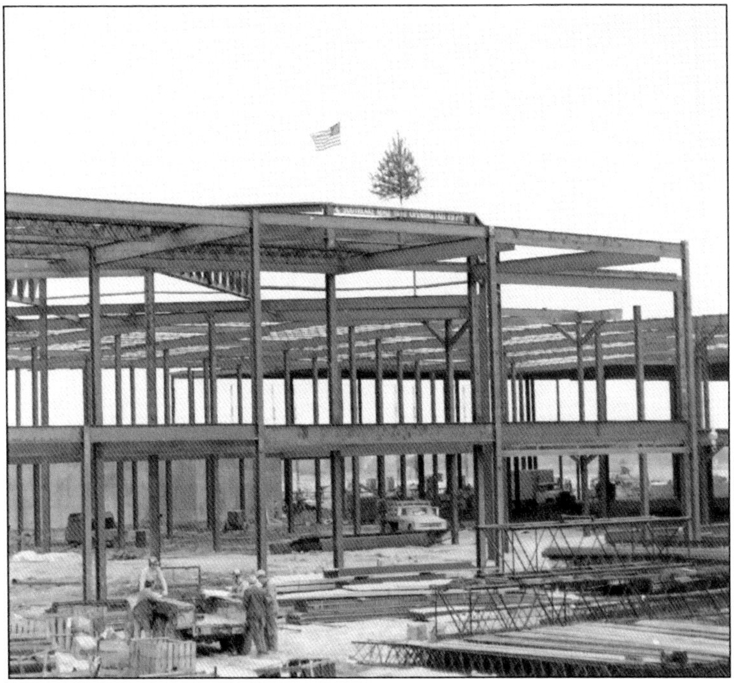

Southlake Mall Construction. The topping-off ceremony is derived from a Scandinavian custom dating to 700 A.D. The custom originated when an evergreen tree was placed on a newly completed house or structure to ward off evil spirits. The placing of an American flag on the last beam is a traditional means of showing patriotism and recognizing the accomplishment of ironworkers. This photograph was taken around 1973. (Courtesy of Southlake Mall.)

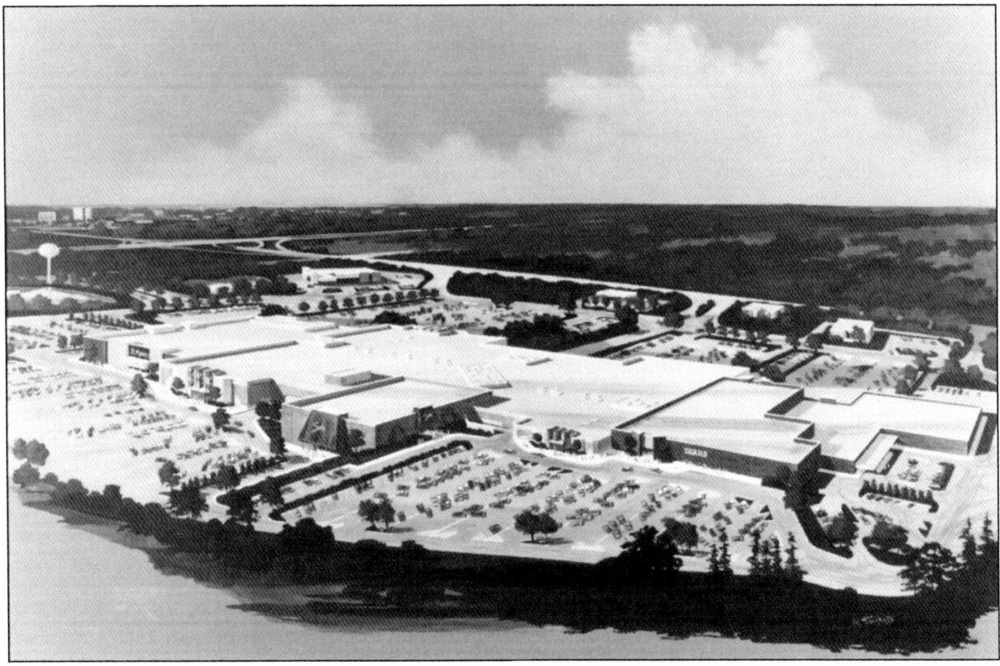

Southlake Mall, Plan View. The grand opening of the regional mall occurred on September 18, 1974. It was scheduled to open with approximately 121 stores and 3 major department stores. The land cover is approximately 80 acres, with 936,000 square feet of retail space. It was anticipated that the new, fully enclosed and climate-controlled shopping facility would employ over 2,000 people. (Courtesy of Southlake Mall.)

SOUTHLAKE MALL, INTERIOR. The enclosed mall, seen here around 1974, originally had varied decorative floors of terrazzo quarry tile and recessed carpeted lounges. Mall officials once boasted that this was the largest mall in Indiana and had contemporary courtyards with magnificent fountains, imaginative sculptures, and natural vegetation of exotic plants. In 2002, Southlake Mall was sold to Westfield Group, which modernized the décor and increased retail space with additional anchors. (Courtesy of Southlake Mall.)

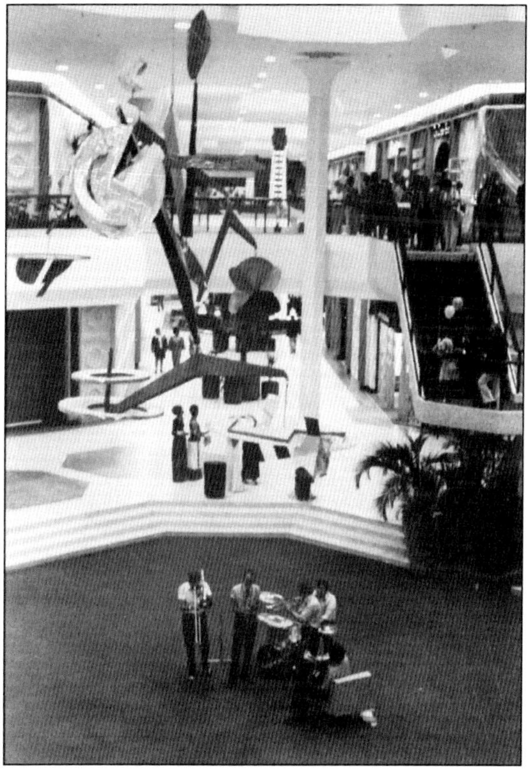

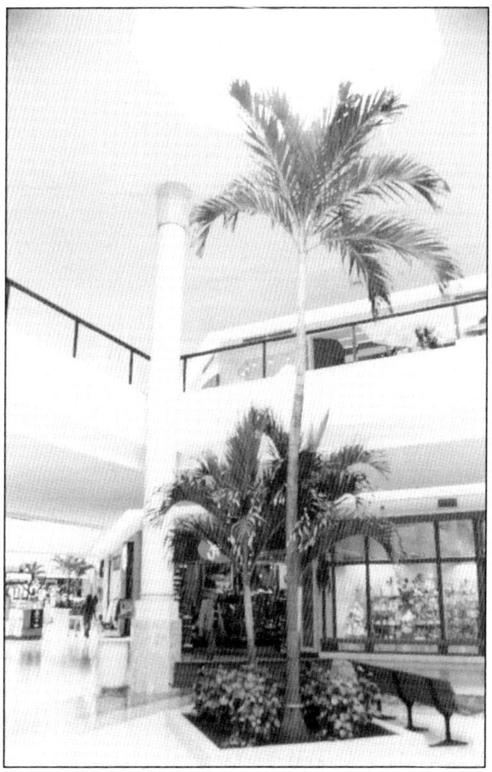

SOUTHLAKE MALL INTERIOR, C. 2000. In the mid-2000s, the mall diversified its uses and increased its retail space to 1.3 million square feet. In September 2013, the mall was sold to an affiliate of Starwood Capital Group, which changed the name back to its original Southlake Mall title. During this transaction, Westfield Southlake Mall was recognized as the second largest mall in Indiana. Nearly 40 years old, this super-regional mall has proven to be a strong attraction, bringing residents from all over Northwest Indiana to the City of Hobart for a premier dining and shopping experience. (Courtesy of Southlake Mall.)

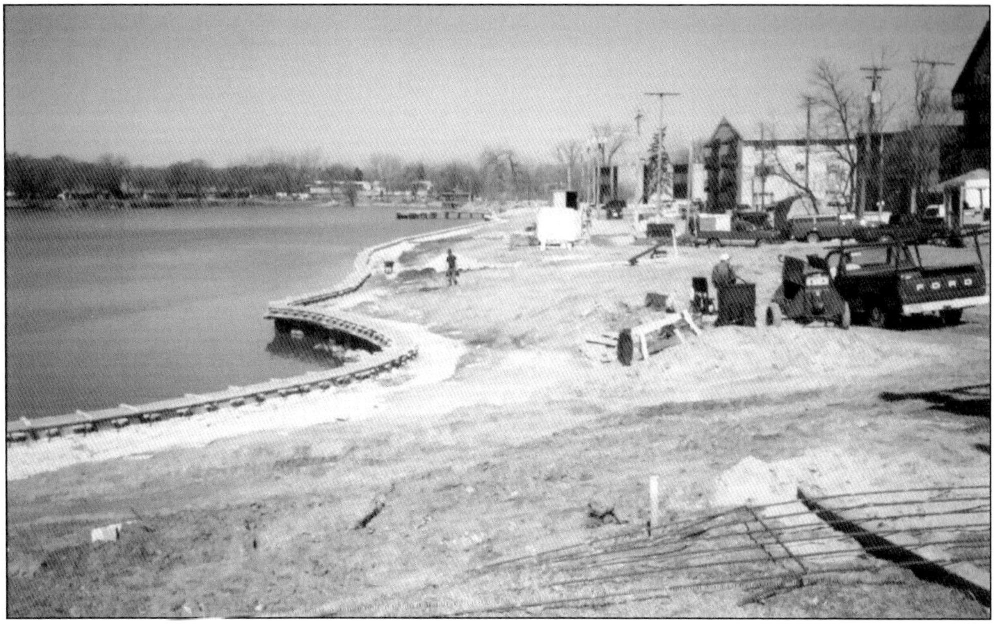

LAKEFRONT GAZEBO. This northwest view of Lake George from Third Street shows the construction phase of the Lake George Lakefront Redevelopment Plan. In 1989, at the request of the city and chamber of commerce, a Ball State University Urban Planning team was asked to conduct a study of downtown and Lake George. The recommendation of the study involved a lakefront promenade. The study called for the collaboration of various stakeholder groups to move the lakefront changes forward. Phase one consisted of the development of Festival Park. Phase two plans were drafted in 1991 and incorporated the lakeshore from the dam to Third Street. The plan called for a seawall, an open public plaza along the shoreline, a fishing gazebo over the lake, and a clock tower. The project was completed and dedicated in 1997. (Below, courtesy of Dana Liss.)

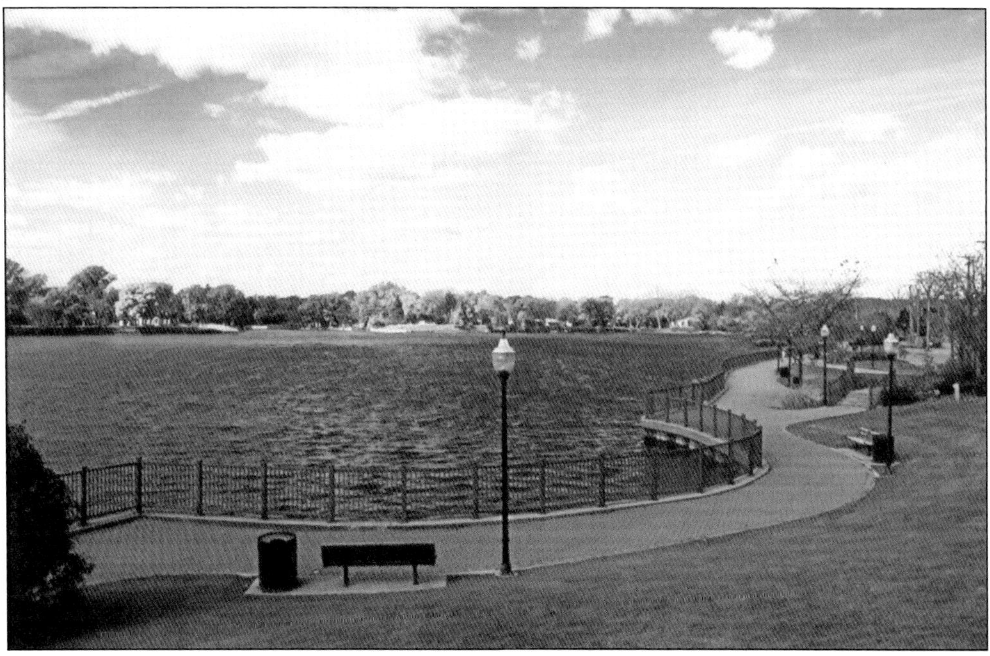

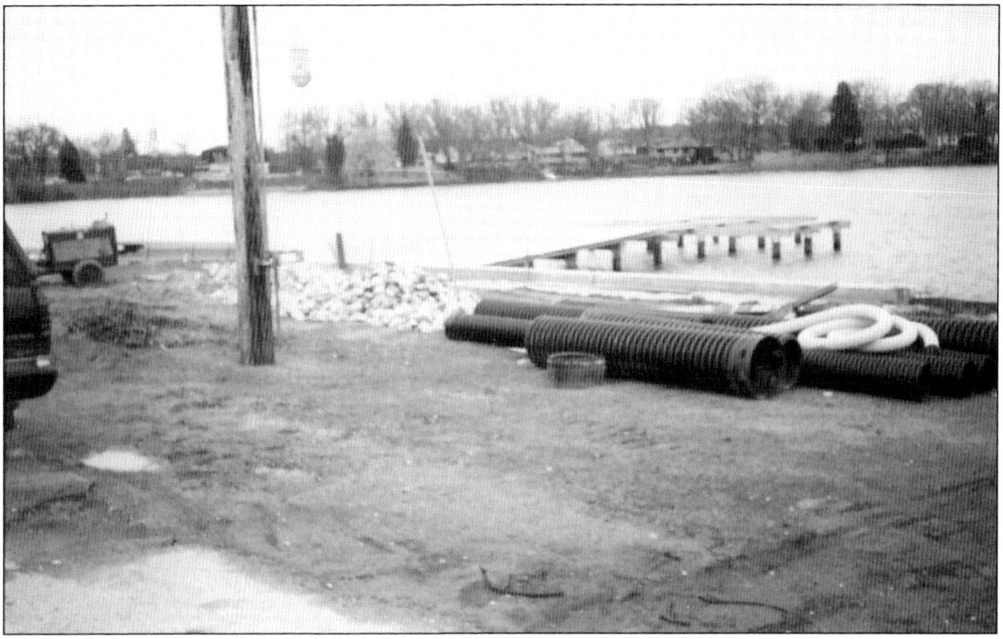

Lakefront Promenade. A southwest view of the Lake George Lakefront Park near Front Street shows the construction of the Lakefront Gazebo (above). Phase three involved the area along Lake George from Third Street to the former Nickel Plate railroad right-of-way. Phase three included a gazebo and a terrace leading to lake access and a floating dock. A walking and biking trail now connects a regional trail constructed on the abandoned EJ&E (Nickel Plate) right-of-way. Phase three was completed in 2008 and dedicated in 2009. In 2004, renovations were done on Main Street, including new sidewalks, benches, period streetlights, and landscaping planters. The redevelopment efforts on the lakefront and downtown have secured the future of Hobart by once again enhancing the natural, social, and economic opportunities of the community. (Courtesy of Dana Liss.)

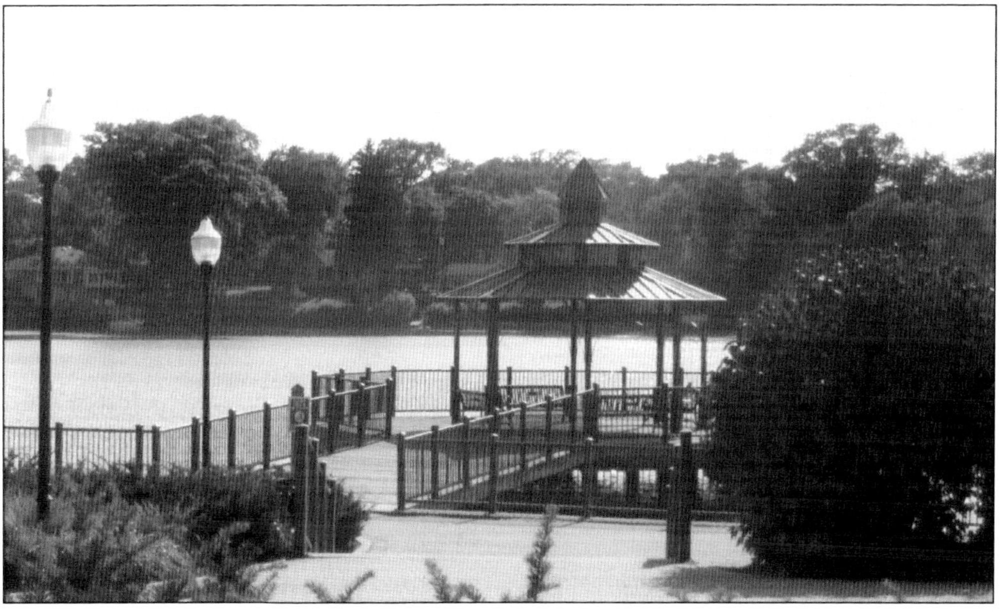

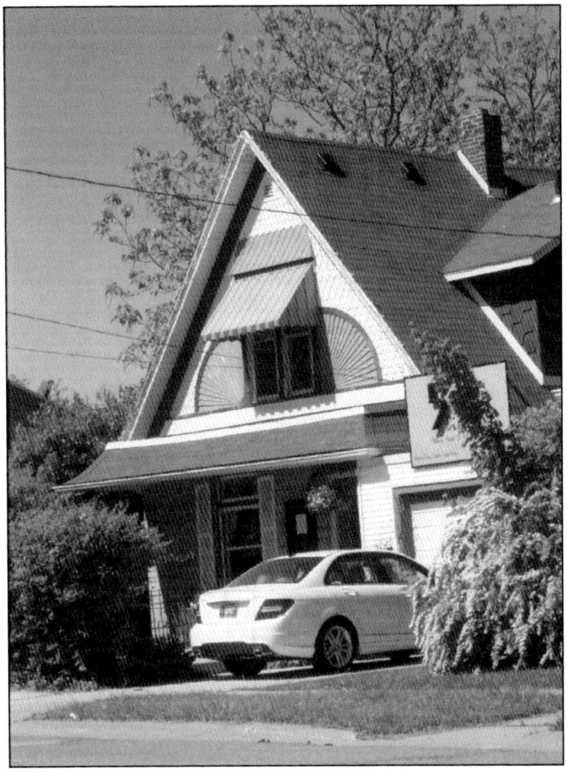

54 Main Bistro. This Victorian cottage constructed in 1895 has the distinction of being the first single-site, local historic district designation by the City of Hobart. The Papp family purchased the home in 2007 and proceeded to open an upscale dining experience with unique views of Lake George, Deep River, and the Kuchta Covered Bridge. (Courtesy of Sergio Mendoza.)

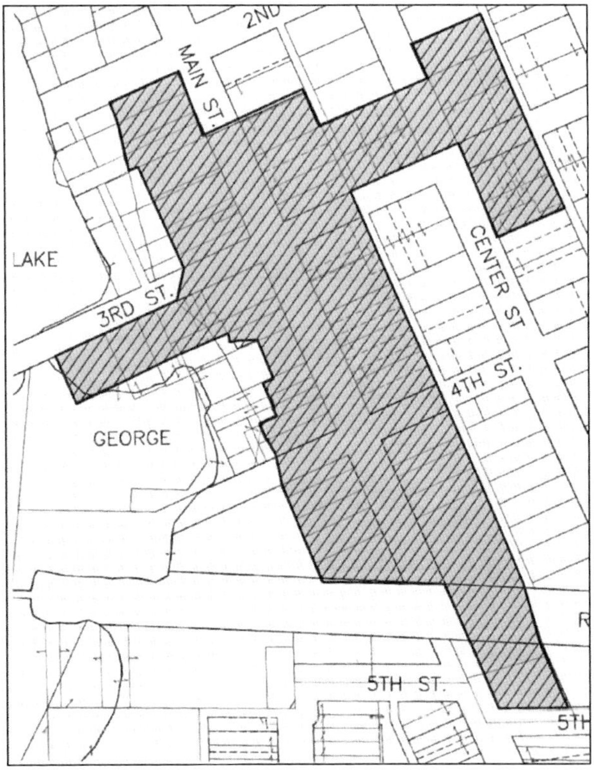

Hobart Historic District. In 2007, Hobart created the Hobart Historic Preservation Commission, entrusted with the responsibility of developing and coordinating historic preservation within the city. Aside from the commission's roles in education and in identifying sites and structures for preservation, the commission established the historic district. The first district was recorded in 2010 as the Lake George Commercial Historic District, and its boundaries were recently expanded, as shown here. The City of Hobart also has a district nomination pending for the National Register of Historic Places. The preservation commission partners with the city's redevelopment commission to assist in facade restoration. (Courtesy of Tiffany Tolbert.)

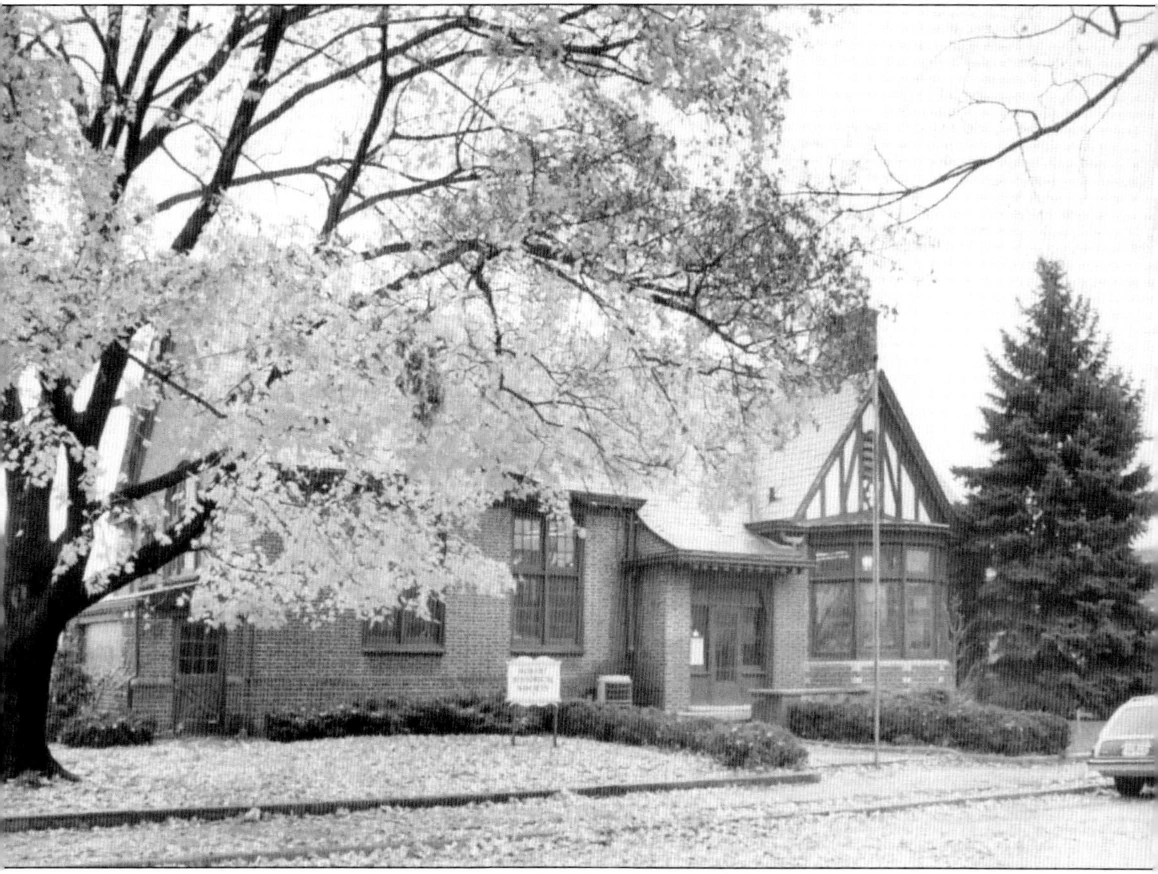

Hobart Historical Society Museum. This Tudor Revival building was constructed in 1915 as the Hobart Public Library. It is now home to the Hobart Historical Society. The society was founded in 1965 to preserve local history for the benefit of future generations. In 1968, the Hobart Historical Society purchased the former Hobart Public library. There are no paid museum employees; over the decades, it has been maintained by a group of dedicated and hardworking volunteers. The building, seen here around 1978, has been listed in the National Register of Historic Places. The interior main floor of the Carnegie building retains the original library plan and has many of the original fittings, including the leaded stained-glass windows. The main floor houses the Mariam Pleak Research Library and exhibits that focus on the history of the Hobart area and on home life in the late 19th and early 20th centuries. Material available for viewing includes fossils and ice-age objects, as well as Indian artifacts. A large area is devoted to 1890–1920 furniture, clothing, linens, and utensils, as well as furnishings brought to Hobart by covered wagon in the 1830s. The lower level has a gallery built as a memorial to Donald B. Ballantyne, whose interest in the early craftsmen of the area brought to the museum its fine collection of wheelwright and woodworking tools. The Donald B. Ballantyne Gallery includes full replicas of a blacksmith shop, a wheel-making and woodworking shop, and an operating letterpress shop. A street scene features shop window displays of early Hobart. Pioneer agricultural implement tools are found in the "In the Alley" Gallery. The public is welcome, and admission is free. The museum is located at 706 East Fourth Street, on the north side of Fourth Street between New and East Streets. The museum is open every Saturday from 10:00 a.m. to 12:00 p.m. For questions, research appointments, or to schedule private tours, please call 219-942-0970. Membership is open to everyone, but appropriate dues apply. Letters of interest or donations can be addressed to Hobart Historical Society Inc., P.O. Box 24, Hobart, Indiana 46342

About the Hobart Historical Society

Over the years, the Hobart Historical Society Museum curators have compiled extensive resource files of pictures and data, which include genealogical material. Some of these resource files are available electronically. The Hobart Historical Society Museum also contains a collection of original and microfilm newspapers dating back to 1889. The society is a 501(c)3 and financially sustains itself through annual membership contributions, public donations, and the sale of souvenirs and commemorative products, including an extensive list of publications expanding on many of the topics briefly mentioned in this book.

Author royalties from this book will be donated: 50 percent of the author's royalties go to the Hobart Historical Society, and the remaining 50 percent will be donated to the City of Hobart, Hobart Historic Preservation Commission.

Products and manuscripts sold at the Hobart Historical Society include postcards, mugs, buttons, memorial bricks, and ceramic tiles. Literary products include *A Century of Hobart Sports*, *Along the Route*, *Gary Railways*, *George Earle and Family*, *Growing Up In Hobart*, *Growing Up In Hobart: the Class of 1965*, *Hobart: As It Began and As We Knew It—The Class of 1965*, *Hobart Historic Buildings*, *Hobart Memories*, Images of America: *Hobart*, *Lake County Communities Past and Present*, *Lake County Interim Report*, *The Nine-day Wonder and The One-month Doodlebug*, and the *Hobart History News* quarterly newsletter. (Courtesy of Sergio Mendoza.)

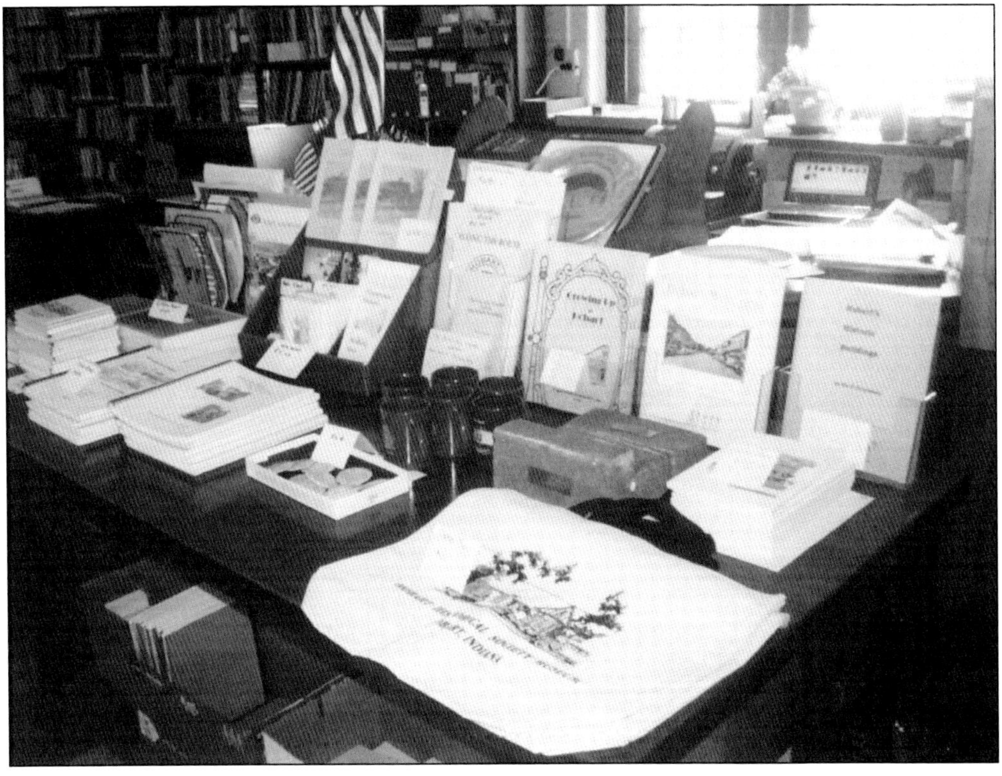

Bibliography

Ball, T.H. *Northwestern Indiana from 1800 to 1900; or, A View of Our Region Through the Nineteenth Century*. Chicago: Donohue & Hennebery Printers, 1900.

Bomberger, Jane. *St. Mary Medical Center—A Mission of Mercy, a Century of Care*. Munster, IN: Community Foundation of Northwest Indiana Inc., 2010.

College of Court Reporting. *History*. www.ccr.edu/index.php/about/history.

Goodspeed, Weston A., and Charles Blanchard. *Counties of Porter and Lake, Indiana: Historical and Biographical*. Salem, MA: Higginson Book Co., 1997.

Hobart Gazette (1889–1930). Hobart, IN: The Hobart Gazette Publishing Company Inc.

Hobart Historical Society Museum. Hobart Historical Society, resource files. Hobart, IN.

McNulty & Brownlee. *Hobart Gazette Souvenir Edition*. Hobart, IN: The Hobart Gazette Publishing Company Inc., 1898.

More, P. *The Calumet Region: Indiana's Last Frontier*. Indianapolis: Indiana Historical Bureau, 1959.

Old Settler and Historical Association of Lake County, Indiana. *History of Lake County*. Gary, IN: Calumet Press.

Pleak, Mariam. *A Short History of Hobart*. Hobart, IN: The Hobart Gazette Publishing Company Inc., 1947.